FALSE PROPHETS

OF

FALSE PROFIT$™

What Every American Concerned about Our Economy &
Their Children's Economic Future Needs to Know about US
High Tech Job Losses and US Stock Market Manipulations

Knowledge Foundation for America, LLC

Lanite Publishing, LLC

Dedication

This book is dedicated to the generations of Americans who worked hard and sacrificed so that their children could have a better life.

Contents

Introduction

This book is a research study and analysis written to help Americans recover economically. It exposes the hidden secrets behind the loss of jobs to foreign workers, the dotcom manipulation of our stock market, and ultimately how both of these were then used to accelerate offshoring by American corporations—resulting in the 2009-2010 economic crisis. Understanding the forces behind these destructive business strategies will allow us to expose the deceptions used by executives to enrich themselves at the expense of American workers, American investors, and the American economy. We will explore the path that led the US into the dotcom crisis and the 2009-2010 economic crisis through a sequence of events that have not received the reporting and media attention deserved. The opinions and theories in this book were developed after extensive research and analyses of information from hundreds of sources. Taken together, the pieces of the puzzle form a disturbing picture. Read the evidence, verify the research, consider the motives and theories, and then work together with other Americans to help restore our economy.

Note: Because of the extensive number of sources, for your convenience the sources reference numbers are provided in [brackets] when quotes are made as well as when no direct quote is used. If a quote is cited followed by additional information obtained from the source, the brackets may be listed at the end of the data, not multiple times. The sources referenced are arranged numerically by the reference number in a list at the back of the book. Certain words and phrases have *italics* added for emphasis in quotations and/or key points.

Chapter 1

Executive Greed

"Bad gains are truly losses."–Ben Franklin

What has happened to America? We are losing our jobs, our insurance, our homes, and our savings. Americans struggle to provide for our children. College costs for our children are soaring yet their future job prospects appear dismal. Banks and major corporations are in trouble. To outsiders it may appear that America is going to collapse. However, Americans have proven to be people of courage who rise to the challenge when confronted by seemingly insurmountable obstacles. Our nation was founded when a few brave colonists dared to challenge an empire to fight for our freedom. Our freedom was defended after the horrific attack on Pearl Harbor when our enemies discovered that instead of crushing us they had "awakened the sleeping giant." Through the Great Depression when all appeared to be lost, Americans persevered. Americans can overcome the current economic crisis. Americans can "fight the good fight" and restore our economy. To do this we need to understand the root causes of the financial crisis, and we need leaders with integrity and intelligence who are dedicated to keeping our nation independent and free.

EXCESS COMPENSATION WARNINGS NOT HEEDED

As our economy declined and our debt to foreign nations grew, US executive compensation skyrocketed to record levels based on financial reports. How were financial reports showing such astounding returns while in reality the companies were being mismanaged into financial crisis? As you begin to investigate, you will discover that executives were getting huge bonuses by bribing US politicians with "contributions," by replacing American workers with foreign visa workers, by using our media to hype stock, by offshoring American jobs to foreign countries, and by other deceptive "cost savings" aimed at artificially inflating financial statements. Millions of Americans lost their jobs to foreign workers, and our stock market was ravaged by corruption. Most Americans know that many of our manufacturing plants were closed, and the work was outsourced to foreign countries. The biggest beneficiary of this outsourcing is China. However, most Americans are not aware of how many of our high tech jobs have been "transferred" to foreign visa workers and foreign countries. Because executives displaced Americans with foreign workers, they plunged our nation into foreign debt. They enabled countries that were technologically decades behind the United States to now compete against the United States. Our nation is facing an economic crisis of record proportions.

Investigating the current economic crisis reveals that the seeds of our economic troubles trace all the way back to 1980. Before this, from the 1950's-1980 the United States enjoyed phenomenal economic success spearheaded by the strategies of leading American management consultants. Then in 1980, American management consultants began to sound alarms about corrupt executives exploiting companies to take excessive compensation. For example, Peter Drucker, a renowned US management consultant and US university professor, warned that the growing pay gap between CEO pay and worker pay in large corporations could lead to exploitation and dishonesty. CEO pay had soared to 42 times the pay of ordinary workers. [3]

Failing to heed the warnings of economic experts, our US government allowed the high ratio of average CEO pay to worker pay to grow more than tenfold, reaching 458 times worker pay by the year 2000, at the peak of the dotcom boom. A study of executive pay from 1980 to 2000 found that the highest paid executives were not the highest performers. The highest paid CEO's unimpressively were below market performance both during the rise and the fall of the stock market. Additionally, many poor performing executives left with "golden parachutes" taking millions of dollars with them after they mismanaged US companies into financial crisis. [2]

In 2002, renowned economist John Kenneth Galbraith, took little satisfaction in seeing his predictions come true. Enron and the other scandals during the dotcom crash epitomized the corruption he had predicted. *Galbraith labeled corrupt executives "financial craftsmen" because they seized control of corporations away from the stockholders by manipulating financial documents to make it almost impossible to monitor and audit their trail of deception.* According to Galbraith, these executives and the people they hired assumed almost absolute power over the corporation, and together conspired to extract exorbitant salaries and stock option compensation. While Galbraith had predicted the problem, what surprised him was the magnitude of the damage done by these "financial craftsmen." [1] Galbraith's economic model probably did not include the multiplier effect from executives transferring US jobs, technology, and money to foreign countries.

While excess executive compensation was bad in 1980, it really got out of hand when executives persuaded Congress to pass the H-1B legislation in 1990. Executives used this legislation to displace high tech American workers with "lower cost" H-1B foreign visa workers who flooded our job market. In the 1990's executives pursuing outsourcing were propagandized as brilliant strategists re-engineering business processes (i.e. outsourcing business processes). Enron was among the companies that employed H-1Bs, engaged in offshoring, and categorized outsourcing activities as "New Economy" strategy. According to one article, in 1997, Clinton praised Ken Lay for the "diversity" that would keep Enron on the "New Economy track." [286] Enron's finance chief later plead guilty to conspiracy. He admitted that senior Enron executives schemed together to mislead investors with financial reports that inflated stocks, so they could enrich themselves at the expense of shareholders. However, Enron's foreign connections received little media coverage. Enron was one among many, yet our government failed to investigate most of the other companies engaged in similar stock deceptions. Americans who lost their hard earned savings in the stock market during the dotcom crash are still waiting for justice.

H-1B visa workers along with foreign investment played a major role in the dotcom boom and bust. The dotcom crash in turn set the stage for the offshoring boom which ravaged the US economy and created the 2009-2010 economic crisis. Executives who got rich from the dotcom stock manipulations used the money to accelerate the offshoring of American high tech jobs and technology, for their own personal gain. Having trained foreign visa workers in the United States; they enabled the offshoring of many American high tech jobs. Executives claimed that employing foreign workers in our high tech jobs is essential for the US to remain globally competitive. The exact opposite is true.

It will not be possible to be competitive when US corporations train our competition and deny US citizens work experience in key technologies of the future. For example, globally the numbers of jobs in the computer industry were growing. Yet, *America's share of these jobs declined dramatically. Not because other nations independently developed competitive IT technologies, but because executives in American corporations transferred US technology and jobs offshore to foreign workers.* By 1998, America had dropped to 70% of the 3.5 million computer industry jobs. By 2001, America had only 60% of the computer industry jobs. By 2002, 45% of our Fortune 500 companies had transferred computer programming jobs to foreign countries doubling the number of jobs they had offshored just three years earlier. [51] We were rapidly losing control of the computer industry we created, an industry vital to our economic future and to our national defense.

YOU GET LAID OFF. THEY GET A BONUS!

Several investigations found CEO pay increases correlated with American citizens being laid off. For example, in 2000, an inequality.org article, "CEO Ponzi Scheme," titled, "Up, Up and Away: CEO Compensation" by Holly Sklar, exposed how executives cashed in while misleading stock investors and employees. Reviewing layoffs and CEO compensation, a 50% correlation was found between mass layoffs (1000 or more employees or 5% of workforce) and within 3 years after the layoffs the CEO being listed in *BusinessWeek*'s top 10 highest paid executives. [2] In 2001, The Institute for Policy Studies (IPS) published a report titled "New CEO/Worker Pay Gap Study" which reported that CEO's in companies that had done mass layoffs (1000 or more job cuts) were paid on average almost 80% more than CEO's in 365 high ranking firms that had responded to a *BusinessWeek* survey. [5]

In September 2004, an article titled, "For CEOs, Offshoring Pays" cited a study by the Institute for Policy Studies and United for a Fair Economy that examined CEO pay of the top 50 offshoring services firms from 2001 to 2003. The study found that layoffs correlated with CEO compensation increases. For example, in 2003 CEOs offshoring US jobs increased their compensation by an average of 46%. One of the biggest pay increases went to the CEO of Intuit who got a 425% pay increase to $22.3 million while offshoring business process outsourcing (BPO) jobs to India. [4]

The Institute for Policy Studies and United for a Fair Economy published its 11th Annual CEO Compensation Survey, titled "Executive Excess 2004—Campaign Contributions, Outsourcing, Unexpensed Stock Options and Rising CEO Pay." This study of the top 50 firms engaged in offshoring US services jobs found CEOs in these firms averaged $10.4 million per year in pay which was 28% above the average large company CEO pay. The report is full of eye-opening research including the names of the executives and details on their pay. Some of the companies where CEO's were reported to have received huge pay increases that correlated with American layoffs included: General Electric, United Technologies (military contracts!), Bank of America, American Express, Oracle, ... India dominated the list of countries getting the jobs. [6] In India the highest CEO pay was $1 million paid to the CEO of Wipro an outsourcing company. [271]

The Institute for Policy Studies and United for a Fair Economy later published an "Executive Excess 2007" report which names executives receiving excessive compensation including private equity hedge funds managers. The report provides a list of proposals on how to remedy the problem of executive excess.

POLITICAL CONTRIBUTIONS YIELDS BIG PAYOFFS

In a June 29, 2004, article published online by pogo.org (Project on Government Oversight) titled, "Government Contractors Wield Influence through Revolving Door, Campaign Contributions," they exposed how government contractors learned to corrupt the system buying influence through political contributions and lobbying. They point out that in 2002; a mere 20 contractors were awarded 40% of the total contracts for that year. [440] *An analysis of contract awards and "contributions" from 1997 through 2004, showed that the top 20 federal contractors averaged receiving approximately $100 in contract awards for every 8 cents they "contributed."* Where else in the world could a company get that kind of sales volume on its marketing expenditures. This is not done directly, for example, if a contractor makes a political contribution, the contribution is not tied to a specific contract award. These top 20 Federal Contractors were awarded federal contracts worth billions from 1997 through 2004: Lockheed Martin got $141.7 billion, Boeing $110.2 billion, Northrop Grumman $61.1 billion, Raytheon $52.4 billion, General Dynamics $35.7 billion, University of California $20.4 billion, United Technologies $22.1 billion, CSC $14.2 billion, Bechtel $14.1 billion, Carlyle Group $9.6 billion, TRW $12.5 billion, Amerisource Bergen $7.0 billion, Honeywell Intl $7.8 billion, Health Net $6.2 billion, British Nuclear Fuels $6.8 billion, and General Electric $13.0 billion. During this same seven year period these top US government contractors spent $436 million on lobbying and political campaigns. Some of the biggest contributors in this group were GE $91 million, Northrop at $64.9 Million, Boeing at $60.7 million, Lockheed Martin at $54.6 million, General Dynamics at $38.0 million, and United Technologies at $31.3 million. [440]

In January 2001, an Institute for Policy Studies (IPS) report exposed that 41 big corporations took advantage of special tax breaks and credits between 1996 and 1998, which exploited US citizens by paying corporations "outright tax rebate checks from the US Treasury." They actually withdrew US taxpayer money. CEOs in these firms increased their pay on average by 69% with the help of these tax rebates. The study also found that six of these CEOs received annual pay increases that completely devoured the entire rebate. [5]

Three years later the 33 page study "Executive Excess 2004 Campaign Contributions, Outsourcing, Unexpensed Stock Options and Rising CEO Pay" published by the IPS and United for a Fair Economy uncovered correlations between CEO pay and political contributions. The study found that the biggest corporate donors to 2003-2004 political campaigns averaged paying their CEOs $17.4 million. This was more than double the average for large company CEOs. The study found that CEOs in companies that sponsored the National Convention for Democrats got a 96% pay increase when compared to average CEO compensation from 2002 to 2003.

The survey also reported that CEOs who personally acted as fundraisers for US presidential candidates received higher compensation. The 38 CEOs who each raised over $100,000 from friends and business associates had average pay of $15.2 million which was 88% more on average that other large company CEO's. US citizens were taxed to help foot the bill for exorbitant CEO compensation. The study estimated that 350 CEO's between 1997-2004 got $9.7 billion in stock options—$3.9 billion of this money came from tax deductions linked to stock options. Shareholders had little control over stock option bonuses, because Corporate Directors approved the stock option bonuses. [6]

CORPORATE TAX WELFARE

The US government gave tax breaks to corporations for "transferring" US technology and US jobs to foreign countries. In an April 2004 *United for a Fair Economy* press release titled "Bush Tax Cuts = Tax Shifts" they exposed how US citizens are trapped into shouldering the cost of the tax breaks given to corporations. From 2002 to 2004 corporations cut their contributions to the federal taxes by 67%. At the same time US citizens saw their share of the tax burden increase by 17%. [155]

US corporations used political "contributions" and legislative maneuvering to avoid paying US taxes. The 2002 tax "stimulus bill created corporate tax loopholes so bad that corporations could deduct more in taxes than they paid in income taxes. A 2002 report by Citizens for Tax Justice found that over a five year period, 1996-2000, ten major American corporations received $50 billion in tax breaks. These highly profitable companies paid only an 8.9% tax rate on over $191 billion worth of US profits. From 2001-2002, these same 10 corporations got $29 billion in tax breaks and paid a 5.9% rate on taxes. *Corporate tax welfare takes the form of tax breaks for executive stock options, offshore corporate tax shelters, and other tax breaks.*

If you look at the list of companies benefiting from the "stimulus" bill, you will see that the list of beneficiaries includes some of the corporations that laid off US citizens and hired foreign workers. For example, the 2002 report calculated corporate tax welfare for the following companies: Microsoft $12 billion, General Electric almost $12 billion, Ford $9.1 billion, WorldCom $5.3 billion, IBM $4.7 billion, General Motors $3.6 billion, and Enron $1 billion. [156] You can read the report online to see how the corporate welfare was computed for these and other companies. The report criticized the 2002 tax "stimulus bill" that was supposed to encourage investment in American businesses. It found that American citizens would be subsidizing corporations by more than $17 billion a year in 2002 and 2003 [156]

CO CONSPIRATORS IN COVER-UP

A January 2002 Special report at *Businessweek.com* titled "Can You Trust Anybody Anymore?" by Bruce Nussbaum noted that executives did not work alone to deceive investors. The very people who were supposed to be protecting Americans from crime compromised their integrity for a piece of the action. Executives recruited co-conspirators including "accountants, lawyers, bankers, legislators, even regulators ..." Together they created complex financial schemes and massive documents designed to obscure the truth from US investors and US workers. [8] Part of the game was to secretly sell company stocks while deceptively inflating the stock prices. [11]

In a 2003 Associated Press release titled "Top Enron Accountant Said Surrendering," Andrew Fastow admitted that he conspired with other senior executives to enrich themselves by deceiving investors. [10]

In his 2004 article "the Great CEO Pay Heist," published by *fortune.com* Geoffrey Colvin criticized how groups of people in fiduciary roles conspired together to take excessive compensation. He faults the "perverse interaction of CEOs, boards, consultants, even the feds." [9]

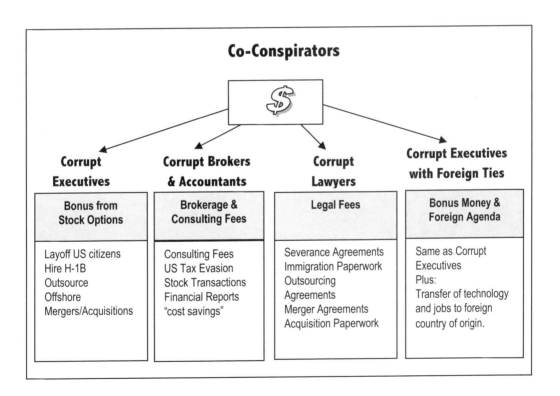

Corrupt Executives	Corrupt Brokers & Accountants	Corrupt Lawyers	Corrupt Executives with Foreign Ties
Bonus from Stock Options	Brokerage & Consulting Fees	Legal Fees	Bonus Money & Foreign Agenda
Layoff US citizens Hire H-1B Outsource Offshore Mergers/Acquisitions	Consulting Fees US Tax Evasion Stock Transactions Financial Reports "cost savings"	Severance Agreements Immigration Paperwork Outsourcing Agreements Merger Agreements Acquisition Paperwork	Same as Corrupt Executives Plus: Transfer of technology and jobs to foreign country of origin.

CONGRESS MEMBERS PROSPER DURING ECONOMIC SLUMP

While American citizens are suffering losing their jobs and their homes, our congressional representatives are quite comfortable according to a June 2008 *USAToday* article titled, "Lawmakers Prosper Despite Economic Slump," [737] They are living large despite the fact that corporate welfare laws, visa laws and other laws they passed are mainly responsible for our 2009-2010 economic crisis.

Chapter 2

American Citizen Job Losses

For decades the credo of American corporations was: "Our employees are our most valuable resource."

The new mantra is train your foreign replacement—you've been outsourced.

If you are an American, you or someone you know, has probably lost their job to a foreign worker. All segments of our society have been affected by the economic attack on America. Among the first casualties were American textile workers and manufacturing assembly workers. Both our Government and Corporate America reassured citizens that Americans would keep the higher paying knowledge-based jobs. They claimed the key to job security was to earn a college degree and fill the high tech and other high skill jobs. Even during the 2008 Presidential race John McCain continued to tell Americans concerned about job security that: "The answer is education and training." He blamed Americans for "our inability to adjust to a new world economy." McCain told Americans that the future jobs are part of "the information technology revolution." [690] How can a US Senator not be aware that as a result of H-1B legislation, well-educated American information technology (IT) workers lost their jobs in droves from 1990 to 2008 as foreign workers took their jobs?

COLLEGE EDUCATED UNEMPLOYMENT

In March 2006, President Bush traveled to India and gave assurances that he would not protect US citizens' jobs from visa programs and offshoring. And, he had the audacity to say Americans just need to get educated. The Americans who were laid off and the new American grads who cannot find high tech jobs are educated. [505] According to the US Department of Labor the 2000-2003 unemployment rate for college educated workers increased 95%. *The long term unemployment for Americans with college degrees increased 300%!* The unemployment numbers for college educated Americans were worse than the unemployment numbers for high school dropouts.

These losses were not from a business cycle downturn, they were permanent losses of high tech jobs, losses that hurt well educated Americans because their jobs were transferred to foreign workers. Yet, so called "experts" advising American executives and politicians still claimed the losses were not important and that the US economy would rebound. [140] By 2007, the US was suffering from unemployment higher than 38 other nations including Mexico. [537]

JOBLESS RECOVERY?

The millions of foreign workers in the US that took citizens' jobs, and the transfer of US citizens' jobs overseas makes the impact of the dotcom crash in 2000 an economic downturn unlike US recessions of the past. Although the recession officially ended in June 2001, most Americans who lost jobs did not get their jobs back. Historically after a US recession three out of four people who lost jobs reclaimed them after a recovery. This time only two out of four jobs were recovered, and half of the recovered jobs were part time. The job market never fully recovered, because US corporations "restructured" into multinational corporations and transferred massive numbers of American jobs to foreign workers both in the US and overseas. [80]

It is deceptive and dishonest for the news media to represent to US citizens that we had a jobless recovery of our economy following the dotcom crash. There is no such thing as a jobless recovery in a nation "of the people, by the people and for the people." Jobs that are filled by hiring non-citizens working in the US are not a recovery. Foreign money used to buy US Treasury Bonds, US land, US houses, and US businesses are not a recovery. An economic recovery occurs when the wealth and safety of US citizens improves. Transferring high tech jobs to foreign workers has left highly skilled US citizens unemployed or underemployed.

An estimated 991,000 foreign workers were admitted to work in the US by our government during 2001. When the government talks about job growth they do not tell US citizens that almost half of the "growth" went to foreign workers. Nor do they tell US citizens that the vast majority of new foreign workers got H-1B *temporary* worker visas that let them work in the US for up to six years. Moreover, while the H-1B was approved by Congress as a non-immigrant visa (NIV), most H-1Bs try to become US immigrants through employer green card sponsorship or other means. Therefore, the H-1B visas not only rob US citizens of current job opportunities, these visas have long term and permanent negative impact on the high tech job market for employing US citizens. [397] (See also the H-1B Job Heist chapter.)

American layoffs continued during the "Recovery." In 2002, the layoffs of high tech American workers continued as unemployment for electrical and electronics engineers reached 4.2%, and the unemployment for computer scientists rose to 5%. Foreign workers were still taking experienced American workers' jobs. As a result thousands of highly educated high tech American workers were suffering from unemployment. Additionally, many young Americans graduating from college with high tech degrees could not find jobs. [62]

FOREIGN NATIONS TARGETED STRATEGIC US JOBS

Maintaining control of our software industry is vital to the US economy and national security. The US software industry is a prime target of foreign nations because of its strategic importance. Foreign workers taking control of computer systems in manufacturing companies gain insider access to US high tech design secrets. Taking control of other business systems provides access to financial data on US companies and Americans, or access to confidential US citizens' medical records ... Furthermore, since 1994, software has become integrated into high tech products. Software innovations and applications are impacting almost all high tech industries [43] from communications devices, to household appliances, to cars, to advanced missile guidance to airplane flight controls.

SABOTAGING US BEST & BRIGHTEST

Foreign governments strategically targeted the jobs of America's best and brightest and most experienced IT workers first, because these workers were America's primary barrier to foreign espionage. These experts had the systems knowledge to uncover technology theft. Because they were the most highly skilled they were the most highly paid. This made these workers vulnerable to the cost savings propaganda of replacing them with much cheaper foreign workers. Throughout Corporate America from the 1980's forward, many of the top experts in the fields of computer software and telecommunications lost their jobs to foreign workers. *Ironically, the Americans who invented US technologies lost their jobs to foreign workers from countries where piracy of US technologies was rampant.* As a direct result of the transfer of jobs from Americans to foreigners you will find Americans with PhDs selling appliances at Sears, and skilled American computer programmers and engineers working at Home Depot.

Our nation turned its back on the very people who invented the technology that made our country the world economic and military superpower. This has many negative ramifications for our country. These Americans are our frontline defense from attacks on the computer systems that are vital to our military, commerce, and infrastructure. Displacing them with foreign workers endangers our troops and all of America. Instead of being appreciated, our society, our media, and executives insulted them with labels like geeks. In contrast, China and India hold their technology workers in high esteem. According to a 2005 survey by Electronic Engineering Times, US citizens employed in high tech professions feel devalued and underpaid. Many are worried that outsourcing creates quality assurance problems, makes projects more complicated, and most of all that it threatens the future of their profession in the US. Only 10% of these technology workers think the US will be able to maintain our technology leadership. [452]

For years American corporations flourished under the leadership of executives who operated under the motto that "our employees are our most valuable resource." Our government and businesses formed a social contract with US citizens to provide a protected work environment with security and advancement opportunities based on achievements. Under this social contract workers assigned patent rights to these corporations, developed profitable business models, and made efficiency improvements, which transformed the US into a powerful economic world leader. US businesses and the US government have broken the important social contract that drove Americans to invent. American electrical engineers have suffered as outsourcing caused layoffs and depressed wages. The loss of these jobs put America's economic prosperity at risk. [122]

An American engineer wrote a commentary about how H-1Bs took jobs that rightfully belonged to Americans: "When a young American decides to enter the EE profession, he makes a well-understood bargain with society." The American engineer invested in his education and worked hard for many years to build our high tech industries only to be displaced and, *watch from the sidelines while some stranger benefits from the very infrastructure he spent his life building.*" The H-1B made no investment in building our society. Ironically many H-1Bs who wrongly took Americans' jobs in the United States experienced the same fate and were laid off as American jobs were offshored to foreign countries. [566] This betrayal of American workers is negatively impacting creativity essential to US competitiveness. A 2003 survey of control and automation engineers found that their primary focus was job security and money. This insecurity about work was destroying interest in seeking out technical challenges.

In July 2005, a US inventor/engineer wrote, "I didn't create jobs out of technology so that they could be moved overseas. I created jobs so that Americans like myself could support their families." For example, he thought our government should investigate the CEO of Intel for transferring "American technology" to India, given the patents and technology invented by US citizens that Intel controls. He noted that Ted Hoff, an American, invented the microprocessor in 1971 while being paid $800 per month at Intel. [461] What Ted Hoff and other American inventors did was assign patent rights and inventions to American companies with the expectations that their inventions would create jobs for themselves and other Americans. However, they would never have agreed to assign their invention rights to a company that would transfer their inventions to foreign countries resulting in job losses for themselves and other Americans. And furthermore, they certainly would never have assigned rights to a company that would transfer the technology to foreign nations that may threaten them or their descendants economically or militarily.

The consequences of educating foreign students who took American jobs is the subject of a 2005 opinion piece in the Electronic Engineering Times, titled "Alarming export: engineers" with the subheading "Failure to nurture U.S.-born engineering students and keep foreign grads here spells trouble for America." When foreign workers took Americans jobs they eliminated much of the American citizen competition. Many demonstrated no loyalty to America, and were intent on helping their country of origin acquire American technology, businesses, and money. While Americans were inundated with globalization and diversity propaganda, many foreign workers from Asia remain primarily loyal to their ethnic group favoring people of their race, religion, and country of origin. Since US corporations built offshore facilities many job opportunities are now better in China and India. [453] After taking Americans jobs and getting years of high tech training and experience in the United States many move back to Asia where they then compete against America.

AMERICAN BRAIN DRAIN

Laying off Americans working in high tech jobs is costing America a tremendous brain drain. [29] This is a major loss to the US and a terrible waste of skills of some of the most talented workers in the world. These are the brains behind the inventions that leapfrogged the US to being the world technology leader. Of course foreign workers in our labs will make some discoveries and inventions. However, this is completely overlooking what the Americans whose jobs were taken could have contributed. What if some of the most important discoveries of our century are never made because we failed to protect American scientists and engineers? Could they have invented a computer chip essential to our national defense, detected and prevented an attack on our infrastructure, ended our dependence on foreign oil, found the cure for a worldwide pandemic, invented a more secure communication system, uncovered false intelligence information planted by a foreign government and prevented a war ...?

Moreover, when foreigners became computer system administrators controlling user IDs and passwords they gained the ability to monitor computers of American scientists, engineers, and programmers who are working on new designs. American inventors could not hope to compete against foreign spies copying their work before they could present their inventions or apply for a patent. American inventors and scientists became casualties when work that took years to invent was copied i.e. stolen in a matter of minutes. Foreigners may be filing patents on US citizens' inventions. Foreigners may be working for the law firms preparing US patent applications. Foreigners may be working for the US patent office.

AMERICAN JOB LOSSES TO FOREIGN VISA WORKERS

In January 2002, the Bureau of Labor Statistics reported 8.3 million US citizens were unemployed. These unemployment numbers had climbed by 2.6 million since December 2000. Many US citizens lost their jobs because US executives with the assistance of lobbyists that work for them got the H-1B quota increased in 2000. [42] In 2003, it was estimated that over 800,000 Americans had been displaced from high tech jobs by non-immigrant (i.e. temporary) H-1B visa workers. [28] In 2005, despite the American layoffs, executives in companies such as Microsoft were pressing the government to approve more H-1Bs, and more basic research money from the US government claiming that both are essential to keep the US competitive. [615]

AMERICAN JOB LOSSES TO FOREIGN OFFSHORE WORKERS

From 2001 to 2006 the US experienced huge losses in vital high tech jobs sent overseas to foreign countries: Communications equipment jobs plummeted by 43%, semiconductors and electronic components jobs plummeted by 37%, computers and electronic products jobs plummeted by 30%. [504] *These are dangerous job losses during a time of war. Particularly alarming, was the foreign takeover of strategic high tech jobs vital not only to our economy but to our national security.* In 2001, during the first four months 51,564 jobs were cut in the Internet sector. [552] According to a March 2002 article, American high tech companies laid off over 520,000 workers by September 30, 2001. During that same period 163,200 foreigners were granted visas to work in the US. [51]

Offshoring propaganda claims that offshoring will benefit America by expanding markets for US exports. For example, a Honeywell spokesman said: "As a global technology leader, we must participate in the worldwide economy and open new markets for our products and services while continuing to recruit and retain a competitive and talented global workforce." [108] The propaganda points to the sale of US computers and telecom equipment in India and other countries. [95] Why would the United States want to "trade" an $80,000 a year programming job to India to get a one time sale of a $3,000 computer, some software, and telephone equipment. That does not sound like a trade anyone with any sense would agree to. The propaganda also claims that offshoring tasks such as reading x-rays will help hold down US health-care costs. What the propaganda fails to mention is that offshoring Americans jobs causes Americans to lose health insurance and that sending sensitive medical information on citizens to a foreign country creates privacy risks and more. [95]

Offshoring rips through America harming individuals, families, communities, cities, states, and our nation. It has harmed American workers from service workers, to medical professionals to computer scientists. One of the biggest targets was offshoring Business Process Outsourcing (BPO), and other jobs that could be done using computers and telephones. Even the American workers who did not lose their job (yet) suffered, because foreign offshoring artificially suppressed their wages. [6]

Following the dotcom crash foreign nations aggressively pressured US corporations to send jobs offshore. The September 11th attack and resulting war on terror diverted attention away from this dangerous shift in high tech jobs. Ironically, the war should have shifted America's attention to the critical need to protect these jobs. Offshoring by American corporations caused record levels of American unemployment in strategic high tech jobs including electrical engineering, computer science, and information technology (IT). For three consecutive years unemployment grew. By 2003, the unemployment rate for these strategic high tech jobs were the highest in our nation's history. Even worse this historic loss of jobs was significantly understated, because the numbers do not count displaced underemployed Americans forced to take lower paying jobs to support their families, nor does it count the number of Americans who left high tech jobs to pursue other professions because cheaper foreign workers had depressed the wages paid for high tech jobs. [88]

American high tech job losses for 2001 and 2002 combined totaled to 560,000. These jobs were lost in vital high tech industries. [61] *In 2002, US labor experts reported a huge increase in offshore outsourcing was causing the US to lose vast numbers of high tech jobs that no one was tracking.* [105] There is no systematic method in place for linking US company job cuts compared to jobs added overseas. Some US companies were keeping job growth flat in the US while adding lots of jobs overseas. [106]

According to some estimates, between 2000 and 2003 the US lost 372,000 information technology (IT) jobs. Many of these job losses resulted from American companies sending IT jobs to foreign owned outsourcing companies in foreign countries—i.e. offshore outsourcing. Software companies are a subset of the overall IT industry. From 2000 to 2004, the US lost 128,000 software jobs, while at the same time India gained approximately 100,000 programming jobs. The new jobs in India were programming software that was sold back to the US. [141] The correlation is striking when comparing US job losses to India's job gains. In 2003, the Gartner Group acknowledged that offshoring was harming American IT workers. [75]

The offshoring of US jobs accelerated during the "recovery." In 2004, experienced US citizens continued to lose their jobs at record rates, and when they were able to find another job the pay was usually less than half their previous salaries. Foreign competition kept wages depressed. The wages for US citizens increased a mere 2%, this is five times less than the 10% expected based on prior US economic recoveries. Despite these trends politicians were claiming that the United States was experiencing a recovery from the recession. [80] By 2004, foreign nations had "moved up the value chain," i.e. many of the jobs lost to offshoring were strategic high tech jobs such as engineering and information technology jobs. During the recovery the job market for high tech American workers grew worse. Electrical Engineers experienced a 6.2% unemployment rate in 2003, which represented a 47.6% increase over the 4.2% unemployment rate in 2002. Gartner estimated that *one in four high tech workers will lose their job to offshore outsourcing to countries such as India by 2010.* [129]

In 2004, the federal Bureau of Labor Statistics drastically cut its projections for US job growth from 2002 to 2012. Because of offshoring, instead of adding an estimated 152,800 information technology American jobs per year, the estimate was revised downward to only 10,600 IT jobs. That was a 70% decline in strategic high tech job growth, which includes job losses in fields such as computer support, software development, and database administration. [140]

According to an October 2005, article titled "Offshoring. Outsourcing. Out of Work." high tech jobs in America were becoming harder and harder to find. These are the most desirable jobs because they pay 84% more than the average job. By 2003 US businesses had cut the number of engineers based in the US down to 70%, and by 2005 it was even worse dipping to 65%. [615] Even with these cuts, the US still was the leader in creating new electronic designs. However the production of these designs was being offshored which enables foreign countries to access leading edge technology and deprives America of much of the revenues, and young Americans of the opportunities to gain the experience necessary to become the designers of the future. The article stated that The Conference Board, a large research business membership, published a report titled, "The New Corporate Reality: External and Market Considerations" warned that prior to offshoring US companies needed to fully examine the impact to determine whether offshoring will destroy their economic and social base at home. Offshoring may ruin the company's reputation, alienate customers, and cause highly talented Americans to shun it as an employer. Why would an American want to design new technology for a company that fails to reward Americans? According to *Electronic Design*'s 2005 Reader Profile Survey the US is at risk of losing its leadership in technology. Most of the US offshore electronics outsourcing jobs were going to China and India. [615] While 60% reported that their companies had outsourced manufacturing operations; a disturbing new trend emerged, 52% reported their companies had begun outsourcing design work. [615] Most of the outsourcing is still done in the US, however about 32% was offshored by 2005. [615]

Forester Research estimated that 3.3 million professional American jobs with combined wages of more than $136 billion will be moved offshore by 2015. It also found that foreign nations were aggressively escalating from taking low level support jobs to higher level jobs such as engineering design. It recognized that American engineers, scientists, and IT workers were all losing jobs to offshore foreign workers. [88]

FOREIGN WORKERS DEPRESSED AMERICAN WAGES

Our nation is treading into very dangerous territory. One survey found that 66.5% of American high tech workers took pay cuts in 2002. And, the negative impact on high tech wages was expected to get worse, as 71.5% of these American high tech workers expected to experience more pay cuts in 2003. Another study found that the average salary paid to high tech professions had dropped dramatically. Some Americans had seen their salaries literally cut in half. Foreign H-1B workers had depressed high tech job salaries in America. Some job search sites such as hotjobs.com, and monster.com had their listing filled with ads recruiting H-1Bs. [144] "Employers use the threat of sending work overseas ..." [141] to intimidate American workers, and to reduce their ability to negotiate compensation and working conditions.

DISCRIMINATING AGAINST US WORKERS

Americans displaced by foreign workers claimed that US corporations used questionable tactics to take jobs away from US citizens. They claimed executives used intimidation to force Americans to accept severance packages; blocked Americans on medical leave from returning to work, eliminated jobs, and then required Americans to find another job within the company or be terminated. They claimed executives lied to the media about the magnitude of layoffs, and threatened to offshore more jobs if Congress did not comply with their H-1B demands. To justify hiring foreign workers executives blamed the US education system. However, Americans educated in America created the technology to which their employer owed its existence and wealth. [392]

Executives have engaged in mass layoffs of US citizens in key technology positions vital to the US economy and national security. Moreover, young American college graduates have been denied the opportunity for valuable work experience in technology and engineering in the US. *It is self destructive for a nation to harm its own citizens, and to favor workers from other countries.* The demographics of high tech American corporations show that executives discriminated against Americans, and in some cases used racist hiring practices. In March 2001, approximately 33% of the engineers in Silicon Valley had ancestry from India. [187] An April 2003 article titled "Lawsuit Slams Sun's 'Bias' for Indian H-1B Workers" said that people of Indian ancestry account for only 4% of the general population in Santa Clara County where Sun Microsystems is headquartered, yet they held 30% or more of the jobs in some of Sun's departments in Santa Clara County. [55]

MILLIONS OF US CITIZENS HARMED

There was no clear concise method being used to track the number of jobs the US has lost to foreign visa workers and foreign offshore workers. Many times the research numbers reported failed to specify which jobs were being counted. For example, do the job losses counted include service jobs, technology jobs, and professional jobs or only a subset of the lost jobs? If counting technology jobs, does it include programmers, engineers, researchers, accountants, medical workers, or others? For this reason when different sources are citied you will see wide variations in the number of job losses reported. However, it is clear that the American job losses number in the millions.

The US has a need for approximately 8.5 million technical workers. When over 3 million foreigners were granted temporary visas for technology jobs it caused massive layoffs of Americans. *In 2001, US corporate executives laid off over a million Americans, while at the same time they were applying for H-1B foreign workers to fill jobs in the United States.* American corporations, universities, and other groups applied for a record 342,035 H-1B visa workers. Despite the economic downturn, executives increased their demand for H-1Bs by 14%. India took about 50% of the H-1Bs while China took less than 10%. [362] [40] In 2001, H-1Bs monopolized the IT job market taking an estimated *9 out of 10 of new computer jobs.* Despite the high unemployment rates for US citizens, the INS granted 312,000 H-1B visas in 2002. [143] In 2003, unemployment for American technology workers continued to get worse. The impact from the flood of foreign workers into the US job market was so severe that 70% of laid off American high tech workers had used up their unemployment benefits and were unable to find jobs. [143]

In 2004 a report referencing studies by the US Department of Labor found that one third of the Americans displaced by foreign workers had been unable to find jobs. It also found that many Americans workers who had found jobs had to take major pay cuts. [81] In 2004, the rate of American technology job losses was worse than expected, and one research firm increased the number of job cuts projected estimating that 830,000 American jobs would move offshore by 2005. This revision was based on expanded offshoring plans by major American corporations. [80]

In 2005, one university study calculated that *14 million American white collar jobs are at risk of being sent overseas to foreign countries.* This enormous estimate may even be underestimating the jobs at risk. The jobs being targeted by foreign nations went well beyond the lower skilled jobs such as call centers, customer service, and back office. This estimate included high tech jobs from information technology (IT), engineering design, and architecture; US media jobs such as news reporting, stock analysis reporting; and even included legal, and medical services jobs. These are many of America's best jobs, jobs of affluence, and jobs of power. These are the jobs that fuel our tax base for funding the government, education, healthcare, infrastructure, and social security. [81] Foreign nations were cutting deeply into the heart of our economy.

By 2006, the US job market saw its fifth year in a row of weak growth. Over the five year period following the dotcom crash, the number of "legal" and illegal immigrants flooding into the US exceeded the number of jobs created by 500,000. [504] US citizens were repeatedly laid off to accommodate the glut of foreign workers invading the US job market.

In April 2009, jobless claims in America jumped to 669,000 the worst in 26 years. [732] And, more job cuts were being forecasted. A *USAToday* article titled, "24 Million Go From 'Thriving' to 'Struggling'," revealed how the American belief that, "those who work hard and play by the rules can get ahead, and that the next generation will have a better life," was being lost. Americans were worried about their children's future. [733] According to another *USAToday* article titled, *"Jobless Rate at 11.2% for Veterans of Iraq, Afghanistan," exposed that veterans who risked their lives for our country were being discriminated against.* One young veteran looking for a job was told that "some employers consider a military record almost like having "a felony."" [743] So Americans who work hard, and those who risk their lives for our country are being denied the just rewards for their work and sacrifice.

RECORD BANKRUPTCY FILINGS

The flood of foreign workers into Silicon Valley caused unprecedented unemployment. Following the dotcom crash, one survey found that 35% of the households in Silicon Valley had one or more people who lost their job and were unemployed for over three months between 2001 and 2002. [73] US citizens employed in service and high-tech jobs bought homes and made other purchases based on expected future earnings. They did not expect that executives would transfer their jobs to foreign workers. The mass layoff of US citizens significantly increased bankruptcy filings which in turn harmed the US economy. Well intentioned US buyers were forced into bankruptcy defaulting on money owed to US businesses. By June 2003, home foreclosures and bankruptcies in the US reached record levels. Almost 1 out of every 100 homes at that time was in foreclosure. And, the ratio was growing with 1 out of every 5 home mortgage payments over 30 days late. [143]

Our government failed to take action. *By 2008, one in 54 homes received a foreclosure filing.* In 2008 bankruptcies hit record levels up 225% over 2006. Banks repossessed 850,000 homes. The rates of foreclosures were growing in 2009. [723]

AMERICAN WORKERS & THEIR FAMILIES HARMED

Americans who made our country the most prosperous nation in the world deserve to be protected from exploitation. It is psychologically damaging to loose a job when you have contributed significantly to your company's success, worked hard, and have a family depending on you for support. Job losses can be devastating. People are rejected and told they are not wanted. Losing a job can cause low self esteem, health problems, broken dreams, broken homes, despair ... When US workers were laid off it harmed their entire families. Unemployed Americans were left to fend for themselves with little hope of regaining their quality of life and security. [49] It put stress on marriages when there was no money to pay bills. It traumatized children when a parent lost a job resulting in lower school performance. Families depend on jobs for food, shelter, health insurance and more. Many families lost their homes. *When parents lose their job, American children not only lose the money needed to pay for college, they lose the belief that a high tech degree will provide them with employment.*

LAID OFF AMERICANS SILENCED

Executives used company funds to pay attorneys to draft severance agreements that required US citizens to train foreigners who were taking their jobs. If the US citizens refused to train their foreign replacements and/or talked to the media they would lose their severance pay. While the executives had lawyers on the payroll advising them, American workers being laid off could not afford legal representation. US citizens desperately needed the severance pay to cover bills while they searched for work in a depressed job market flooded with H-1Bs. US citizens were trapped into deciding whether to buy food for their children or to expose the corruption. For example, laid off Bank of America employees claimed that they were required to sign severance agreements that would cut off their severance pay if they talked to the media. They were put in the awkward and degrading position of being required to train their replacement before their final day. [90] Americans who did try to bring this to the media rudely discovered that the media in the US was being controlled by multinational corporations also implicated in transferring jobs from US citizens to foreign workers. Therefore *Americans who lost their jobs to foreign workers had no place to turn for media coverage.*

SURVEY—AMERICAN OR FOREIGN ENGINEERS?

A 2006 online survey of offshore outsourcing by *Electronic Engineering Times* included a quote from an American: *"It has forced me into bankruptcy and destroyed my family."* [528] Another American engineer implored: "I regularly call my congressional and senate representatives to dissuade them from giving jobs away via H-1B, L1 and equally pernicious visas ... I also regularly respond to any such idiots publishing material that H-1B is good for America. I mention the issue to anyone who will listen, but unfortunately it often falls on deaf ears." [529] The survey surprisingly tallied that 77% of US respondents did not object to outsourcing. However, digging deeper, you discover that foreign visa workers participated in the survey, and that the survey apparently allowed anonymous responses that relied on foreign workers to identify themselves—so foreign workers could skew the survey by falsely claiming that they were Americans. H-1Bs have a vested interested in protecting the jobs they took from Americans, so of course they are pro-outsourcing. Only 6% admitted to being H-1Bs, and only 4% admitted to being born in India [529]—percentages well below their representation in overall US high tech job statistics reported by many other studies. This makes the reported percentages highly questionable. Note that American engineers who lost their jobs to foreign workers probably are not responding to engineering surveys when they are no longer employed as engineers. If surveyed they would probably respond 100% against outsourcing. The survey found that engineers in India took American engineers' jobs because they were paid $38,300 less; however, once they had the jobs they were "anxious for better pay." [529]

AMERICAN STORIES

The stories of harm to US citizens caused by the H-1B foreign worker visa program and outsourcing are many. These are just a few examples. In 2000, an American company replaced a Senior IT executive with an H-1B visa worker. When the foreign H-1B visa worker took over as an IT executive he immediately fired the American employees and outsourced the projects they were working on to Tata Consultancy. Tata then used H-1B foreign visa workers brought into the United States to work on the company's software development projects [28]

Another outsourcing story reported in 2001, Charlotte, NC based Bank of America outsourced its Human Resources (HR) management to Exult. As part of the outsourcing agreement Exult hired the Bank of America HR employees. Exult then turned around and outsourced computer programming jobs to HCL and Hexaware. Both of these outsourcing companies were H-1B foreign worker "bodyshops." The former Bank of America employees lost their jobs to foreign H-1Bs brought into the United States who they were forced to train to get severance pay. [37] According to *rescueamericanjobs.org*, in 2003, "Amazing Facts and Statistics: Non-immigrant (Temporary) Foreign Work Visa Programs," Siemens required American employees to train their foreign replacements. The Americans were then laid off, and the foreigners settled in to live in Florida. [28] Another report claimed that Cigna insurance company fired American workers then outsourced its high tech jobs to Satyam an India outsourcing company. US citizens could not even get a chance to compete for any of the consulting jobs, because Cigna gave Satyam the right to screen out consultants. [63] (See also where Satyam was debarred by the World Bank and imploded in an accounting fraud.)

Chapter 3

US Economic & Tax Losses

They call losses profits.

Executives in US corporations and the US media represented that displacing US workers with foreign workers was good for Americans. They claimed lower costs would benefit US consumers and the US economy. Even leaders in our government claimed that replacing US workers with foreign workers was good for taxpayers because it lowered costs. They asserted that American workers were freed from these jobs, so that they could focus on the new technologies of the future such as nanotechnology. [72]

INDIA DOMINATES THE H-1B VISAS

As stated earlier, India dominates the H-1B program taking almost half the visas, followed by China with about ten percent of the visas. In July 2003, India used a McKinsey & Company "study" released by NASSCOM to claim that the H-1B program and outsourcing would continue, because H-1Bs from India working in the United States paid $500 million a year into US Social Security, and spent $1.8 billion a year benefiting the US economy. [123] The McKinsey study failed to mention that one month earlier in June 2003, India pressured the US government to refund Social Security taxes to the growing number of H-1Bs forced to return to India because of the economic slowdown in the United States. [86] Ironically, much of the slowdown was caused by offshoring US jobs to India. India also acknowledged that vast numbers of H-1Bs obtained green cards and may collect Social Security benefits. [123] *The study also failed to mention that non-immigrant visa workers from India transferred $10 billion a year in remittances from the US to India.* [28] If half of these money transfers ($5 billion) were sent by H-1Bs to India, and H-1Bs were spending only $1.8 billion in the US, then H-1Bs were transferring about 74% of their US pay to India. This seems impossible until you learn that often outsourcing companies provide H-1Bs with free apartments and food, and pay them cash or a check with no US taxes withheld. Some

H-1Bs have their paychecks automatically deposited in a bank in India while they live in the US on a spending allowance and pay no US taxes. [154]

SOCIAL SECURITY JEOPARDIZED

There is a lot of concern about US Social Security being solvent. The best way to protect Social Security is to protect US citizens' jobs. Unemployed Americans do not pay into Social Security. Furthermore, our government needs to stop awarding green cards to visa workers who paid little or no US taxes. Many H-1Bs evade paying US taxes while working six years in the United States and then are awarded green cards entitling them to US Social Security benefits when they retire. Our government, which aggressively pursues collecting taxes from US citizens, makes no effort to collect those six years of back payroll taxes. [154] Our government also needs to reject attempts by foreign countries to exempt visa workers from paying US taxes. If H-1B workers from foreign countries are exempted from paying Social Security taxes this would give H-1Bs an insurmountable competitive cost advantage over US citizens for jobs in the United States.

OFFSHORING DEPRESSED WAGES & LOWERED TAX REVENUES

Foreign workers depressed American wages which in turn reduced taxes collected by our government. A study by the Bureau of Labor Statistics evaluated the impact of offshoring from 1979 to 1999. They reported that 55% of Americans who lost their jobs because of foreign competition took substantial pay cuts. About a quarter of the people lost 30% or more in their level of compensation. [129]

Tax revenues fell as worker pay fell from $6.35 trillion in 2000, to about $6 trillion in 2002, a 5.1% drop. At the same time, the flood of immigration and visa workers caused explosive population growth that cumulatively depressed the overall American economy. The government had more people to provide services to, and the government had less money to provide the services. The income of Americans adjusted for inflation dropped 9.2% from 2000 to 2002. *Hardest hit were the high tech professional jobs.* [142]

In 2005, another study also found that the American standard of living was being lowered. New jobs being added were paying 21% lower wages and were providing less health insurance or none at all. *The hardest hit professions were US software jobs.* [141]

INDIA DOMINATES HIGH TECH OFFSHORE OUTSOURCING

India dominated high tech offshore outsourcing. In a February 2001 forbes.com article titled, "Can India Retain Its Reign as Outsourcing King?" by Todd Jatras, he names US corporations involved in outsourcing to India. The US executives in these corporations had begun transferring strategic research facilities not just maintenance of legacy systems. [91] According to the report India had $6 Billion in software exports. China was in a distant second place with $1 billion in software exports. Pakistan was also in the outsourcing market with $120 million in software exports. [91]

A September 23, 2002 report, "Offshore Upstarts" by Paula Musich on *eWeek*, claimed *India was the number one source for offshoring with 85% of the software outsourcing market*. The report also claimed that Russia and China were trying to catch up with India. [774] A 2004 report titled, "Will India Price Itself Out of the Offshore Market," exposed that the wages for programmers in India were rapidly growing. However, it claimed India still had 80% of the offshore market. [301]

Just months prior to the 2004 US Presidential election, a March 2004 article titled, "American IT Pros Sue, Bangalore Shivers," reported that thirty five laid-off American IT professionals filed a class-action lawsuit against the US government, because American programmers who lost their jobs to India did not have the same unemployment benefits as American manufacturing workers who lost jobs to China. Laid-off American IT workers demanded that the US government expand the "Trade Adjustment Act" to help them recover from job losses to foreign workers. Under this program, displaced American workers who lose jobs to foreign competition can receive up to 2 years of unemployment coverage, plus assistance with job training, job searches, and health insurance. India "shivered" because this lawsuit exposed some of the deceptions in the claimed offshoring cost savings. India was worried that the US government upon realizing the magnitude of the unemployment costs would pass legislation to stop executives from transferring American jobs to India. [71]

ECONOMIC REALITY CHECK

If the claims of cost savings benefits were real, then areas with high concentrations of foreign visa workers would have the greatest prosperity in America. California is the litmus test state because it has the most foreign IT workers. California's state budget deficit, the largest in our nation, climbed to $35 billion by January 2003. [197] By the end of 2008 California's budget deficit had risen to almost $41.8 billion. [711] California's budget deficit shows the real economic impact. Prior to the influx of foreign workers Silicon Valley, California was one of the most prosperous areas in the US. California was well positioned to maintain its prosperity and our nation's high tech leadership. Instead, California has now been decimated by layoffs of US citizens and the hiring of foreign workers. This pattern of economic decline followed in other states as H-1B workers arrived to displace US workers. For example, North Carolina went from a prosperous state to a multi billion dollar budget deficit when it was flooded by foreign workers.

Transferring jobs from Americans to foreigners does not benefit the US economy. The US economy is declining and the US Government is losing essential tax revenues as executives in US corporations and government offices replace American workers with foreign workers. Bottom line, Americans fund the US Government by paying a percent of their income in taxes. Diminishing Americans' income weakens the US Government because it has less money for defense, less money for research, less money for Social Security, less money for education, and less money for other programs.

There have been a lot of misleading financial manipulations claiming that globalization benefits America. Americans who have witnessed the harm of job losses have been looking for an economic model that will educate the public on how globalization is harming our economy and government. A January 19, 2004, cbsnews.com report, "Outsourcing Backlash Brewing," by Rachael Konrad for the Associated Press wrote: *"Despite that daunting economic logic, outsourcing opponents say they hope to educate the public about the true cost of globalization."* [72]

US ECONOMIC LOSSES CAUSED BY HIGH TECH WORKER VISAS

The following Economic Circulation Model™ was created to help the American public understand the "true cost of globalization." It computes US tax and business economic losses caused by displacing one American IT worker we will call Sam, with a foreign visa worker from India. In this analysis, Sam is paid $80,000 per year compared with an H-1B or L-1 visa worker paid $50,000 per year.

The model estimates the tax and economic impact per American job taken. Rarely are Americans able to reclaim their jobs. More likely, their job after being taken by foreign visa workers in the United States will later be transferred to offshore workers in a foreign country.

First we will compute the economic and tax impact of Sam's job; and then we will compute the economic and tax impact if Sam loses his job to a visa worker.

Sam's Direct Economic Impact in the United States	
Salary	$80,000
State Taxes	$5,600
Federal Taxes 28%	$22,400
After-Tax Income Spent (Circulated in the US)	$52,000

If Sam pays 28% in federal taxes that is $22,400 plus $5,600 for state taxes equaling a total of $28,000 in US tax revenue. (While not all states collect income taxes; all do have some method for collecting money from US citizens to fund schools, roads, and other infrastructure.)

After Sam pays his taxes he has $52,000 in after-tax income which he spends in the United States. When Sam spends the $52,000 it becomes income for other people. The after tax money circulates and is shown as recycled income. First, the money Sam spends goes to Group A. (Group A includes all the Americans who would have made money from selling goods and services to Sam such as his mortgage lender, his grocer, his doctor, his barber, restaurant owners, and other US businesses.) Group A Americans who received money from Sam, pay their taxes on the money and then spend the remainder putting it in circulation in the US when they buy from Group B, etcetera. (Note when the after-tax income fell below $9,000 the calculations were stopped to fit the chart on the page.) The following chart shows income put into circulation by Sam. Each time the money changes hands in the United States, the US government collects more taxes.

Economic Circulation Model™ of Sam's Job
Money Circulated Generating US Taxes & US Business Income

	Group A	Group B	Group C	Group D	Group E	Totals
Income Circulated	$52,000	$33,800	$21,970	$14,281	$9,282	$131,270
State Tax	$3,640	$2,366	$1,538	$1,000	$650	$14,793
Federal Tax	$14,560	$9,464	$6,152	$3,999	$2,599	$59,173
After-Tax Income to Recycle	$33,800	$21,970	$14,281	$9,282	$6,034	

So Sam's money, circulated in America, would generate approximately an additional $74,000 in taxes ($14,793 in State Tax + $59,173 in Federal Tax), which when added to the $28,000 in taxes Sam paid, brings the total taxes collected to $102,000. *The amazing fact is that when the money circulates in our economy it is taxed over and over again, and the US government collects more in taxes than Sam's total pay.* The impact from

Sam's circulated income for US businesses is even greater, pumping $131,000 into the US economy. So the overall economic and tax benefit of Sam's $80,000 salary is $102,000 in taxes plus $131,000 for a total impact of **$233,000**.

Next, compare the tax and economic losses to America from displacing Sam with an H-1B visa worker. The H-1B paid $50,000 a year is supposed to pay 40% in US taxes or $20,000. [30] [46] However, many body shops and the H-1Bs they employ find ways to pay little or no US taxes. [30] [46] [153] For example, some H-1Bs are paid minimum wage salaries while they are paid separately for US living expenses which are not taxable. [28] A tax treaty exempts Chinese teachers or research assistants in US universities from taxes. [58]

L-1 visa workers are regarded as employees of a foreign owned company, so even though they take jobs in the United States they do not have to pay US income taxes. [28] [143] The "high paid" Americans like Sam who pay 28% or more in taxes frequently bring home less pay than foreign workers who evade paying taxes. American citizens need higher base salaries than foreign workers, because they are not eligible for the tax breaks exploited by foreign visa workers such as deducting their living expenses.

As noted earlier, the money transfers that visa workers send back to India appear to average about 74% of their salary. For the sake of simplicity, we will assume that if a visa worker from India pays 40% in US taxes they only transfer 40% of their salary to India; and that if they pay no US taxes they transfer 80% back to India i.e. we assume the money they did not pay in US taxes is transferred to India. (The average of 80% and 40% = 60% which is 14% below 74%.)

If the H-1B who is paid $50,000, sends a 40% or $20,000 money transfer back home to India and pays $20,000 in US taxes, that leaves only $10,000 to spend in the United States. If the visa worker paid no US taxes and transferred 80% to India that also

	H-1 B Visa Worker	H-1B or L-1 Visa No Taxes Paid
Salary	$50,000	$50,000
US Taxes Paid 40%	$20,000	$0
Transfer to India	$20,000	$40,000
Money to be Circulated in the US	$10,000	$10,000

leaves only $10,000 to spend (i.e. circulate in the US economy).

The following table shows that feeding $10,000 into the economic impact model, the visa worker's circulated money generates only about $16,500 in the US economy and about $6,000 in US tax revenue ($1,155 in State Taxes + $4,620 in Federal Taxes).

Note that with Sam's example the money circulation benefit calculations were stopped when the after-tax income reached $9,282, but in the visa worker's example the computed benefits were allowed to continue until the after-tax income reached $6,500 which comparatively slightly inflates the visa worker's contributions.

Economic Circulation Model of Foreign H-1B or L1 Visa Worker
Money Circulated Generating US Taxes and Business Income

	Group A	Group B	Group C	Group D	Group E	Totals
Income Circulated	$10,000	$6,500				**$16,500**
State Tax	$700	$455				**$1,155**
Federal Tax	$2,800	$1,820				**$4,620**
After-Tax Income to Recycle	**$6,500**	**$4,225**				

If the H-1B visa worker paid US taxes, add the $20,000 they paid plus $6,000 generated when their $10,000 circulated and the total US tax revenues are only $26,000. If the visa worker paid no taxes, then the US tax revenues are only $6,000.

Next the yearly losses from displacing Sam with a visa worker are computed.

	Sam's Tax & Economic Contributions	H-1B's Tax & Economic Contributions	US Tax & Economic Losses from Displacing Sam with an H-1B
Taxes Paid Directly	$28,000	$20,000*	
Taxes Generated by Money Circulated in US	$74,000	$6,000	
Total US Taxes	**$102, 000**	**$26,000**	**$76,000**
US Economic/US Business Income from Circulated Income	**$131,000**	**$16,500**	**$114,500**
Total Tax & Economic Impact	**$233,000**	**$42,500**	**$190,500**

*If an L-1 Visa worker or an H-1 that evaded US taxes delete this amount, increasing the yearly loss to **$210,500**.

The US government should note that while Sam would have generated $102,000 in taxes, a visa worker would have generated only $26,000 for a net tax loss of $76,000 per year; or worse, $102,000 minus $6,000 for a net tax loss of $96,000. And,

US business owners should note the economic damage caused by displacing Sam with a visa worker. Sam's $131,000 minus the H-1Bs $16,500 and the US economic loss is $114,500. Finally, the total estimated US tax and economic loss is $190,500 per year from displacing Sam with an H-1B visa worker; or, if the visa worker paid no taxes then the loss to the United States is $210,500 per year. *The amazing fact is that the indirect loss from transferring money out of circulation in the United States is much greater than the direct loss. And this economic loss of $190,500 or $210,500 is the impact from replacing just one American worker with a foreign visa worker.* So hiring "cheaper" visa workers may pad the pockets of a few executives, but it greatly harms our government and overall economy.

The next question is how many high tech American workers lost their jobs to foreign visa workers in the United States? US corporations and even our government replaced American workers with cheaper foreign visa workers. [154] It is difficult to get an accurate count of the number of foreign workers in the United States on H-1B visas, L-1 visas, and other high tech visas, not to mention the number of visa violators working in the US illegally. By 2001, the number of H-1Bs in the US was estimated between 2-4 million. So to be conservative if we take 3 million job losses to H-1Bs at an estimated average economic and tax loss of $190,500 each, the total economic and tax loss ($190,500 * 3 million) is $571.5 billion per year. Next, we need to add an estimate for L-1 and other visa workers and illegal aliens taking high tech jobs in the United States. If all these combined total another 3 million jobs, then $190,500 * 3 million would result in an additional $571.5 billion per year loss. Adding $571.5 billion plus $571.5 billion would bring *US economic and tax losses from Americans losing high tech jobs to foreigners working in the United States to over $1 trillion per year.*

The real losses are even greater, because the model does not include layoff costs such as unemployment payments to laid off US workers, uninsured US citizens, the costs of retraining workers who lost their jobs to foreign workers, welfare costs, and more. Nor does the model include the costs of layoffs that force US citizens to default on mortgage payments, car payments, credit card payments ... When citizens file bankruptcy, the government is again impacted by lost tax revenues, because US businesses are unable to collect the money owed for products and services. Nor does the model include the environmental and economic costs from millions of foreign workers flooding into the US causing increased pollution, strained water supplies, increased demand and prices for gas and other resources. Moreover, visa workers use US infrastructure, roads, parks, and other taxpayer financed facilities. [154] Also, when non-citizens buy real estate the US property becomes foreign owned. There are many more costs which will be exposed. The visa damage is enormous and unsustainable. If these visa programs continue ultimately our government and economy will collapse.

CALCULATING US ECONOMIC LOSSES FROM OFFSHORING

Replacing Americans with offshore foreign workers is even worse than the visas. When Sam is displaced by an offshore foreign worker it impacts all the people in the US who would have sold products and services to Sam such as: the restaurants where he eats, the grocery stores where he shops ...

The offshore foreign worker would pay no US taxes, and would spend no money in the US.

Economic Damage From Offshoring Sam's Job
No Taxes Collected and No Money Circulated

	Group A	Group B	Group C	Group D	Group E	Totals
Income Circulated	$0	$0				$0
State Tax	$0					$0
Federal Tax	$0					$0
After Tax Income to Recycle	$0					

All $102,000 in taxes Sam would have generated are lost. And, the full $131,000 Sam would have generated by spending money circulated in our economy are lost. So the overall loss to the US from Sam losing a job to an offshore worker is the full $233,000 (and that estimate is for just one job loss).

This economic model shows the criticality of keeping Americans employed to both the US government and the US economy. The $60,000 in "cost savings" from replacing Sam with a "cheaper" $20,000 offshore worker is a deceptive illusion.

When Sam's IT job is lost approximately two support jobs are also lost. On a larger scale this phenomenon can be observed when a factory in a small town closes. It is not just the factory workers who loose jobs. The whole town suffers; from grocery stores, to clothing stores, to home builders, and other businesses.

The following graphic provides a visual to help grasp the damage caused by transferring American jobs to foreign workers. Offshoring literally flat lines our government and economy.

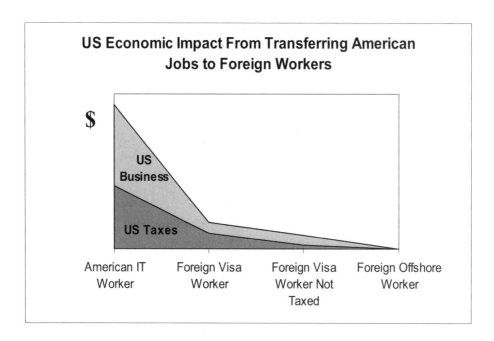

The next question is how many American jobs have been offshored and how big are the projections for offshoring? Surprisingly our government has not been tracking the number of these job losses. Offshoring accelerated dramatically after the dotcom crash. If the current number is around 3 million, then $233,000 * 3 million would be a yearly economic and tax loss of about $699 billion.

Multiple sources were projecting that 14 million US white collar jobs were at risk of being offshored. If offshoring is not stopped and 14 million US jobs are offshored, then $233,000 * 14 million would result in future US economic and tax losses of about $3.3 Trillion per year. This is a big bite out of the annual $14.4 trillion GDP for the entire US. Note that these are the high paying jobs. The financial loss of one $80,000 per year job is equivalent to losing four $20,000 per year jobs.

Offshoring is even more damaging to our economy than the effect of foreign visa workers. This offshoring damage is enormous and unsustainable. If the offshoring of American high tech jobs continues our government and economy will soon collapse.

Critics will argue that Sam can find another job which will offset some of the loss. However, job searches are taking longer and longer as the number of American jobs taken by foreign workers grow. Also, many Americans are forced to take jobs for which they are overqualified and paid significantly lower wages and less medical insurance. The important point is that this economic model focuses on the impact for each individual job taken. Once a foreign worker takes the job, displaced Americans rarely are given the opportunity to reclaim the job.

This Economic Circulation Model™ is a useful tool that provides a systematic method that disproves the cost savings claims, and shows how replacing Americans with foreign workers is devastating Americans, our economy and our government. The above projections focused on just high tech job losses. The same economic model can be used to estimate the costs of other American job losses. For example, manufacturing jobs have been transferred at alarming rates as have business processes (BPO) jobs such as customer support, insurance claims processing, and more.

Chapter 4

Americans Taxed To Educate

Competition

Our Government taxed American Citizens to fund educating foreign workers who took their jobs.

Where did all these foreign visa workers taking US citizens' high tech jobs come from? We educated them in our universities. According to a September 30, 2004, "War Outsourcing and Debt Delusion Rules," by Paul Craig Roberts, *US universities had educated enough people from India and China to take every high tech job American corporations needed.* [255] Foreign student graduates took entry level high tech job opportunities away from young Americans, and as they gained work experience, they "moved up the value chain" taking high tech and management jobs from experienced American workers.

Americans were taxed to subsidize the education of millions of foreign students when many could not afford to send their own kids to college. [230] US colleges are subsidized by taxpayers, because tuition and other bills paid by students do not usually cover the full costs. For example, in 2002, it was estimated that Americans subsidized students attending public universities on average $9,200 per student. An estimated 275,000 foreign students in public funded US universities drained $2.5 billion that year from American taxpayers. [230] However, the actual cost is much higher because most foreign students do not have the money to pay for their tuition, room and board, and more. The National Center for Education Statistics reported that 59% of all foreign graduate students got financial assistance. Even more significant 40% received grants that they do not have to repay. [252] [143] According to an online advice sheet published by a professor at the University of California, *a foreign graduate student in a 4-6 year PhD program costs about $120,000 to $220,000 in grant money.* [549] While Americans are taxed to fund foreign students, many foreign students are exempt from paying US taxes. For example one study reported that, "Students from India are given an exemption from paying taxes ..." [143]

And furthermore, Americans were even taxed to recruit foreign students. The US State Department set up over 450 centers in foreign countries to recruit foreign students, and it funds EducationUSA which provides information on how to get visas, and how to apply for financial aid. [477] According to an April 2005, newsletter, our US National Science Foundation encouraged US universities to recruit foreign graduate students. [186]

ARE FOREIGN STUDENTS GOOD FOR AMERICA?

Are foreign students good for America? Not according to an evaluation by George Borjas who in June 2002 wrote two articles, "Rethinking Foreign Students— A Question of National Interest" [230] and "An Evaluation of the Foreign Student Program." He found that the foreign student visa program was "riddled with corruption" and "ineptly run." [254]Proponents of massive student visa programs claim that it benefits the US by creating alliances with foreign countries. Yet there does not appear to be much evidence to support this claim. Foreign students take one out of every twenty openings in American colleges and universities. They take seats that should go to Americans. From 1955 to 2004 foreign student enrollment in US colleges climbed 1,572%. Foreign students in this volume pose a major economic drain and national security risk to America. [252] Another dramatic jump in foreign student enrollment occurred in 2005, dominated by Asians who took 58% of these student visas. [531] From 1990 to 2004, the number of foreign born computer scientists and mathematicians educated in US universities almost doubled. [221] This dramatic increase traces back to the 1990 H-1B visa legislation.

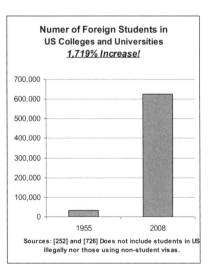

Numer of Foreign Students in US Colleges and Universities
1,719% Increase!

Sources: [252] and [726] Does not include students in US illegally nor those using non-student visas.

In 2008, a record 623,805 foreign students were enrolled in US colleges. The increase was credited to efforts by our government and universities to recruit foreign students. An immigration researcher challenged the claimed financial benefits and found that the costs of educating foreign students are understated. He reported that US universities provide financial aid to 90.7% of foreign graduate students and only 64% of American graduate students. He warned that foreign students depressed wages and discouraged Americans from pursuing graduate studies in certain fields. [726]

THE US GOVERNMENT APPROVED EXCESSIVE VISAS

To qualify for a student visa a foreigner must be accepted by an INS-approved school. The INS approved 73,000 schools! In addition to the expected universities, the list includes beauty schools, English language schools, acupuncture schools, etcetera. There was not enough oversight to ensure against visa fraud. [230] The INS did not control the number of foreign students flooding into the United States, nor did it know how many and what type of students were admitted. [252]

Our government approved multiple types of student visas. *The F1 visa is a temporary non-immigrant visa (NIV) granted to enroll fulltime in academic or language programs. They were required by law to exit the U.S. within 60 days of completing their studies.* The M1 visa is a temporary NIV granted for foreign students to attend trade and vocational schools. It is valid for only one year then they must return to their country. The J1 visa is a temporary non-immigrant exchange visitor visa that is used by students who seek academic training in the US that is "not available in their home country." The J1 admits students in secondary and university programs, professors, research students, teachers, physicians, and more. Recipients of the J1 visas are required to return to their country for at least two years prior to applying for a permanent residence visa to live in the U.S. However, many obtained waivers. [611] [612] [613] Who was granting all these visas and waivers?

WHY OUR UNIVERSITIES SEEK FOREIGN GRADUATE STUDENTS

US universities, profit in the short term, by displacing experienced Americans with H-1Bs because it increases the demand for high tech classes [224] [47] and by using low cost foreign graduate students to teach undergraduate classes. Additionally, outsourcing firms provided financial incentives. For example, the founder of a consulting company set up a program with the Dean of George Mason University that offered scholarships, housing allowances, and paid internships for students from India. [256]

Americans should know that *the biggest financial incentive to recruit foreign students came from US government taxpayer financed research money.* According to Dr. Norman Matloff, the science and engineering reputation of a US university is based on how much research money it is awarded, particularly from the US government. The research money is mostly used to pay graduate students to conduct research. To get the money, US universities need to get graduate students. Apparently there is no requirement that students doing government funded research are US citizens. The US overproduced PhDs, yet US universities still recruited foreign graduate students to get more US taxpayer funded research money. [186]

WHO'S A MINORITY?

American affirmative action goals were implemented to help descendants of Native American tribes and of slaves who were historically disadvantaged American minorities. US universities set affirmative action goals because these American minorities were demographically underrepresented. For example, a group that comprises approximately 10% of US citizens demographically would be underrepresented if that group had less than 10% of the seats in our colleges. US university administrators used non-citizen, non-immigrant foreign born students to claim affirmative action goals: "these foreign graduate students are particularly attractive to universities when they can use them to meet affirmative action goals." [252]

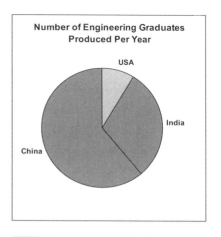

Number of Engineering Graduates Produced Per Year

USA

India

China

Consider the following statistics to understand the absurdity of counting students from China and India as minorities. In 2008, it was estimated that China produced 600,000 engineers per year, India 350,000 per year and the United States only 70,000 per year. [687]

In 2005, it was estimated that China produced 50,000 computer scientists, India 68,000, and the United States 30,000 annually. [766] [161] [484]

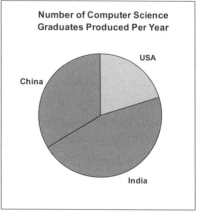

Number of Computer Science Graduates Produced Per Year

USA

China

India

Asians are not underrepresented in our universities. Demographically it would be expected that Asians would represent about 3% of our college students. Yet the University of California, Berkeley undergraduate program was 40% Asian in 2007. [627]

Americans are being warned that we may lose our technology leadership to Asia, because Asia is producing more engineers, programmers and other high tech graduates than the United States. So why are critical educational opportunities in our universities going to foreign students? [264] (Some people assert that China and India inflate their numbers by counting people with certificates not just four year degrees. However, even if the estimates from China and India are inflated, it appears they are producing significantly more than the US.)

In 2004, India, China, and Russia each produced more engineering bachelor degrees than the United States. [301] In a September 2004 interview on the Charlie Rose Show, India's Prime Minister Manmohan Singh claimed India produced around 250,000 engineers a year which combined with India's low wages gave India a unique competitive advantage against the United States. [422] How ironic for American universities to categorize students and faculty from China and India as minorities when in the global community people from China and India outnumber US citizens approximately 5 fold each. [252]

DANGEROUS FOREIGN TAKEOVER OF US GRADUATE SCHOOLS

Working on federally funded research educates the next generation of technology workers. [170] Such jobs should go to educate US citizens, not to educate people that may one day pose a threat to the US economically and/or militarily. US universities seek more US taxpayer money to fund research; however, the research they want funded is largely done by foreign graduate students and foreign born professors. The media has done little to inform Americans of this dangerous foreign takeover. [44]

Between 1985 through 1996, foreign students from China, India and Taiwan combined took 62% of the total science and engineering doctoral degrees awarded by US universities. Universities in California awarded engineering degrees to Asians at more than double the rate of other US universities. [372] For a group that comprises about 3% of our population to take over half of the doctoral degrees in US graduate schools shows something is highly askew. In 2001, foreign students dominated US graduate schools taking 60.4% of the computer engineering master's degrees, 68.9% of computer science master's degrees, and 51.8% of the dual computer science/engineering master's degrees. [363] In 2001, US universities granted 37,000 doctoral degrees in electrical engineering, 54% of these graduate degrees went to foreign students. [226] [770] Also in 2005, China increased the number of its graduate students attending US universities by 20% reaching 62,582 student visas. And, in 2005, India increased the number of graduate students sent to study in US universities by 32% to take 76,503 student visas. [531]

Asians are more than 1500% overrepresented in American university high tech doctoral programs. These US doctoral programs are the prime source for producing our college professors who define our college curriculum, oversee research, and act as expert advisors to our government and business leaders. Either Asians are racially superior as some argue, or something very sinister is going on in US college admissions and financial aid. The racial superiority argument is not credible given that the US for decades was technologically advanced far beyond China and India. In the 1970's when foreign students from Asia began to flood into US universities, the United States was the undisputed world leader in software and computer information systems. In contrast, both India and China were notorious for pirating US software and technology.

A November 2005, report by the Council of Graduate Schools (CGS), an organization of 450 US educational institutions, claimed that the enrollment of foreign students in US graduate schools increased in 2005. According to CGS it is imperative that the US have foreign students to do the research to keep the US globally competitive. [477] If it were true that foreign students doing research made the United States globally competitive, then the US technology leadership would have been growing by leaps and bounds given the vast number of foreign graduate students in our universities. However, just the opposite was occurring. *The foreign nations supplying these foreign students were rapidly acquiring US technology which is more indicative of foreign spying or "knowledge transfer."*

In 2006, the US government was relying more on university based research. Many US government agencies channeled taxpayer funded research money to universities including the Defense Advanced Research Projects Agency (DARPA), and the National Science Foundation (NFS). Your taxpayer dollars are funding military research on security, communications, biological, decision support systems, and more. For example, according to an article titled, "Military R&D 101," US university research labs were working to create humanoid robots with muscles 100 times stronger than humans. [621] These robots are being developed to fight and would be very dangerous if the technology was obtained by a foreign government. Universities are also conducting R&D for military aeronautics research, advanced communications research, and satellite surveillance systems. US universities argued that foreign student graduates should stay in the US because sending them back to their own country would create economic and security threats. So if they knew this education was dangerous, why were they recruiting foreign students?

PROFESSORS WITH FOREIGN AGENDAS

US Universities have a responsibility to hire educators who want Americans to learn, to excel and to prosper. The demographics of our professors ought to match the demographics of our citizens. Yet, the demographics of many US universities' faculties are vastly different. Because most colleges require professors to have a PhD, the foreign takeover of our graduate schools paved the way for the foreign takeover of our universities. When foreign students graduated with PhDs in our universities, many used their degrees to obtain US university faculty positions.

Often foreign born professors are difficult for Americans to understand. And, some foreign born professors promoting globalization may discourage Americans from pursuing technology degrees. When US citizens protest "globalization" the mantra of the foreign born professors is, "there is no turning back". They want Americans to think that outsourcing cannot be stopped. When of course not only can it be stopped, it must be stopped. Globalization has enriched a few greedy men to the detriment of people around the world.

Foreign born professors can abuse their faculty positions to increase student recruitment from their country of origin. As faculty members they influence the distribution of US taxpayer funded research work by selecting who works on advanced university research projects and most importantly who is recognized for the research and any patents awarded. The academic credentials, grades, degrees and references they confer determine who is considered the best and brightest and who gets hired in US management and high tech jobs. Most US business and government executives rely on college records for hiring high tech workers, because they lack the technical knowledge to compare potential job candidates. [45]

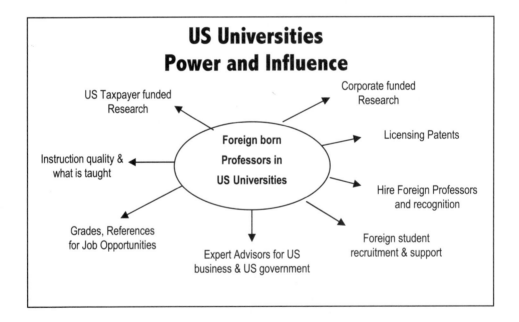

US University faculty jobs gave foreign born professors a platform for creating studies to promote visa worker programs, outsourcing, and offshoring. US faculty positions also position them to select which business partners will benefit from turning American taxpayer funded university research discoveries and patents into products.

FINANCIAL AID MISAPPROPRIATED

Some US university administrators misappropriated financial aid that was meant for US citizens and channeled this money to foreign students. They deprived many deserving young Americans of the opportunity to attend college which in turn denied them career opportunities. For example, one article reported that in October 1997, the United States government was investigating allegations that *administrators at a college awarded grants to foreign students who were not qualified and redirected federal money meant for American students to foreign students instead.* [252] How many other colleges did this? In June 1998, a group of Americans challenged billing the US government millions of dollars for foreign student graduate school tuition waivers that were used to help foreign PhD students get jobs in top university research programs. [252] This is one of many reasons foreign students outnumber Americans in our graduate schools. Americans had to pay tuition; while many foreign students attend tuition free by taking money from American taxpayers to which they are not entitled.

US universities also misappropriated alumni contributions and American corporate matching funds to pay for foreign student tuition, housing, H-1B visa workshops and even social networking activities. During the 2009 recession US universities continued calling American alumni to raise funds for graduate programs where much of the money sought was to benefit foreign students who would compete against Americans for jobs. US Universities should be required to disclose to alumni how much money they channeled to foreign students. Alumni displaced by H-1Bs especially have a right to know.

In 2007, foreign students from India arrived with almost no resources yet they planned multi-year stays attending US universities and living in the United States. So who is paying for their education? How can they afford to attend an American college when so many Americans cannot? They were part of a new trend where students from India were coming to the United States to obtain high tech training, so that they could return to India to fill offshored American jobs. India had 75,000 students studying in the United States. NC State was a school of choice, because it offered a graduate degree in computer networking. During the 2006-2007 school year, 450 people from India were attending NC State, and they expected to reach almost 800 the next school year. They kept a low profile and clustered together for living and socializing and formed a support group called Maitri. There were so many students from India that one Indian said that he thought Americans felt out of place in NC State engineering classes. [626]

In 2008, China had 67,723 students studying in the United States, with 557 of these students attending Duke University which is financially out of reach for most Americans. In April 27, 2008, a freshman student from China with "full financial aid" admitted that it was, "Not my academic records" that got her into Duke. When she became embroiled in a campus controversy over Tibet, "she lectured Chinese students in English about being more tolerant and open to dialogue with the pro-Tibet side." However, in a letter to the Duke Chinese Students and Scholars Association she wrote in Chinese that she was not for Tibet's independence and: "The Americans want to roast us in hot coals ... Be sure not to let them take advantage or show off their cleverness." [693] If she is anti-American why is she in our country, and why are we educating her? What is the source of her financial aid?

US TAXPAYERS PAID RECORD LEVELS OF STUDENT AID

The number of "minority" students applying to US colleges skyrocketed due to the flood of foreign students, amnesty, chain immigration, and growing numbers of illegal aliens. As Americans lost high paying jobs to foreign visa workers and offshoring, their children needed financial aid to attend college. The dual negative impact of depressing American wages while at the same time increasing the number of student "minorities" meant that *even though American taxpayers paid a record $105 billion in student aid in 2002, the number of students applying for aid dramatically increased resulting in a decrease in the amount of aid received per student.* For example, taxpayers paid $11.7 billion in 2002 for Pell grants, but the money was divided among 4.8 million students. Which meant the average Pell grant received was only $2,421. [264] In April 2009, Congressman Tom Tancredo was invited to UNC by a chapter of Youth for Western Civilization. He was threatened and called a racist and not allowed to speak by a group of protestors, because he opposed providing instate tuition discounts to "undocumented immigrants." [740] The report never revealed how many of the protestors were foreign. Nor did it address the cost to US taxpayers of providing instate tuition discounts to non-citizens.

US CITIZENS' COLLEGE COSTS SOARED

The growing number of foreign students caused Americans' college costs to skyrocket. Compounding the problem, when foreign students graduated they took Americans' jobs and depressed Americans' wages which decreased the taxes collected by our state governments. Growing state deficits in turn forced states to cut back on the money they gave to state universities. To offset this decline in state financing, US colleges increased student tuition costs even higher. [264]

American college costs increased much faster than general inflation. [263] From the mid 1980's to 2000, United States college costs grew at almost 3 times the rate of the median family income. A 2004 independent investigation of college costs titled, "U.S. Flunks Higher Education Affordability" compared average family income with net college costs state by state. For example, New Hampshire college costs ran 32% of average family income contrasted with 23% the prior decade. [262] Many Americans did not have the $60,000 - $120,000 needed to pay for their child's four years of college. In 2004, the United States Department of Education reported that 170,000 qualified students could not even afford the cost of a community college. [264]

Squeezed by rising college costs desperate American parents resorted to home equity loans to finance their children's college. This precarious financial position of putting the family home up as collateral for a college loan created substantial stress on young Americans attending college. It is hard for students to focus on studies when worrying about family financial problems and when working one or more jobs in addition to taking college classes. *Even with help from their families, and working summer jobs the average American college student had to take out loans and work 23 hours a week to pay for college. In 2004, on average they graduated owing $17,000 in student loans.* [264]

It got worse, a May 2009 article, "College Graduates Struggle to Repay Student Loans," reported that many students had to resort to both federal and private loans. *From 1998 to 2009 the amount of federal student loans doubled to $85 billion, and private loans tripled.* About two thirds of young Americans graduated burdened with big college loans to repay. They could not find jobs in the area they studied because of visa workers and offshoring. During the economic crisis their relatives could not help them. They could not buy a home. They could not even get bankruptcy relief, because student loans were not eligible. Ironically people who recklessly ran up credit card debt or even gambling debt could get bankruptcy relief—but not young Americans who invested in getting an education and owed student loans. [743]

MANY STUDENTS IN ASIA GET A FREE EDUCATION

Students in India and China enjoy a distinct advantage over American students, because they can focus on studies and not worry about college expenses. It costs about $3,000 per student per year to attend the Indian Institute of Technology (IIT) and the government of India picks up the tab. [303] India's diaspora living in the United States also made major contributions to fund educating students in India. (See Indian "Mafia" in the United States) By 2002, the Chinese government had paid to educate huge numbers of computer information technology (IT) workers. [774] Moreover, executives in US corporations used corporate money to fund educating foreign students in China and India in preparation for offshoring American jobs.

SHOULD QUALIFIED AMERICANS GET A FREE EDUCATION?

According to a 2006 article, "Should H-1B Employers Pay for U.S. Students' Degrees?" The Programmers Guild wanted the US government to increase US employers' H-1B fees to $5,000 per H-1B per year. The fees would fund educating Americans in programming and engineering areas companies claimed the US had shortages. Industry lobby groups objected saying that since the H-1B program began they had paid over $1 billion in H-1B fees to provide scholarships and training for Americans. However if it costs $60,000 for a four year degree, $1 billion would have only paid to educate less than 16,000 Americans over the sixteen years the H-1B program had been operating. [741]

WHITE AMERICANS DISCRIMINATED AGAINST

The "traditional" students (white Americans) were discriminated against in US college admissions in favor of "non-traditional students" (any race but white). Moreover, "traditional" students were discriminated against financially as the "non-traditional students" were heavily financially subsidized. The children of non-white new immigrants and people granted amnesty get preferential educational opportunities.

Some American colleges set aside money for foreign students, and some students had expenses paid by foreign governments and other organizations that favored foreign students. Many "non-traditional" students got a free college education not based on merit, but rather on "minority" status (i.e. race). Bottom line, people should not be discriminated against, because they have white skin. The descendents of the majority of American soldiers who fought and died for this country, and the scientists, inventors, farmers, teachers, and other Americans who built America are discriminated against in our universities. Can you imagine Chinese universities giving preferential admissions and financial support favoring non-Chinese students? Or, can you imagine Indian universities giving preferential admissions and financial support favoring non-Indians? Is China educating 70,000+ students from India and vise versa?

President Bush requested $11 million for the 2003 budget to fund scholarships to encourage US citizens to become computer experts for protecting the US from cyber attacks. These scholarships were to be administered by the National Science Foundation and the Office of Personnel Management. [208] Do the demographics of the students receiving the technology scholarships reflect the demographics US citizens?

AMERICAN GRADUATES DENIED JOB OPPORTUNITIES

Corporate executives hired foreign graduates and claimed it was justified, because America invested in their education, and because if the foreign students returned to their country they would compete against America. They denied job opportunities to young Americans graduating with college degrees in science and engineering. [47] [88] Without entry level high tech job experience young Americans will not develop the skills necessary to design the computer systems of the future. [255] These entry level jobs are the foundation jobs, and the foreign governments grabbing these jobs from Americans know it. The most critical job fields during war today are computer programming, microprocessor chips, communications, and biotechnology. By channeling these jobs to foreigners, executives in American corporations are endangering US national security. It is vital that these jobs go to US citizens loyal to the United States. Because US corporations hired several hundred thousand foreign workers, US citizens who graduated in 2003, faced a dismal job market. [63]

By 2005, because of job losses to foreign workers, US citizens in the engineering fields were advising their children not to pursue engineering degrees. In 2008, the job market was so bad, and American students were so burdened with debt that after graduating from college 48% had to move back in to live with their parents. Because of high college costs, 42% owed student loans of $25,000+, and 33% owed more than $5,000 to credit card companies. When they found a job the pay was often less than expected, 42% of employers planned to offer new college graduates less than $30,000 per year. [704]

DANGEROUS DROP IN AMERICAN ENROLLMENTS

The 1990 H-1B legislation that allowed foreign workers to flood the US market caused dramatic drops in the enrollments of young Americans into engineering and computer science degree programs. The combination of depressed wages and the lack of job opportunities discouraged young Americans from pursing high tech degrees.

The first big drop in undergraduate electronic engineering degrees occurred in 1995. In 2001, the US experienced a steep decline in the number of undergraduate students enrolling in computer science programs. This correlates with the increased offshoring of high tech US jobs following the dotcom crash.

The decline continued with another dramatic drop in the number of Americans enrolled in computer science programs in 2004. A 2004 National Science Board (NSB) report found that *the US had dangerously dropped in the proportion of 18 to 24 year olds pursing degrees in engineering and natural science. While the US was 3rd in the world in 1975, by 2004 we had fallen to 17th.* [221] A 2004 study reported that young Americans had the qualifications and were prepared for college. So excessive costs, not the quality and availability of qualified American students were the reason for declining enrollments of US citizens. [261]

Again in 2005, the US experienced dramatic drops in the number of Americans enrolling in science and other technology degree programs. In 2005, over 400,000

American engineers had been laid off. During that same period, executives persuaded Congress to expand the H-1B program. American students are too bright to pursue a degree in a profession where the wages have been depressed by foreign workers and executives are channeling the jobs to foreign graduates. [45] [250] [615] [255] [81]

According to a March 2007, article titled "Where are the Programmers?" the US was experiencing a very low interest in computer science studies at a time when solutions were needed for highly complex parallel programming for multi-core processors. [619]

DISINCENTIVES FOR AMERICAN TO PURSUE PHDS

Many US citizens qualified to enter US graduate school programs choose not to do so, because doing research for $16,000 a year compared to getting a job in industry does not make financial sense. [186] Foreign students artificially depressed the pay which means most US citizens lose money if they pursue a PhD. Additionally, many US citizens are saddled with a large undergraduate college debt to repay, so they cannot afford to attend graduate school. In contrast, many of the foreign students got a free undergraduate college education. Moreover, many US corporations do not offer good job opportunities to Americans with advanced degrees, so there is little incentive for Americans to invest their time and money in graduate programs. On the other hand, foreign graduate students eager to stay in the US and who do not have the pressure of repaying massive college debt are more likely to pursue PhDs. And, they have greater jobs opportunities, because executives know they will work cheaper and longer hours to stay in the United States.

STUDENT VISAS DOORWAY FOR ILLEGAL IMMIGRATION

US universities were misused as a doorway for illegal immigration. [41] To obtain approval for a visa to study in America, foreign students had to sign a written agreement that legally bound them to return to their country of origin after completing their studies. [230] A US consular official could not approve a foreign student visa application if there was any reason to suspect the student would attempt to stay in the United States. [252] However, "many foreigners want to study in the U.S. precisely because a student visa buys them a ticket into the country." [230] It is a very important point to remember each time you read that someone entered the United States using a student visa that it was illegal to misuse student visas to attempt to immigrate to the United States. If they stayed after their visa expired they became illegal aliens.

When the US government granted amnesty to 3 million illegal aliens in 1986, almost 10% of the people receiving amnesty had entered the US using student visas then stayed illegally after their visa expired. [230] The INS granted 65,000 foreign student visas in 1971, and kept increasing the number year after year despite knowledge that foreign students were staying in the United States illegally after their visas expired. From 1971 to 1991, the US granted more than 3 million foreign student visas. Although these students were not supposed to seek employment in the United States 393,000 managed to obtain green cards (permanent-residence visas). Approximately 87% remained in the US illegally. [230] Another study found that 80% of science and engineering doctoral students from China and India who obtained student visas from 1988 to 1996 planned to stay in the US. Half of these foreign students claimed they already had job offers that would enable them to stay.

Of the 1990-1991 doctoral recipients, 79% of the doctoral recipients from India were still in the US, and 88% of the Chinese were still in the US. [249] How many of these got H-1B visas? The Institute for International Education reported that for the 1993-1994 school year over 575,500 foreign students were in the US. However, this was underreporting the total because it did not include foreign students in the US illegally, nor did it include foreign students who entered the US using other types of visas. [252]

For many years China sent the most foreign students to study in the United States. In 1999 alone, over 50,000 visas were granted to students from China. [252] By some estimates, 99% of students from China tried to stay illegally in the US instead of returning to China. It was so bad that one former US official who did not want to be identified commented that: "An honest evaluation would virtually end (student) visa issuance (to Chinese applicants)" [246] In July 2000, it was estimated that 90% of India's IIT graduates headed to the US. [30] According to the 2000 census 38% of workers in the US with Science and Engineering (S&E) doctoral degrees were foreign born, 29% of workers with S&E master's degrees were foreign born, and 17% of workers with bachelors degrees were foreign born. [221]

The failure of the US government to enforce immigration laws emboldened these foreign students. They formed the National Association of Foreign Student Advisors (NAFSA) lobby to pressure our Congress to grant them US citizenship. By 2001, more than half of the students in US university computer science and engineering graduate programs were foreign born. [221] In 2001, India surpassed China in the

India arrests foreign students who overstay. According to an article titled, "Hyderabad Police Arrest 25 Foreign Students for Overstaying." The students arrested were Ethiopians, Somalians and Djiboutian. [716] Does India discriminate based on race and nationality?

number of US student visas. By 2002, India had more than doubled the number of students it had sent to the US in 1993. In 2002 China sent 64,765 foreign students to US universities and colleges, and India sent a record setting 74,603. The majority of these students sought employment in Silicon Valley. [321]

STUDENT VISA APPLICATION FRAUD

According to a January 17, 2010, news announcement in India's www.telugudreams.com US consular officials investigated a student visa applicant in India who submitted documents showing high scores on the TOEFL certifying high level English skills, yet during the interview the applicant was unable to answer basic questions in English. The applicant admitted to buying fraudulent documents. The report exposed that business centers in India were selling high priced "forged academic degrees," and "the US government believes that any funds collected ... for fraudulent documents may represent proceeds of a crime which may be sizable..." [754]

This student visa fraud is big business that has been going on for many years. A 2000 report by *www.americanvisas.com* reported that: "So prized are U.S. student visas that the deceptions used to acquire them can be elaborate ... Because visa officers conduct as many as 200 interviews per day, they've no time to verify documents or confirm stories." [246]

According to a March 2006, article "Education: Why Everyone Cheats Now," universities in Asia posted the answers to the English language test relied upon by American universities as the basis for foreign student admissions. [634] No wonder we have so many foreign students in American colleges. If someone cheated to get admitted to college, they can be expected to cheat to get a degree. Scores on SAT exams are used for awarding college admissions and scholarships. The Internet and small cameras, and other devices were used to cheat on tests such as the SAT. One standardized exam had to stagger test times and change questions each time the test was administered, because students taking the tests in California were photographing the test and posting it on the web to help students in Hong Kong cheat. [634]

According to a June 17, 2002, *National Review* article, "Rethinking Foreign Students, A Question of National Interest," by George J Borjas the demand in Asia for US student visas was so strong that falsifying visa applications became big business. The article reported that in China "consulting" firms charged $10,000 to supply false reference letters, *fake documents showing economic support*, and even an actor for the required interview at the US consular office. And it reported that in India the Foreign Studies Service Bureau guaranteed a US student visa for only about $800. [230] When foreign students lied about having economic support—guess who picked up the tab.

DRAMATIC RISE IN CHEATING

Our culture is being morphed from a culture that values honesty, fair play, and integrity into a culture of lying, cheating and stealing. Seeing corrupt executives in power is teaching American youth that working hard and being creative just makes you a target for exploitation. The moral fabric of our society is being torn apart. Many students now believe you have to cheat to be successful. [634]

Cheating in our schools is on the rise: "Large-scale cheating ... has hit US Campuses in recent years." [628] An analysis of cheating found that in 1963 about 26% of students cheated, in 1993 the percentage more than doubled reaching 56%, and by 2007 over 70% of students were cheating. [634]

According to national surveys, "cheating is widespread among graduate students." [635] Imagine a student with a thick college textbook and 50 pages of notes with no idea of what questions will be on the exam, competing against someone who has an illegal copy of the exam and got help finding the answers. Unchecked cheating allows cheaters to rise to the top. The smartest student may well be the one with the lowest score who did not cheat.

America is going through a catastrophic shift in culture that is shaking the very foundation of trust essential to the successful functioning of our schools, government, and stock market. When many students cheat, it puts pressure on other students to cheat to remain competitive. Apparently cheaters are more likely to be admitted to our universities, and cheaters are more likely to be promoted to management, and cheaters are more likely to get rich investing in our stock market. Yet, no one wants a surgeon that cheated his way through medical school. No one wants to ride in an airplane designed by an engineer who cheated his way through engineering school. No one wants to make investments based on financial reports prepared by someone who cheated to get an MBA.

According to March 27, 2006, *Newsweek International* article titled, "Education: Why Everyone Cheats Now," by Emily Flynn Vencat, technology has made cheating easier. For example, students can buy essays on the web. Some of this cultural shift may be because of the growing number of foreign students. According to the article cheating on university entrance exams was common in India and China. It claimed that entrance exams to attend universities in India were stolen then sold to students. Pre-medical exams sold as high as $15,000. In China it claimed that gangs supply "look-alikes" to take Chinese university entrance exams for a fee. [634] The article claimed that overcrowding of our labor pool "is the real culprit" driving the increased cheating. More college students are competing for a limited number of jobs. Almost one third of Americans now have college degrees. [634]

The flood of foreign students into our universities, and job markets increased the pressure to cheat. This could get much worse because China's university student enrollments from 1998 to 2005 increased 300% soaring to 16 million. Many of these students may enter US graduate schools then look for work in America, or take offshored American jobs.

The cheating problem is widespread. For example, in April 30, 2007, article, "Duke Business School Hit by Cheating Scandal," on *tmcnet.com* reported that a professor noticed some students' answers on a take home exam were suspiciously similar. This triggered an investigation that caught thirty-four MBA graduate students in a network of cheating. Students had obtained unauthorized access to the files containing the test answers, made copies of the answers, then distributed the answers and collaborated with other students to find answers and cheat on the test. This violated the Duke Honor Code that requires students to be honest and trustworthy. The MBA program involved had 40% foreign students. The article acknowledged that some of the cheaters were foreign students but did not provide details. This MBA program costs about $60,000 per year. [628] Who was paying?

Ohio University also had a cheating scandal where over 20 mechanical engineering graduate students cheated on their master's thesis. This triggered a broader investigation that resulted in students being dismissed and a master's degree revoked. The investigation was ongoing. [635] Because of ethnic network collaboration, some groups of foreign students who cheat have a big advantage over American students who cheat.

LOWERING EDUCATION QUALITY

Americans are paying more for college, yet the quality of education their children receive is declining. Many foreign graduate students obtain jobs as teaching assistants, despite American college students' complaints that they provide poor quality instruction. Comparing grades and test scores of Americans taught by foreign assistants to those taught by US citizen professors supports their complaints of inferior instruction. [230]

Recall that many foreign graduate students used fake credentials to obtain their visas—therefore many are not qualified to teach. Moreover, since the majority of foreign graduate students planned to seek employment in the US in violation of their visas, *they had an inherent conflict of interest to be teaching the children of US citizens.*

THE GOOD NEWS

Outsourcing promoters warn that the US only produced 70,000 engineering graduates in 2004 well below the numbers produced in China and India. This sounds bad until you discover that from January 2001-2006 the US only created 70,000 engineering jobs. [504]

While the number of engineering graduates produced by foreign universities sounds daunting, Americans should not lose heart because engineering skills are not a numbers game. What we need are a few outstanding inventors. Most of our greatest inventors never had PhDs. [491]

Finally, creating a glut of engineers and scientists does not encourage inventiveness, but rather hinders it as engineers and scientists vie for a limited number of jobs and worry about job security. Over and over again US citizens have proven that they have fantastic invention skills. What is needed is to get US citizens in US R&D labs, reward the inventors with recognition and job security, take appropriate measures to protect the intellectual property they invent, and the US will do wonders again. The US is capable of producing all the programmers and engineers that we need.

Chapter 5

Studies Mislead Congress

Prior to "globalization" university studies helped position the United States for success.

Now many studies are propaganda tools promoting visas, outsourcing and offshoring.

Our universities turned into propaganda machines when executives commissioned university studies to sell visa programs, outsourcing, and offshoring to our government. There was an "understanding that the outcome of the studies will be in industry's favor." [24] These studies persuaded the US Congress to pass the H-1B visa program and to repeatedly increase visa caps. It appears to be a conflict of interest because universities receive industry research funding, and cannot afford to alienate executives. Moreover, by supporting the claims of a high tech labor shortage, US universities could get more research money from Congress by flooding graduate school programs with foreign students from China and India. [494]

An April 8, 2004, article on *economictimes.indiatimes.com* titled, "US Professors: New Age Ambassadors for India Inc." explained how professors from India on the faculty of major US universities were working with India's outsourcing firms to generate studies promoting and defending outsourcing US jobs to India. According to the article, two of India's largest outsourcing companies, Infosys and Wipro, wanted to keep it "under wraps" that they were working with US professors to develop pro-outsourcing case studies. The goal was "that academicians will strike the right balance" in the outsourcing debate to, "help the Indian IT industry, against the ever increasing backlash." They also arranged travel to Bangalore because: "Welcoming academicians into their campus is the best bet for the Indian IT sector." [245]

OUTSOURCING = "FOOL'S GOLD"

It would be wrong to assume that all professors originating from India promoted outsourcing. An article titled, "Outsourcing: A Greater Threat Than Terrorism," by Paul Craig Roberts reviewed a book published in 2005, titled *Outsourcing America* by college professors Ron and Anil Hira. According to his review of the book, the authors called the expected savings "fool's gold," and poked holes in three pro-outsourcing studies: 1) They said the 2004 Global Insight Study done for ITAA was propaganda used to lobby for outsourcing, and that ITAA required reporters to write about the study without investigating the merits of the claims. 2) They criticized the Catherine Mann study as being overly optimistic, using flawed logic, and not understanding the strategic implications of outsourcing technology jobs. 3) Finally, they dismissed the McKinsey study as a lobbying tool to help sell outsourcing. [81]

Previously in 2004, Professor Ron Hira questioned the assumption that the outsourcing "cost savings" would be invested back in the United States. He thought it was more likely that the money would be invested in expanding offshore facilities or pocketed by executives. He also questioned the assumptions that America's lost jobs would be replaced by equal jobs, and that the US technological edge would not be lost. [129]

STUDIES CONCOCTED TO GET LEGISLATION PASSED

It is difficult to find US university professors willing to criticize the H-1B visa program, outsourcing, and offshoring because of the lure of money and the threat of personal attacks. Nonetheless, one critic is Dr. Norman Matloff, a Professor in the Department of Computer Science at the University of California, Davis. In April 21, 1998, Matloff presented his research findings to the US House Judiciary Committee Subcommittee on Immigration. His paper, "Debunking the Myth of a Desperate Software Labor Shortage," exposed how studies were concocted to support passing the H-1B visa legislation: "These lobbyists know very well how to play the political game. They know, for example, that politicians like to use academic 'studies' for cover." He explains: "Industry lobbyists know that they can count on academia to produce seemingly unbiased studies which in fact are designed from the outset to produce results supportive of industry's position." [24] In 2000, there were a series of articles published calling Matloff the "Scourge of Silicon Valley." Matloff warned that it is foolish to think that entry level programming jobs can be transferred to foreign workers and the US still retain our high level design jobs. [255]

In November 2004, Matloff wrote, "Globalization and the American IT Worker: Exporting IT jobs and importing IT workers not only harms U.S. IT workers, it also harms U.S. firms and the broader economy." [745] In 2005, Matloff wrote, "Offshoring: What Can Go Wrong?" "Distance, cultural differences, inexperienced programmers, and other obstacles might make you wish you'd kept that IT project at home." [746] Offshoring problems he identified ranged from intellectual property risks, to low quality, and more.

Defending American jobs made Matloff a target. For example, in an H-1B/L1/Offshoring e-newsletter Matloff wrote that the National Association of Foreign Student Advisors (NAFSA) lobby "is one of the most aggressive lobbying groups on immigration issues on Capitol Hill ... they once had the audacity to try to pressure me not to testify before Congress." [186] An even more threatening example, Arthur Hu set up a website titled, "Norman Matloff, the Hatchet Man of Asian Immigration." (Recall the H-1B was supposed to be a non-immigrant temporary visa.) On his website Hu criticizes Matloff and posts: information on how to contact Matloff, a list of who has quoted Matloff, and derisive comments such as "even the lowest Indian engineers is better that the huge proportion of whites who are not even engineers in the first place." He lashes out at Matloff writing: "Matloff convenient dismisses all evidence of Asian superiority over the general population..." He complained that Matloff criticized Asian networks because they "only hire their own"; and, that Matloff exposed how Asians had brought their elderly parents to the US then put them on SSI for Americans to support. Hu goes on to say Matloff's "report on immigrants in Silicon Valley is nothing but an academically veiled and vicious racist attack on what are the most disproportionately important ethnic groups in Silicon Valley, if not the entire US." [747] Matloff's wife is a Chinese immigrant. Matloff was attacked because he is an American who uncovered the truth, and stood up for fellow Americans.

"GROUNDBREAKING STUDY" OR PROPAGANDA?

AnnaLee Saxenian, Dean of the School of Information Management and Systems at the University of California Berkley, wrote: *Regional Advantage: Culture and Competition in Silicon Valley and Route 128.* (1994), *Silicon Valley's New Immigrant Entrepreneurs* (1999), and *Local and Global Networks of Immigrant Professionals in Silicon Valley* (2002). [330] She is frequently quoted by people promoting student visas, H-1B visas, outsourcing, and offshoring. For example, just before the dotcom crash a February 23, 2000, article, "Where Integrated Chips Means Indians, Chinese," quoted Saxenian's "groundbreaking study." [330] The title of the article is erroneous, because neither Indians nor Chinese invented the integrated chip for computers.

The "Silicon Valley's New Immigrant Entrepreneurs" working paper of May 2000, hyped the "superior educational attainment" of people from India and China working in Silicon Valley reporting that 55% of the workers from India held graduate degrees, 40% of the workers from China held graduate degrees, yet only 18% of their white counterparts held graduate degrees. [372] It failed to acknowledge that these racial differences were not due to racial superiority, but rather because people from China and India used US graduate schools to bypass US immigration controls, and because for most Americans advanced degrees rarely yielded better job opportunities.

Interestingly, it told how outsourcing American jobs got started: *"The pool of people that came to the US and went to school and then ended up often in places like Silicon Valley has paved the way for this outsourcing."* She explained that when foreign students chose to find jobs in the US they established "brain circulation" connections with their country of origin. [372] US citizens' protests of foreign born workers taking their jobs were dismissed claiming that foreign born scientists and engineers were creating jobs in the US by starting up new businesses. Supposedly immigrant entrepreneurs created economic wealth—that must explain the record California budget surplus—oops deficit. The math is interesting. If 150,000 jobs were created by these immigrants in Silicon Valley from 1975 to 1990, and during that same time period the foreign-born worker population more than doubled to 350,000, i.e. they took more jobs than they created. [372] This study quoted an immigrant named Satish Gupta, claiming that the immigrant networks are successful because of trust based on factors such as caste, mannerisms and culture. [372]

Saxenian explained that immigrants used their contacts and knowledge of Indian culture and institutions to establish the offshore outsourcing links between Silicon Valley in the US and India. [379] Saxenian lauded H-1Bs as "agents of global change" who circulated US technology discoveries to India and China. Despite all the hype by Saxenian, an examination of the immigrant startups revealed that most did not create breakthrough leading edge technologies. [329]

After the US economy was devastated by the dotcom crash Saxenian continued to promote hiring foreign workers and offshoring US jobs. Saxenian was listed as a speaker for a 2000 *The IndUS Entrepreneurs* (TiE) Conference that was held in Bangalore, India shortly after the dotcom crash plummeted the United States into an economic downturn. (TiE is sometimes referred to as the Indian "Mafia") In a September 2002 article, Saxenian advocated open environments where information flows "across traditional boundaries." [378] If she is advocating the flow of US technology secrets, that may involve breaking US intellectual property laws and may break other laws protecting national security and the US economy.

Saxenian protested when the US Department of Defense attempted to prevent foreign nationals from working on sensitive US defense research. She warned that without foreign nationals, there would not be enough high tech workers to staff defense projects. Nor, would the US have companies qualified to do defense work, because she asserted that every company in Silicon Valley had 10% to 40% foreign nationals as employees. [389]

Saxenian, while advocating foreign access to sensitive defense technology, has also advised and/or provided input to multiple US government agencies including the National Academy of Sciences, and National Research Council and the National

Science Foundation. [482] A truly groundbreaking study would be one that exposed how foreign nationals penetrated so deeply into American defense contractors.

"GLOBAL ADVANTAGE" OR PROPAGANDA?

Vivek Wadhwa entered the United States in 1980, co-founded TiE Carolinas (See also Indian "Mafia"), started two US software companies, and was teaching at Duke University. [685] In January 2007, he released a study titled "America's New Immigrant Entrepreneurs" which was "an expanded and updated version" of Saxenian's 1999 study. [685] According to Wadhwa, his students at Duke collaborated with AnnaLee Saxenian to produce the study that claimed foreign visa workers gave the US a "global advantage," created jobs and led our innovation. [632]

The same day the report was released a website named Indolink.com proclaimed this study "confirms and extends the earlier findings by AnnaLee Saxenian" that, "first generation Indian-Americans have become a significant driving force in the creation of new businesses and intellectual property in the U.S. since 1990." [685] Wadhwa is a first generation Indian-American, so how can anyone expect his study to be objective. While Wadhwa was the primary author, Ben Rissing a Research Scholar, and Gary Gereffi a Sociology professor also helped lead the research conducted by the Masters of Engineering Management program at the Pratt School of Engineering at Duke University. The Masters degree students credited for doing the research were Indian-Americans including: Ramakrishnan Balasubramanian, Pradeep Kamsali, Nishant Lingamneni, Niyanthi Reddy, and Batul Tambawalla. [685] If any non-Indian students contributed, they were not named in the article.

The threat to US competitiveness created by the "growing momentum of outsourcing critical research" was the reason given for the study. Wadhwa said that to "understand the sources of the U.S. global advantage" they decided to study the contribution of foreign students who stayed and worked in America. So it appears his students may be studying their parents and/or themselves. His conclusion: "After analyzing the data, my view is that America doesn't need more temporary workers it needs more immigrants." His advice that America should increase immigration "received worldwide attention and acclaim." [685] It is not surprising that people in other countries who want to immigrate to the United States would praise a study produced at a US university that claimed we need more immigration.

Wadhwa's 2007 study reported that from 1995 to 2005 25.3% of technology companies started in the United States had one or more foreign-born founders. By 2005, immigrant startups had $52 billion in sales and employed 450,000 workers. The vast majority of the startups were concentrated in software and services for manufacturing and research. [632] US manufacturing and research computer systems are a prime target for foreign espionage. The study claimed that people from India founded more high tech companies in the US from 1995-2005, than immigrants from Britain, China, Taiwan and Japan all totaled. Wadhwa *acknowledged that these foreign students/workers came from countries that were becoming a growing competitive threat to the United States.* Yet, he asserts that granting them permanent status will "likely lead to greater economic growth and create a greater intellectual property and competitive advantage." [632] However, to determine what is "likely" to happen, we should compare the competitive position and intellectual property status of the US to their countries of origin prior to 1970, when they began to flood our universities for high tech educational degrees. Prior to 1970, neither India nor China posed a competitive economic threat to the United States, because both these countries were many decades behind the United States in technology advances.

Wadhwa Received Excessive Media Coverage

Wadhwa was "featured in thousands of articles ... including The Wall Street Journal, Forbes Magazine, Washington Post, New York Times, U.S. News and World Report and Science Magazine." And he has received TV coverage on ABC, NBC, CNBC, CNN, and BBC. [686] Following are some media coverage stories done to support his 2007 new study.

January 3, 2007, *BusinessWeek* published his article titled, "Open Doors Wider for Skilled Immigrants." He argued that the US needed to "bring in more of the world's best and brightest" to slow the outsourcing of critical research which threatened US competitiveness. He did this study because earlier studies were based on immigrant entrepreneur "contributions" founding companies during the dotcom boom. [687]

In an *EETimes* August 24, 2007, article titled, "Green-card Red Tape Sends Valuable Engineers Packing," Wadhwa said that 500,000 foreign visa holders who had been trained in US companies were in line for green cards, but only 120,000 per year were available. He warned that if they do not get green cards to continue working in the United States: "they become our competitors. That's as stupid as it gets. ... *How can this country be so dumb as to bring people in on temporary visas, train them in our way of doing business and then send them back to compete with us?*" [703] That is a very good question.

In a 2007 article titled, "America's New Immigrant Entrepreneurs," Wadhwa wanted visa holders to be granted permanent residence green cards without waiting six years. *He pointed out that temporary visa workers could not start businesses.* He acknowledged that H-1B visas had been misused to bring in foreign workers who did not have exceptional skills, and had depressed wages harming Americans. Yet, he argued that the 140,000 per year limit (Where did the additional 20,000 come from?)

be lifted, because this did not accommodate the massive numbers of people from China and India on visas who wanted to immigrate to the United States. [632]

Skewed Non-citizen Patent Claims

Wadhwa's 2007 study also claimed that non-citizens (foreign graduate students, foreigners with green cards, and visa workers) living in the US were named as inventors or co-inventors on 24.2% of the 2006 US international patent applications. This contrasted with 1998 when they were named on only 7.3% of these patent applications. Wadhwa thought this was impressive since people from India and China make up less than 1% of the population in the US. [632] Wadhwa was in a position to know that students from China and India take about 50% or more of the seats in US graduate school research labs. Therefore, if they only account for 24.2% of the patent applications this would not be impressive. A patent application does not mean a patent will be awarded. Many of these may be frivolous patent applications. Furthermore, patents are not a numbers game. One really significant patent may be more valuable than thousands of others. Also, some US colleges began teaching engineering students as teams. [662] The team approach may have forced American inventors to list multiple non-citizen co-inventors even if the foreign students made little or no contribution.

One of the biggest factors skewing the patent application statistics was caused when millions of highly skilled and experienced American programmers, scientists and engineers were displaced by foreign visa workers. This dramatically decreased the number of Americans working on research and filing patents. Additionally, young American graduates were denied technology research jobs where many patents are generated. Furthermore, immigrants received more venture capital to fund startups doing expensive research and patent applications.

On a sinister note, many H-1Bs obtained jobs in American companies as programmers, system administrators, and even as security experts. This correlates with escalating foreign corporate espionage targeting US technology. Such access to corporate computers would make it easy to copy and steal inventions being worked on by American scientists and engineers who have their patent ideas and research stored on company computers. How many H-1Bs and other non-citizens are employed in our US patent and trademark office?

Wadhwa's Startup—Step one to Offshoring

According to an article titled "Indian Owns a Goldmine," Wadhwa's software company, Relativity, has made millions transferring computer files storing decades of private information on American citizens' including credit histories, insurance claims, medical data, and property records to the Internet. Putting this data on the

Internet was the first step required to enable offshoring America BPO jobs to India and other countries. One of Relativity's three main competitors, Tibco, was also founded in America by an immigrant from India. [688] It would be interesting to learn how many of the people working for Wadhwa's company are from India, and how many of his clients outsourced and/or offshored BPO to India after his company transferred their data to the Internet. He has stated that he was one of the first CEOs to hire H-1Bs. [780]

GLOBAL IT ACM STUDY

The 83,000 member Association for Computing Machinery (ACM) conducted a study of outsourcing and reported its findings in 2006. ACM emphasized that its report was not from a "United States-centric perspective." [557] The goal was to provide a study of globalization of the software industry to help members be successful globally. *The study found that most of the growth in offshoring had occurred in "the past five years," i.e. following the dotcom crash while America has been at war.* It acknowledged that globalization created national security risks for the US and jeopardized US technology leadership. Yet, it concluded that these risks would not deter the growth of offshoring. The study reported that education was the key enabler of offshoring to countries such as India and China. The historic advantage held by the United States in technology and research has shifted *due to US graduate schools*, and because young Americans were losing interest in pursuing science and math degrees. Curiously, the report then claimed that the US leadership in technology research was at risk, because it is unable to recruit as many foreign student researchers as it had previously. The ACM recommended: "eliminate barriers to the free flow of talent."

The study reported that the US had more IT jobs in 2006 than it did during the dotcom boom. It failed to report how many of these US jobs went to visa workers. This study predicted that *IT jobs would be among the highest growth jobs for the next decade, and that 12-14 million US jobs are at risk of being offshored over a 15 year period.* The report downplayed these American job losses claiming the losses were small compared to the yearly job loss/job creation cycle in the US. The economic downturn caused by the dotcom crash was used to justify offshoring. And, according to the study, some venture capital companies required as a condition for funding that US startups use cheaper offshore workers to reduce the "burn rate" of the money invested. [557]

Chapter 6

India's Management Thinkers

Pre-globalization: "Our employees are our most valuable resource."

The New Mantra: US employees are our most expendable resource.

Americans dominated successful business management strategy for many generations which made the United States the most prosperous nation in the world. [372] At the very foundation of this American success was the core premise that "our employees are our most valuable resource." Then American business leaders were led down the path by a new mantra "our employees are our most expendable resource." High tech American workers were displaced at alarming rates by foreign workers using H-1B visas, outsourcing and offshoring.

THINKERS "CHANGING THE FACE OF AMERICAN BUSINESS"

A 2005, article titled "The Indians are Coming—How Management Thinkers from India are Changing the Face of American Business," by Des Dearlove and Stuart Crainer in *The Conference Board* provides insight into how "thinkers" from India, aimed for the not too subtle goal of "changing the face of American business." Ironically their propaganda promoted "diversity" which they themselves do not appear to practice. Although they obtained US citizenship, many maintained close ties to India, and showed little or no allegiance to America. Some made negative comments such as: Americans "monopolized business wisdom" and "colonized" the Japanese business practices. The typical profile of these "thinkers" is they were born and raised in India. They entered the United States using non-immigrant student visas. Several of these "thinkers" attended Harvard. Instead of returning to India, the "thinkers" stayed in the US and sought out jobs as professors and advisors. [240]

In the United States our universities are revered as sources of expert knowledge. These "thinkers" used their affiliation and credentials with US universities to get articles and books promoting outsourcing and offshoring published. When they are on the faculty, they refer to US universities as the "world's most prestigious B-schools." Armed with Masters degrees and PhDs from US universities, they promoted themselves as "management thinkers," "superstars," "strategy gurus," "executive coaches" who brought "refreshing diversity" to Corporate America boardrooms and US university MBA programs. During the 1990's many US businesses and even the US government were lured into outsourcing and offshoring by "globalization" propaganda these immigrants spun to benefit India. Paradoxically, they advised US corporations to offshore to India's chaotic business environment that they struggled to escape. [240]

According to the article their new management philosophy aside from "globalization" i.e. sending US jobs to India, was to advise that when people "are adding the most value" they should be seen as investors, because they "invest their human capital in the company, will expect a return on it, and expect growth of that capital." [240] This was the same as "our employees are our most valuable resource" which was the American management philosophy pre-globalization. Indian thinkers persuaded American companies to break the social contract with Americans who had invested their "human capital" in American companies and were the reason America was the most advanced and prosperous nation in the world. Instead of being rewarded, Americans were denied a fair return on their investment.

How could these "thinkers" achieve so much influence considering the US far surpassed India in business, technology, and economic achievements? The article *provided the answer: "India's collectivist culture offers a ready foil to America's rampant individualism."* [240] According to this statement, they acted as a collective, not as individuals in business dealings—including those who were granted US citizenship and swore allegiance to the United States. Note that foil is defined as "to prevent from being successful; thwart, and to obscure" or to confuse a trail to avoid being caught. In the article, they unwisely used Enron as an example to berate American individualism. Enron was a poor choice, because it was a collective deception by co-conspirators, and also because part of the Enron deception involved misappropriating millions of US taxpayers' dollars to fund building a power plant in India—a project the World Bank rejected. After the plant was up and running, India refused to pay and locked the gates which made it appear that there was never any intention to repay US taxpayers. This power plant may one day fuel competition against the US.

IMPACT OF "THINKERS" ON US ECONOMY

The "thinkers" claim that, "While no one can predict the Indian thinkers' long term impact on American businesses, there is no question that they are bringing refreshing diversity to boardrooms and MBA programs." [240] Although the "thinkers" claim that it is not possible to foretell the long-term impact of their advice on US businesses, this is simply not true. [140] The impact from these "thinkers" was exposed by the enormous US budget deficit and high unemployment that resulted from H-1B visas and outsourcing and offshoring. And it is spread across the US devastating our economy, American workers and their families.

WHO ARE SOME OF THESE "THINKERS"?

Who are some of these "management thinkers" promoting outsourcing and offshoring to India? Well, there is Ram Charan an "executive coach" who was a confidant to Jack Welch while he was leading GE. This is the same Jack Welch that was nicknamed "Neutron Jack" because he laid off so many US citizens when he offshored work to India. [66] There is C.K. Prahalad a University of Michigan professor, and Vijay Govindarajan a professor at Dartmouth College's Tuck School of Business. [240] The "rising stars" among the "thinkers" are: M.S. Krishnan a professor at the University of Michigan; Rakesh Khurana, Nitin Nohira, and Krishna Palepu on the faculty at Harvard; Deepak Jain and Mohanbir Sawhney on the faculty at Northwestern's Kellogg School; Jagdish Bhagwati on the faculty at Columbia; Raj Reddy on the faculty at Carnegie Mellon; and many more. [240] The following provides more detail on a few of these "thinkers."

Vijay Govindarajan—Tuck University Professor

Vijay Govindarajan was born and raised in India. He entered the US as a student to attend Harvard Business School. [240] Around 1985, Govindarajan became the first person from India to obtain a faculty position at Tuck University. Govindarajan used his US professor credentials to become one of the highest paid executive coaches in Corporate America. He proudly claimed that India "thinkers" have had unprecedented influence over US business management, *"there is no doubt that Indians have had a disproportionate influence on management thinking and practice. As a percentage of the U.S. population, they are miniscule—less that a single percent—but then look at their representation in business schools."* [240]

American executives may have been a lot less receptive to his "advice" if they knew Govindarajan was also quoted as saying "the center of gravity cannot simply be the United States." He then acknowledged that by persuading American corporations to transfer American jobs, technology, and money to India he was personally profiting, "my market value is going up." [240]

By 2005, Govindarajan estimated that 20% of the faculty at Tuck originated from India. He stated that 40 students from India entered Tuck's MBA program in 2005. Why would Americans want to fill our business schools with foreign students who will be competing against Americans for jobs and resources? There is something very disturbing about a group that comprises less than a "single percent" of the US demographically controlling 20% of the teaching positions in a US university. Govindarajan even took 50 young American executives to India. One of the Americans asked an Infosys executive if he was concerned IBM or Accenture may try to acquire Infosys, an Indian outsourcing company. Govindarajan proudly recalls the Indian executive responded that maybe Infosys might acquire IBM or Accenture. Because of globalization, American companies like IBM were no longer held in such high esteem. [240]

How brilliant is Vijay Govindarajan? Well, he argued that overpopulating created more smart people. His logic—intelligence is the same from country to country, and in each country he estimated that 20% of the people are smart, therefore since there are a billion people in India, there are 200 million smart Indians. [240] If this thinkers' logic were true, then India would have been more prosperous than the US, and we would have spent the past couple of decades mass immigrating to India. The truth is overpopulation drags down creativity; it drains scarce resources, which in turn interferes with a nation being able to focus on R&D and provide quality education.

M.S. Krishnan —University of Michigan IT Professor

M.S. Krishnan a "top new thinker" graduated from the University of Delhi in India in 1987. He was admitted to Carnegie Mellon University where he obtained a Masters degree in 1993, and a PhD in 1996. M.S. Krishnan became a professor at the University of Michigan. Krishnan serves on the boards of multiple academic journals and has published about 40 articles. [649]

In 2004 he persuaded the University of Michigan to set up an offshore research center at IIT in Bangalore, India. He was quoted as saying: *"If you look at globalization the wheel is not going to stop. ... If U.S. companies compete globally, it's unavoidable that they will have manufacturing in China and Taiwan, design and software in India, probably marketing and strategy in the United States. ..."* [253]

If our leaders are gullible enough to listen to this, then they need to be replaced by intelligent Americans. Krishnan may be surprised at how quickly Americans can stop the "globalization wheel". Krishnan should know that the United States successfully competed globally for many years without offshoring to China or India.

C. K. Prahalad—University of Michigan Professor

C.K Prahalad was born in India. He became a US citizen and a professor at the University of Michigan. [240] He also worked on the side as a "business consultant" promoting outsourcing and offshoring to India.

In 2004, he collaborated with M.S. Krishnan to persuade the University of Michigan to set up a research center in Bangalore, India. The University of Michigan's India center was to arrange for US faculty and students to take trips to India and work on research projects. Was this center in India financed by US taxpayers and US college tuition? *This "management thinker" was quoted as saying that people were caught off guard by "the rate at which China and India are acquiring a world-class technology base and the speed at which they are beating others."* And, he claimed that divisions of American companies located in India had filed over 1,000 US patent applications in 2003. [253] Prahalad appeared in a 2006 ABC News piece that promoted offshoring to India as "the destination for American business outsourcing." [513]

Mohanbir Sawhney—Northwestern Kellogg School Professor

Mohanbir Sawhney obtained a Ph.D. from the Wharton School at the University of Pennsylvania. [235] Sawhney stayed in the United States after completing his studies and obtained a faculty position at Northwestern's Kellogg School. [240] Sawhney used his position with the college to become a business advisor to American executives. Sawhney also co-founded a consulting company for startups that he claimed, "pretty much locked up the Chicago-area deal flow." [237]

Sawhney is a member of The IndUS Entrepreneurs (TiE) often referred to as the Indian "Mafia." In an April 2000 article, Sawhney talked about being a "market maker" because he advised both buyers and sellers when negotiating deals. He jokingly called it "my scam." Sawhney was on the board of directors for 5 companies and on 16 advisory boards. Most of these 21 companies were Internet startups preparing for IPOs. *Sawhney did not invest in the startups, yet he demanded 1% equity or more for his help.* [237] He was also advising Presidents and CEOs of major US corporations. [191]

A July 2000 article raised concerns of conflicts of interests by some US professors who were engaged in startup business ventures. One of the professors named was Mohanbir Sawhney who taught an Internet marketing course at Northwestern University Business School while being involved with 19 companies. According to the article, although it is common for US university professors to do consulting work on the side and serve as experts on the boards of US corporations, there are serous conflict of interest issues in the case of entrepreneurial startup ventures where university research projects are involved and students are recruited. Some US professors earning in the mid $50,000's leverage their university connections and suddenly become millionaires. [238] *Unlike many professors who kept low profiles while engaged in such activities, Sawhney sought publicity.*

By 2001, some of the fruit of Sawhney's practice became evident. Sawhney and Sanjay Kumar of Computer Associates were high profile members on the board of publicly held Divine interVentures that funded many dotcom startups. During the dotcom boom Divine was considered a shining example of cunning management know how. But, by January 2001, the stock plummeted to around $1 per share and both Sawhney and Kumar resigned. [236] How much money did US citizens lose investing in the startups they helped launch? So why were Sawhney and Kumar still touted in the US media as brilliant "management thinkers" in 2005? *BusinessWeek* selected Sawhney for its list of the 25 most influential people in e-Business. [235]

The list of large corporations Sawhney advised is strikingly similar to the list of companies hiring H-1Bs, outsourcing, and offshoring. A partial list of the companies he advised included outsourcing services companies such as Accenture, Infosys (India), and IBM Consulting Services; financial institutions such as Bank of America and Goldman Sachs; American software companies including Adobe and Microsoft; American technology leaders including Boeing, Cisco Systems, Dell, Motorola, Rockwell Automation, Dow Chemical Company, DuPont, Ericsson, Honeywell; and other corporations including Hallmark, Kraft Foods, and Sony. [235]

Sawhney advised US corporations to "go global" i.e. outsource and offshore their business. Sawhney told US business executives and students that outsourcing cannot be stopped. He used GE Capital as an example claiming that they employ 10,000 programmers in India to provide support services around the world. [51] In 2003, Sawhney published "*Getting to Global.*" He advised American executives that the Internet enabled going global, and that even if they only sell to a small town in the US, they should consider using foreign workers to produce products or manage office operations. [108]

Some of the companies Sawhney advised were US government contractors. He advised Honeywell, a company that builds jet engines and electronic control systems, to offshore. In 2004 Honeywell began replacing American employees with cheaper foreign workers in 95 countries. [108]

Moreover, according to Sawhney, he met with 300 senior executives at Boeing. Although Boeing was a global business, he claimed its executives agreed with him "that the company had a long way to go before it can consider itself a truly global company." [239] The problem with Boeing according to Sawhney was that Boeing's products were designed in the United States, primarily manufactured in the United States, and most of its employees were located in the United States. Sawhney wrote a paper: "Getting to Global" which had a four stage plan for getting Boeing and other American Corporations to go global. "Stage 1–Global Sales" marketing and sales promotion—this despite the fact that markets such as India and China failed to provide the big markets promised. "Stage 2—Global Sourcing" US corporations are advised to setup offshore manufacturing to "take advantage of cheaper labor...and to overcome export restrictions." "Stage 3—Global Processes" advises US corporations to offshore business processes such as: customer support, marketing research, managing networks, R&D and more. He gave IBM as an example claiming it *offshored strategic development from data mining, to supply chain management and ecommerce.* In "Stage 4—The Capability Network" the US corporation morphs into a network spread out across the globe. [239]

Boeing followed Sawheney's advice. The production of its 787 was expected to "revolutionize the way Boeing manufactures planes" by outsourcing development to "partners around the world." Boeing expected to reduce its $10 billion development costs. However in December 2007, Boeing was "facing the gloomy prospect of shelling out millions of dollars in penalties" due to delays. Instead of a testament to Sawheney's advice, Boeing's experience appears to discredit him. According to Ann All's December 10, 2007, post on *ITBusinessEdge*, "Boeing's problems are a testament to the risks and limitations of outsourcing and global supply chains." [670]

MCKINSEY & CO. MANAGEMENT CONSULTANTS—RAJAT GUPTA

McKinsey and Company was proclaimed to be the largest management consulting firm in the world. [334] After immigrants from India entered the upper ranks of the McKinsey & Company, it began to produce studies and advise American corporations to convert to multinationals, to hire H-1B foreign visa workers and to outsource and offshore—particularly to India.

Rajat Gupta, who was born in Calcutta, India, became the managing director of this giant consulting company. [187] Rajat Gupta claimed that "Offshoring work will spur innovation, job creation, and dramatic increases in productivity that will be passed on to the (American) consumer." He advised American managers to cut costs by replacing American engineers paid around $80,000 a year with engineers in India who would work for only $10,000 a year. [300]

McKinsey worked with the National Association of Software and Services Companies (NASSCOM) India's powerful software lobby. Members of NASSCOM included India's technology companies and IBM's services unit in India. [100]

According to a 1999, article titled, "Making of a Software Superpower," "NASSCOM has played a key role in propagating India as the destination for software services and development." [228] In 1999 there was a much hyped NASSCOM-McKinsey "study" that predicted India's software and services then 2% of India's GDP would jump dramatically by 2008. [176] This "study" was used as a marketing tool to sell offshoring to India to the US government and US businesses. This study predicted that India's IT services industry of only about $2 billion in 1998, would jump to almost $40 billion by 2008, and, India's software products, business services and e-business which were less than $1 billion were forecasted to jump a combined total of about $50 billion. That means overall India's information technology industry growth was targeting a jump from about $3 billion in 1998 to $90 billion by 2008. [124] This was to be accomplished by persuading American corporations to offshore our jobs to India.

In 2000, McKinsey employed many consultants in India, so it is not surprising that they promoted India as the ideal outsourcing location for technology jobs such as engineering, financial jobs such as accounting, database management jobs such as data processing, customer support, transcription and more. In 2000, McKinsey predicted that outsourcing service jobs to India would grow 50% annually from 40,000 jobs in 2000 to 700,000 jobs by 2008.

An essential component of India's offshoring plan was the placement of H-1B visa workers in high tech jobs in the United States. A July 2003, *EETimes* article titled, "India's Tech Industry Defends H-1B, Outsource Roles" by K.C. Krishnadas, India was worried the US may end or cut back on the H-1B visa program. India counts these high tech visas as "India's software exports industry."

By March of 2003 India had already "exported" 120,000 H-1B visa and 15,000 L1 visa workers to the US. India was particularly concerned with maintaining these exports to the US, because Germany had decided to restrict the number of green cards, and the United Kingdom was reconsidering its "fast track visa scheme." *Parliamentary delegates from India traveled to the US to "lobby against bans on outsourcing."* Moreover, the article asserted that NASSCOM used a "study" by McKinsey to declare as "fact" that outsourcing by the US to India would continue. NASSCOM claimed that India had around 170 IT companies employing almost 60,000 people operating within the US. [123] How can a foreign country lobby the US Congress that is supposed to represent American citizens?

A 2003, *BusinessWeek* story, "The Rise of India," by Manjeet Kripalani and Pete Engardio, reported that intense pressure from the American public caused the state of Indiana to cancel an outsourcing contract with India's Tata Consulting. Rajat Gupta at McKinsey & Co defended offshoring asserting that it creates more jobs and innovations. Yet the article appears to contradict his claims reporting McKinsey Global Institute acknowledged that in the past 20 years only 36% of Americans displaced by foreign workers found jobs that paid the same or better. And, around 25% of the Americans displaced experienced a 30% or worse drop in their income. [300]

In an effort to squelch the growing US backlash and influence the US Congress in 2003, NASSCOM commissioned another "study" by McKinsey Global Institute to put forward the argument that offshoring was good for the US economy. In 2003, IBM referenced this report to justify offshoring plans. [100]

In 2003, NASSCOM made bold claims of offshore cost savings benefits for the US economy, and quoted McKinsey & Co.'s forecast that offshore services in India would grow to $142 billion by 2009. *NASSCOM claimed these same services cost $532 billion in the US, therefore it asserts the net savings for the US economy is $390 billion.* [123]

In 2003, India's NASSCOM claimed that American banks, financial services companies, and insurance companies saved $6-$8 billion over the last four years due to offshore outsourcing IT to India. According to NASSCOM these billions in saving prevented layoffs and created 125,000 more US jobs. [67] The 2009 US banking financial crisis appears to contradict these claims of benefits to US banks.

There is some formidable criticism of McKinsey & Company. Critics claim that it operates in secrecy making it difficult for the public to scrutinize its performance; because, it does not disclose its list of clients, nor its involvement with clients, making it difficult to determine its success rate. Critics also claim that it conceals its pricing which may be more than $10,000 a day for a team of consultants.

> Bobby Jindal worked for McKinsey & Co. in the early 1990s, advising our Fortune 500 companies during the time H-1Bs caused massive numbers of Americans to lose their jobs. Later he became a US Congressman, and then Governor of Louisiana in January 2008.

Enron was headed by McKinsey alumni, and some sources claim that *Enron was one of McKinsey's biggest clients when it collapsed.* Two books were written about McKinsey's management consulting: *The Witch Doctors* by John Mickelthwait and Adrian Wooldridge, and *Dangerous Company: The Consulting Powerhouses and the Businesses They Save and Ruin* by James O'Shea and Charles Madigan. [696]

In 2004, McKinsey & Company was continuing to assert that offshoring US jobs to low wage countries would cut costs by 45% to 55%. *They claimed huge profits would result since 14 million US service jobs could be offshored.* [6]

2005 Technology Without Borders Global iit2005 Conference

In 2005, a "Technology Without Borders Global iit2005 Conference" held in the US was co-chaired by Rajat Gupta Managing Director of McKinsey & Company. The conference encouraged the collaboration of IIT Alumni to help other IIT graduates use the India network to advance their careers, find business partners, obtain access to US university research, *obtain subcontracting from the US government, to lend a hand to the India government,* and more.

Several sessions were focused on promoting US-India business collaborations. One speaker at this iit2005 Conference talked about a May 2002 meeting at McKinsey & Company offices in Connecticut where *they hatched the idea to promote "brand IIT" as a "household name in USA."* He explained how US media such as *BusinessWeek* and even cartoons such as Dilbert were used to promote the "brand IIT" to Americans because, "in the USA, increased globalization is threatening decades of high living standards." They went further to plan a major PR campaign for "brand IIT." [523]

This 2002 meeting of 50 IIT graduates decided to form Pan-IIT as a non-profit United States corporation umbrella organization with the goal set forward by India's Prime Minister Jawharlal Nehru "Service to the nation" to transform India by "Giving Back." The first Pan-IIT conference was held in October 2002 in Washington, DC. Pan-IIT's annual meetings were to alternate "between the United States and India." They were pleased with the *"excellent media coverage"* including CBS's "60 Minutes" promoting IIT as a "world-class brand." By the time of the 2005 conference Pan-IIT had 12 Chapters in North America.

This iit2005 Conference proudly displayed the House Resolution 227 passed in April 2005, by the US Congress under pressure from the Indian network. In an unusual move Congress formally recognized India's Indian Institute of Technology (IIT), a foreign university, lauding the contributions of immigrants from India and encouraged Americans to appreciate their contributions. It is unlikely that Americans will applaud their contributions with regard to visa programs, outsourcing and offshoring that have caused millions of high tech US citizens and office support workers to lose their jobs harming American families and communities.

In 2005, Congressman Bobby Jindal and Congressman Tom Davis co-sponsored the IIT recognition resolution which the Indian network planned to use to promote "brand IIT" to encourage hiring H-1Bs, outsourcing, and offshoring to India. [342] Jindal was born to graduate students from India a few months after they arrived in the United States to attend college. Jindal was recommended as a potential Vice President for McCain in the 2008 presidential election.

PAN IIT—RAJAT GUPTA

In May 2007, the PBS program, "Foreign Exchange with Fareed Zakaria" ran a TV show segment, "Sizing Up the Competition" where Zakaria interviewed Rajat Gupta the former head of the McKinsey outsourcing firm, and the current Chairman of Pan IIT Global.

According to the show, Pan IIT was formed to promote linking India's Indian Institute of Technology (IIT) to US research universities to benefit India. Zakaria in his introduction of Gupta refers to India's (IIT) as the "MIT of the East." Then he mentions that they both grew up in India.

Zakaria wonders how India was able to fund IIT because of the poverty (apparently he does not know that US aid helped finance building engineering schools in India). He asks if it's a waste of money to educate American scientists when India can produce scientists cheaper.

He and Gupta talked about how India's IIT has produced about 150,000 graduates and that 50,000 of these graduates were living in the United States. Gupta claimed that these IIT graduates living in the US had formed "the backbone of the tech industry" in America.

Gupta said IIT graduates "tremendously contributed to this (United States) economy, and created a tremendous number of jobs." The companies Gupta named were Sun Microsystems, Sycamore, Info USA. [640]

America was the world technology leader and competed globally well before any IIT graduates came here to be educated in US graduate schools. He fails to mention that many of the "created" jobs in these companies went to H-1Bs from India who displaced American workers.

Gupta talked about how globalization has broken down barriers (access to US technology) and mentions huge market opportunities in Asia. This is misleading because most American companies that offshored to India were primarily selling products and services back to America. Few people in India had the money to buy products or services when American companies first offshored.

Moreover, Zakaria and Gupta echoed the claims that the transfer of US technology and jobs to India cannot be stopped and declared we should not stop it, because living standards were improved in other parts of the world.

Gupta talked about how 15 years earlier (1992) he had used his consulting services to persuade American companies to offshore research to India. *Gupta referred to outsourcing as a "revolution" and asserted that thus far only 3% of the jobs that could be outsourced had been outsourced. Zakaria asked if America had only seen the "tip of the iceberg with outsourcing?" And Gupta responded, "Yeah."* [640]

Chapter 7

H-1B Job Heist

Entry level high tech jobs used to go to young Americans graduating from college.

Now many entry level high tech jobs are being channeled to foreign H-1B visa workers.

The H-1B legislation was passed because, "corporations make political contributions to assure the passage of legislation" that lets them import cheap foreign workers. [63] Your tax dollars finance the government, but CEOs buy influence that overrides your interests. CEOs buy legislation to get laws passed that benefit them to the detriment of most American citizens. A Senator from Utah exposed the truth of how executives wield power over H-1B voting in the US Congress, "*There were in fact, a whole lot of folks against it, but because they are tapping the high-tech community for campaign contributions, they don't want to admit that in public.*" [24]

Given the fraud and deceptions executives used to get H-1B legislation passed, the "transfer" of high tech US citizens' jobs may be viewed as a theft of these jobs.

1) False claims that the United States had a "desperate shortage" of high tech workers were used to persuade the US Congress to pass the H-1B visa bill. These shortage claims were contradicted by the mass layoffs of Americans.

2) False claims that foreign workers were the "best and brightest" and were needed to create a "world class" workforce. This was not credible given the United States' was the world's technology leader.

3) False claims of "cost savings" from replacing Americans with foreign workers. The Economic Circulation Model and the US trade deficit both prove the cost savings claim is false.

It is appalling that if someone steals your wallet you have more legal protection than if they steal your job. Americans are told that we cannot do anything to stop this transfer of US jobs to foreign workers. However, united we can reclaim our jobs and protect our country.

1990 CONGRESS PASSED H-1B BILL HARMING AMERICANS

If you are an American you probably never heard of the H-1B—that is unless you lost your high tech job to one. However, it is very important for US citizens to know about the H-1B visa program and how it has been used to threaten US technology leadership in computer information technology (IT), engineering, and other high tech areas. [47] The H-1B is a controversial temporary high tech worker visa program approved by the US Congress in response to extensive bipartisan lobbying efforts primarily from executives in Silicon Valley, California. Executives represented to Congress that the US had a serious shortage of high tech workers and they were desperate to fill open positions temporarily with foreign workers until enough Americans were trained to fill the jobs. Executives assured Congress that they would only hire foreign workers if they could not find qualified Americans. [63]

The US government did not seek an independent investigation to verify the high tech worker shortage actually existed prior to passing the legislation. Bowing to the pressure from lobbyists, in 1990, under the first Bush administration, Congress passed the H-1B non-immigrant visa (NIV) program which allowed executives to temporarily fill open high tech jobs with foreign workers.

Congress permitted H-1Bs to work in the United States for up to six years. When their visas expired H-1Bs were required to return to their country of origin. Congress did not require businesses hiring H-1Bs to show they attempted to hire Americans first. However, Congress did require that H-1Bs must be paid the prevailing wage to protect US workers from being replaced by cheaper foreign workers. This wage requirement shows that the US Congress suspected the motive was cheaper workers not a worker shortage. The US Congress set a 65,000 a year H-1B visa quota cap. Imagine 65,000 Americans a year losing their high tech jobs to foreigners through an act of Congress.

The entire premise of the H-1B program was contrived. It took two years to educate a foreign student in a US graduate school to become qualified to fill an H-1B visa job. Logically an American student could have been trained in the same two year time period. Moreover, how could Congress justify granting a six year foreign work visa when an American could have been trained and ready to fill the job in just two years? [63]

WORKER SHORTAGE FRAUD

Several investigations found that the claims of a US high tech worker shortage were fraudulent. In 1999, Dr. Gene Nelson testified before the US House of Representatives that the H-1B was harming high tech American workers. Nelson traced the shortage claims back to the National Science Foundation (NSF) which he said made the claims to increase its budget. He found that at the time the H-1B bill was passed, the US had 13 million people trained in science and engineering and only ¼ were employed in their field. Therefore, the US had a high tech job shortage, not a high tech worker shortage. [47]

In 2000, the H-1B program was ten years old and yet the high tech American worker shortage propaganda continued. For example, the Information Technology Association of America (ITAA) claimed that 800,000 computer jobs went unfilled. [289] However, the US Department of Commerce found no proof that a shortage of American programmers existed, and that an alarming 28% of new programming jobs were going to H-1Bs. [26]

Dr. Matloff surveyed University of California-Davis computer science graduates and found that less than half were able to get programming jobs. [63] In December 2000, he criticized the computer industry for hiring public relations (PR) firms to fill US media with claims of severe programmer shortages. Matloff noted that H-1Bs were hired because they were cheaper, not because any shortage existed. Moreover, he believed that the US Congress had ample evidence that the shortage did not exist. [26]

By 2003, the H-1B "temporary" program had been displacing Americans for thirteen years. The fraud behind the foreign worker visas and outsourcing was exposed by The Phyllis Schlafly Report in its June 2003 issue titled: "What the Global Economy Costs Americans." The six page report lists the following subtitles: "The Scam of the H-1B Visas," "The Scam of L-1 Visas," "The Scam of Outsourcing," and "Comments from the Engineers Replaced by Foreigners." [63]

On May 16th, 2006, Vivek Wadhwa, an engineering professor at Duke University, testified to the U.S. House of Representatives Committee on Education and the Workforce that the US did not have a shortage of engineers—30-40% of graduates with Masters degrees took jobs outside their profession. He said the 2004 reports that China produced 600,000 engineers, India 350,000 and the United States only 70,000 were flawed, because the Chinese Ministry of Education and India's NASCOMM inflated their numbers by counting people who only had certificates. *He warned against the US graduating more American citizen engineers saying it could cost the US its competitive edge, because it would reduce salaries and cause unemployment.* He asked: "If a certain type of engineering job can be done more cost effectively in India or China, why should we invest in graduating more of those types of engineers?" [779] This is bad advice. Because of the wage gap just about any job can be done cheaper in India or China. The US should not give up control of engineering to Asia. When Wadhwa testified, did the US Congressional Committee know that he was one of the first CEO's to hire H-1Bs, and said that he hired H-1Bs because they were cheaper? [780] In

2007 he wrote an article "Open Doors Wider for Skilled Immigrants" that appears to contradict his warning about the risks to the United States from having too many engineers.

"BEST AND BRIGHTEST" PROPAGANDA

H-1B sponsors claimed that H-1Bs were the "best and brightest." For example, in 2000 an article, "The Indians of Silicon Valley", by *Fortune* claimed, American engineers "typically aren't as talented as those from India." [289] Another article said that "of course" it was a programmer from India who set up the database used to track bodies from the September 11th terrorist attack. [319] Propaganda deceitfully equated attending graduate schools to the "best and brightest" to justify preferential hiring of H-1Bs over Americans. [49] Multiple investigations found the claims were false.

In 1998 Senator Dianne Feinstein, reported that few H-1Bs were highly skilled, instead 85% of H-1Bs took entry level programming jobs that should go to young Americans, and frequently H-1Bs were paid less than prevailing wages as required by law. Nonetheless, despite misgivings, under industry pressure, and going along with her peers she voted to approve a 1998 H-1B quota increase. [15] [12]

In 2000, an INS audit discovered that many H-1Bs used fake credentials. Foreign born computer programmers received less than 8% (9 out of 115) of the Electrical and Electronic Engineers awards while Americans earned over 92% of the awards. [44] This was ten years into the H-1B when 25% of the scientists and engineers working in Silicon Valley were foreign born. [372] [272] If they were the "best and brightest" they should have received more than 25%, yet they received only 8% which indicates that American scientists they displaced were actually the "best and brightest."

A 2003 study also found that many H-1Bs were not qualified, and were paid less than $58,000. Of the 2003 computer technology awards, only 6 out of the 34 winners of the prestigious Turing Award were foreign born, and only 1 out of 50 winners of the System Software Award were foreign born. [63]

In May 2006, the U.S. House of Representatives Committee on Education and the Workforce was deciding if the United States needed to invest more to keep American engineers ahead of the competition. *In an endeavor to assuage their concerns and convince them this was not necessary, Wadhwa testified that: "all available data indicates that the vast majority of Indian and Chinese graduates are not close to the standards of US graduates."* And he reported that the IIT graduates who came to Duke to study were "only as good as the average American student." [779]

EXPOSING THE REAL REASON BEHIND H-1B DEMAND

There was no worker shortage, the "best and brightest" claims do not hold up, and the Economic Circulation Model™ disproves cost savings claims. So what was the truth? *The H-1B was not driven by any need the United States had, but rather by foreign nations that wanted access to strategic US technologies; and, by foreign students and illegal aliens who wanted high tech American jobs.* From 1971 - 1991, the US granted more than 3 million foreign student visas. Although they were not supposed to seek employment in the US, 393,000 obtained green cards. About 87% remained illegally. [230] They worked for low wages because they were illegal and because they were not burdened with huge college debt. This glut of illegal foreign workers tempted unscrupulous executives in US corporations to inflate earnings in the short term by replacing Americans with cheaper foreign workers.

Once the H-1B bill was passed in 1990, the demand for foreign student visas soared. Linking H-1Bs to huge executive bonuses was the lure. When you put side by side the growth in foreign student visas and the H-1B visas it all becomes clear. *The H-1B legislation was sought to legalize hiring foreigners educated in the US.* If you compare a chart of student visas, allowing 2-4 years to graduate, it is striking how the increase in foreign students tracks to high tech visa workers. For example, by 1998 about six million foreign students had been awarded visas, allowing that it took two to four years to complete their studies; you can see that by the year 2000 almost six million foreigners had been granted high tech worker

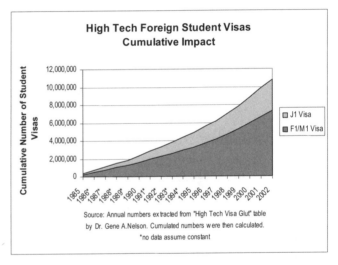

**High Tech Foreign Student Visas
Cumulative Impact**

Source: Annual numbers extracted from "High Tech Visa Glut" table by Dr. Gene A.Nelson. Cumulated numbers were then calculated.
*no data assume constant

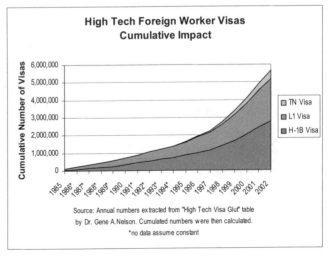

**High Tech Foreign Worker Visas
Cumulative Impact**

Source: Annual numbers extracted from "High Tech Visa Glut" table by Dr. Gene A.Nelson. Cumulated numbers were then calculated.
*no data assume constant

visas.

In 2000, an estimated 53,300 foreigners already living in the US received 40% of the H-1B visas granted that year. A little more than half of these were in the US on F-1 student visas. The other half included illegal aliens such as foreigners who stayed when their student visas expired. Surprisingly, visa violators were not screened out when applying for H-1B visas to work in sensitive US government jobs, US universities, US banks, and high tech US companies. H-1B programmers were entrusted with access to confidential data. Many H-1Bs sought employment implementing SAP and Oracle database systems [335] which gave insider access to strategic databases containing data on design secrets, customers, suppliers, employees, and more. [41] If a foreign worker can break a US law and not be screened out, then it should be illegal to screen out Americans for equivalent or lesser infractions such as a bad credit history caused by a layoff.

INDIA DROVE H-1B LEGISLATION

H-1Bs are predominately computer programmers. Almost 74% of the computer related H-1B jobs went to people from India. [41] In 2000, the government of India lobbied to increase the H-1B visa program, so that they could "export" more Indians to the US. They were also trying to persuade Germany and other countries to approve similar visa programs. At that time the IT jobs offshored to India were lower skilled jobs. India saw US high tech jobs being done by H-1Bs and L-1s as positioning to later move these high tech jobs offshore to India. [30] In 2005, India managed to get H-1B bills sponsored in the US Senate. Using the World Trade Organization, the Indian government lobbied to eliminate the H-1B cap, and eliminate the requirement to pay H-1Bs the prevailing wage. [615]

40% OF ILLEGAL ALIENS SECRET

The news media tends to only show illegal aliens from Mexico. However, millions of illegal aliens entered the US on non-immigrant visas (NIVs) then stayed after their visas expired. [143] While for the 1986 amnesty 10% of illegal aliens were visa violators, by 1996, there were so many visa violators in the US that a law was passed requiring the INS to track visa holders. In early 2000, the INS estimated 8 million illegal aliens were in the United States, and that 3.2 million were visa violators. This means that student visa violators, H-1B violators, and other visa violators comprised 40% of the illegal aliens covertly in the US. These illegal aliens were predominantly Asian not Mexican. By 2003 the INS had spent $31.2 million of our tax dollars to build a computer system to track visa holders and identify violators. Yet, the system was not ready. The INS wanted $57 million more to continue development. [143] Were visa workers employed to program the system that would track them? American IT workers would have a strong incentive to protect their jobs—it is hard to imagine they would not have gotten this system up and running in 1996, much less seven years later in 2003.

H-1B VISA APPLICATION FRAUD

The applications of foreigners getting the H-1B visas were often fraudulent. H-1Bs were supposed to have earned high tech college degrees and have specialized work experience and skills. The US consular office verified that 21% of the H-1B applications submitted in India had fraudulent information. And, an additional 29% of the claims were suspected of being fraudulent. This meant that up to 50% of the H-1B visas granted to India may be fraudulent. [34] [302] Some of the H-1Bs taking high tech American workers' jobs only had a couple of Java programming classes. [24]

Recall also the statistics on foreign student visa fraud—this means many of the H-1Bs who did have the US education credentials claimed may have obtained their degree through fraudulent college applications.

CONGRESS PROTECTED VISA WORKERS BUT NOT AMERICANS

The US Senate unanimously approved an amendment that provided protection to foreign workers who filed complaints against the H-1B visa program. [14] Americans were taxed to investigate and award money to H-1B workers who were abused. Yet, our Congress failed to protect Americans who lost their jobs due to the fraud used to get the H-1B legislation passed. And when unqualified H-1B workers using fake credentials took Americans' jobs and health insurance, American's were not awarded any compensation. Congress even made it illegal to favor keeping US citizens over H-1Bs during a layoff. [31] This is unconscionable given that the H-1B was only granted as a temporary visa to fill jobs where there was a shortage of Americans.

Oracle, Cisco Systems, Intel and Sun Microsystems in Silicon Valley were in the list of companies hiring the most H-1Bs in 2000. The following year these same companies were doing massive layoffs of US citizens. February 1, 2002, AsianWeek.com carried an Associated Press story "H-1B Visa Demand Rises," that said the INS could not produce a count of the number of H-1B applications filed by these companies during the layoffs. [40] During the recession caused by the dotcom crash, many H-1Bs and other visa holders who lost their jobs stayed in the US illegally competing with US citizens for hard to find high tech jobs. The US government not only failed to deport visa violators, but during 2001, in the midst of a recession, it granted over 715,000 work visas and permitted 110,000 foreigners on visitor visas to work in the US. [74]

CONGRESS APPROVED HARMFUL H-1B VISA QUOTA INCREASES

Not only did Congress pass the original H-1B bill in 1990, it repeatedly compounded the harm to American workers by raising the annual H-1B visa quotas.

1998 H-1B Quota Increased to 115,000

In February 1998, Senator Spencer Abraham sponsored a bill to increase the H-1B quota. Executives from major US corporations, including a VP from Sun, a VP from Microsoft, and the President and CEO of Cypress Semiconductor testified to Congress that this increase was essential to fill jobs and protect the US leadership in the computer industry. [123] [13] [54]

> As a Senator from 1995-2001, Abraham was chairman of the Senate Immigration Committee, chairman of the Manufacturing Competitiveness Committee, and he wrote the "H-1B Visa in Global and National Commerce Act." [517]

The White House Office of Management and Budget criticized the bill for focusing on providing job opportunities for foreign workers and failing to protect and provide work opportunities for US citizens. [12] [13]

Americans who found out about the proposed H-1B increase did not believe there was a shortage nor did they believe that foreign workers were more skilled than Americans. A 1998 IEEE-USA/Harris Poll of 1,000 people found that 82% of Americans opposed any visa increases. [36] The president of the Institute of Electrical and Electronics Engineers (IEEE) told the Senate that companies misused the H-1B to try-out foreign workers including illegal aliens, foreign students and foreigners with visitor visas. [54] In April 1998, Dr. Norman Matloff, presented his research findings of H-1B fraud to the U.S House Judiciary Committee's Subcommittee on Immigration in a report: "Debunking the Myth of a Desperate Software Labor Shortage." [24] This in-depth report published on the web was updated in 1999, 2000, and 2001.

Silicon Valley executives engaged in intense lobbying to get the quota increase passed. The Technology Network PAC (TechNet) hosted more than 70 informational meetings and fundraisers including meeting with our President, Vice President, Speaker, House Representatives and Senate leaders. The influence money began to flow. In June 1998, H-1B critics said Abraham received money from Sun Microsystems and fundraising even though he would not be up for reelection for two years. [22] Other sources claimed that executives of Syntel, Mastech, Microsoft, and the American Immigration Lawyers Association (AILA) all made advance donations to Abraham's campaign fund. [468]

Despite opposition, Congress stealthily passed the 1998 visa quota increase, "... but only when hidden within the budget bill." [46] According to a May 1998 article, "Senate Passes Bill Increasing Foreign Worker Visas," the US Senate defied the objections of the Clinton administration and voted to expand the H-1B program. [13] Later President Clinton did a flip flop and signed into law the huge 1998 H-1B quota cap increase to 115,000 visas per year. After signing, Clinton "went on a major fundraising tour of Silicon Valley and some other high-tech regions." [24]

2000 H-1B Visa Quota Increased to 195,000

In March 2000, an article titled, "India's High-Tech Hopes," by a writer in Bombay India, extolled how Clinton's visit to India would be an opportunity to obtain H-1B concessions from the United States. India wanted Clinton to grant almost a 100% increase in H-1B visas yearly quota allowance. [288] Another article, intended for the Indian audience, stated that Clinton hosted a "mother of all official state banquets" in honor of India's visiting Prime Minister. The banquet was touted as the most lavish state dinner hosted by Clinton during his presidency. There were almost 700 guests predominately people who originated from India. [281] How many of the attendees hosted at taxpayer expense were involved in the H-1B visa fraud, outsourcing, and offshoring of US jobs?

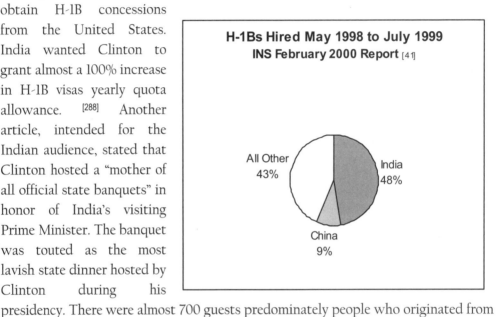

H-1Bs Hired May 1998 to July 1999
INS February 2000 Report [41]

All Other 43%

India 48%

China 9%

Aside from India and China, H-1B visas went to other countries including: the UK, Canada, Philippines, Korea, Taiwan, Japan, Pakistan, Russia, and many more. Each of these countries received 4% or less of the H-1Bs granted. [41][59]

In October 2000, despite warnings of fraud, and strong American public opposition, US Senators voted 95 to 1 to increase H-1B quotas. [26] However, the House wanted to require protections for American high tech workers. In a deceptive maneuver it was announced that there would be no vote on the H-1B that day. When only 40 out of 435 representatives remained, they secretly voted to approve the quota increase without adding protections. [24] A Representative from Virginia in reference to the vote said: *"This is not a popular bill with the public. It's popular with the CEOs ... This is a very important issue for the high-tech executives who give the money."* [24] President Clinton signed the bill: "In one of his last acts as President, Bill Clinton passed the American Competitiveness in the Twenty-First Century Act." This act increased the H-1B quota limit to 195,000 per year. So under Clinton's watch, the H-1B quota tripled from 65,000 to 195,000 per year. [42] (Also see H-1B quota exemptions were granted dramatically increasing the number of H-1B visas issued during his administration.)

2006 Pressure to Increase H-1B Quota to 600,000!

Despite evidence to the contrary, claims of shortages continued. [491] In March 2006, an article, "Congress Considers Massive H-1B Visa Expansion, Gates Tells Congress It's Microsoft's Top Priority," claimed that Congress was considering granting 600,000 H-1B visas in a single year! Senator Arlen Specter drafted the immigration "reform" bill. Bill Gates traveled to Washington DC and spent "his own personal political capital on this issue." Skeptics observed that if a shortage existed, Microsoft wages would have been growing, instead they had been mostly "stagnate for several years." [565] The top ten US technology companies that hired H-1Bs in 2006 listed in order included: Microsoft, IBM, Oracle Corporation, Cisco, Intel, Motorola, Qualcomm, Yahoo, HP and Google. [665] Fast-forward to May 2009, and FoxNews.com reports, "Microsoft Lays off Thousands, Hints at More to Come". [739]

ERRORS AND EXEMPTIONS ALLOW H-1BS TO EXCEED QUOTAS

Errors and exemptions allowed H-1Bs to far exceed the quotas; taking high tech jobs from American programmers, engineers, scientists, medical workers and more at an alarming rate. In 2000, "errors" in a computer program let thousands more H-1Bs into the US than the law allowed. These were convenient "errors" for companies hiring H-1Bs and for H-1Bs wanting American jobs. The INS hired KPMG Peat Marwick, a Big 5 accounting firm, as an outside auditor to find these H-1B errors. However, KPMG was a major employer of H-1Bs, which appears to be a potential conflict of interest. [27] The audit found over 22,000 excess visas were illegally granted. [34] These excess H-1Bs were not counted against the next year's quota, because executives objected and the INS apparently just overlooked the excess H-1Bs illegally granted. [27] So, 22,000 more Americans lost their jobs.

Moreover, the 2000 H-1B quota increase signed by Clinton exempted certain H-1Bs from the quota cap including H-1Bs hired to teach or do research in US universities, H-1B researchers in US government labs, and H-1Bs employed by non-profit organizations. [42]

In a December 30, 2002, article, "H-1B Visas—A Time to Cut Back," by Tom Tancredo for the AWC he claimed that the INS concealed the number of exempted H-1B visas it issued. [29] February 1, 2002, AsianWeek.com carried an Associated Press story "H-1B Visa Demand Rises," that reported the US Congress put no limits on the number of H-1Bs universities could hire. [40] The top ten US universities hiring H-1Bs in 2006 included: University of Michigan, University of Illinois, University of Pennsylvania, Johns Hopkins University School of Medicine, University of Maryland, Columbia University, Yale University, Harvard University, Stanford University and University of Pittsburg. [665]

In 2002, President George W. Bush signed bill, H.R. 2215, increasing US immigration to record levels. The House voted 400 out of 422 representatives to approve the bill. This bill allowed H-1Bs to stay beyond the six year limit, and it allowed foreign medical students to stay in the US as H-1Bs after they graduate, provided they set up practice in rural communities. This means acceptance into a US medical school became an avenue to bypass US immigration controls. [60] No mention was made as to background checks on these foreign workers taking sensitive computer and medical jobs.

When the H-1B visa cap reverted back to 65,000 in 2004, it did little to remedy the damage because of the huge number of H-1B's already in the US, the visa extensions, the quota exemptions, the alternate visas, and the acceleration of offshoring. That year in the midst of rising layoffs, executives lobbied for more exemptions claiming H-1Bs were essential to keeping the US globally competitive. Andy Grove, the Chairmen at Intel wanted foreigners who received graduate degrees to be exempt from quota caps. [404] (In 1999, Intel had a hiring freeze while aggressively lobbying to increase H-1B quotas. [31])

In 2005, Americans were pressuring Congress to reform or end the H-1B. The ITAA fought against any requirement for companies to prove they did not displace Americans, or that they made an effort to hire Americans first. ITAA was pleased when President Bush approved 20,000 new exemptions to the H-1B cap for foreign students who obtain graduate degrees from US universities. *ITAA claimed that because foreign students take over 50% of the graduate degrees in science and engineering that it is good for America to keep them here, because sending them home would deprive America of its public investment in educating them.* It said that American companies should have the first opportunity to hire them. [65]

The high tech job losses for Americans number in the millions. Multiple sources claim that our government failed to keep an accurate count of H-1B visas it granted. So, there are wide variations in estimates. For example, according to a report titled, "Amazing Facts and Statistics: Non-immigrant (Temporary) Foreign Work Visa

Programs and Workers," posted by Rescue American over 4 million H-1B visas were granted by the INS from 1998 to 2001. [28] In contrast, Representative Tom Tancredo's statistics reported to the House showed about 1.4 million H-1B Visas were granted from 1998 to 2002. [603] Some counts may only include computer workers and not count engineers or medical workers. Note the H-1B legislation was passed in 1990, so the first eight years of the program are not included in either of these estimates. [603]

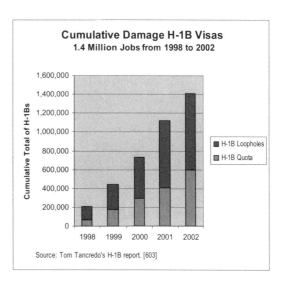

Source: Tom Tancredo's H-1B report. [603]

Tancredo emphasized *H-1Bs were "not supposed to be able to dislocate any American worker*," and the 90 day rule between the layoffs and hiring of H-1Bs should be extended six months. He reported a study found that 45% of the work experience claims on H-1B applications from India were fraudulent, and that H-1Bs stayed in the US illegally after they lost their jobs. Tancredo submitted bill H.R. 2688 to repeal the H-1B program saying Congress is obligated to tell Americans the truth and that the need for H-1B workers was based on lies. [603] The US India Political Action Committee (USINPAC) claimed that it blocked Tancredo's bill to end the H-1B program.

In 2003, the INS acknowledged that the number of H-1B visas issued were more than double its official count. The INS did not count H-1Bs who got approved for extended stays, nor the H-1Bs issued to universities and to non-profit organizations because they are exempt from the quota controls. [63] Nor did the INS track the number of layoffs of US citizens caused by the visas. [16] The INS has a mandate to deport H-1Bs immediately if they are laid off or fired. Yet the INS informed H-1Bs that they would not be deported and that they could stay in the US to look for jobs. [28]

EXECUTIVES TREATED H-1BS LIKE INDENTURED SERVANTS

Executives preferred to hire H-1Bs because H-1Bs were bound by restrictive work contracts executives misused to treat H-1Bs like indentured servants that they could overwork and underpay. If H-1Bs complained executives could threaten to send them back to their country. In December 2000, an H-1B programmer from India complained that their status was like a "modern-day slave." [26]

Although employers were legally required to pay H-1B visa workers the going wage, multiple studies found that H-1Bs were paid significantly less. One article reported that by using various schemes, executives were able to pay H-1Bs about a half of what they paid US citizens. [63] Other reports estimated that H-1Bs were paid 15% to 33% below normal or about $20,000 to $25,000 less. [34]

An Indian manager with a green card who helped companies hire H-1Bs explained that companies liked hiring H-1Bs, because they would work for low pay and put in fourteen hour days and not charge for overtime. [31]

SECRET H-1B HIRING PRACTICES

Much of the H-1B hiring was done secretly. Congress did not require companies to advertise the jobs or give US citizens an opportunity to apply. [31] So, companies hired H-1Bs to fill high tech jobs that were never even posted. [35] Executives became adept at modifying job requirements to favor hiring H-1Bs. [49] For example; executives may hire H-1Bs first, and then write the job requirements. [468]

In 2007, the underhanded truth about H-1B hiring was caught on a video titled, "H-1B Video Shocker: 'Our Goal is Clearly Not to Find a Qualified ... U.S. Worker." A lawyer was recorded giving tips on how to hire H-1Bs. It was proof that US employers secretly discriminated against hiring US citizens. [666]

INVESTIGATIONS OF H-1B HIRING

The INS and the US Department of Labor initiated investigations into H-1B visa fraud and abuse by some of the biggest American high tech companies. [34] In March 2003, the President-Elect of the IEEE-USA requested a legal investigation of H-1B and L-1B hiring practices. He claimed that during a time when over 500,000 high tech jobs were cut, almost 800,000 new or renewal H-1B visas were issued, and in 2001 there were 329,000 L-1 visa workers in the US. He asserted that outsourcing companies used the *H-1B and L-1 visas to fill jobs that Americans needed and were qualified to fill.* [62]

Also in 2003, Dr. Matloff reported that executives in several major corporations admitted that they had misused H-1B and L1 visa workers to replace American workers. He proposed several reforms including a required 6 month waiting period before hiring H-1Bs after a layoff. [329]

According to a June 2006, article, "Tech Worker Group Files Complaints Over H-1B Job Ads" The Programmers Guild was filing legal complaints against companies that advertised specifically to hire H-1B visa workers. The group alleged that companies in the US were in violation of the U.S. Immigration and Nationality Act that requires jobs inside the US must be available to American workers. Some of the ads not only required H-1Bs, but even specified that they must be from India. [594]

SUN MICROSYSTEMS DISCRIMINATION

In 2003, Sun Microsystems laid off more than 2,500 US citizens. The discrimination appeared blatant. People from India made up 30% or more of Sun's employees yet in Santa Clara Country people from India comprised only 4% of the overall population. [55]

Sun co-founder Vinod Khosla in a 2003 interview with "60 Minutes" *stated that H-1B workers from India "are favored over almost anybody else."* [125] Khosla said, "If you are a WASP (White Anglo-Saxon Protestant) walking in for a job, you wouldn't have as much pre-assigned credibility as you do if you're an engineer from the Indian Institute of Technology." [55] Khosla was born in India, and came to the United States as a student. [188] The superiority claims were bogus—Java, Sun's leading software for the Internet was developed by James Gosling—a white guy. In 2005, Gosling was Sun's CTO for creating products for developers. [478]

GOVERNMENT INVESTIGATING THE ULTIMATE IRONY

While the H-1B was supposed to be temporary, H-1Bs applied for green cards to allow them to work in the US indefinitely. A June 2008, article reported that the Labor Department was auditing pending foreign worker green card applications. The investigation centered on compliance with US law when converting temporary visas (i.e. H-1Bs and other visas) to green cards. While to get H-1Bs companies did not have to prove they tried to hire Americans first, US law does require that before sponsoring a foreign visa worker for a green card, a company must first attempt to recruit and hire qualified American workers. The jobs involved pay $80,000 on average and applicants from India dominated the applications being audited. The ultimate irony is that H-1Bs took American jobs by working well below the prevailing wage, but once they had job experience they were trying to use attorneys to lock the jobs in at about the same pay level as the Americans they displaced. The Labor Department wanted to make sure that Americans get access to jobs they are qualified for and that their working conditions are not negatively impacted by visa workers. [709] The audit was closed a few months later in the fall of 2008.

CONGRESS PASSED MORE FOREIGN WORKER VISA PROGRAMS

Congress also approved the TN visa that allows Canadians and Mexicans to work in the US under a program similar to the H-1B visa. Congress approved the L-1 visa for intra-company transfers of executives or employees with specialized training.

Large outsourcing firms that had become "gatekeepers" for personnel management hit the jackpot with the approval of the L-1 visa. By 2001, outsourcing firms had brought 328,480 L-1 visa workers into the United States that they then contracted out to take American jobs. [63] Executives ordered Americans to train the L-1s who took their jobs. [52] A March 2006, article for people in India, "Worried about H-1B visa? Take the L1 Route," reassuringly claimed that a visit from President Bush to India was "a shot in the arm for Indians aspiring to work in America." The article explained that the L-1 visa had no cap and could be used to get around H-1B limits, and did not require paying the prevailing wage. [567]

In 2002, Congress passed the Trade Promotion Authority (TPA) previously known as Fast Track which empowers the President to negotiate trade agreements with open border visas. These visas allow the free movement of foreign labor into the US job market. The TPA was sought by foreign nations who "do not have goods to trade, but they do have vast supplies of labor." To open up their markets to US companies they required that international companies be able to bring foreign workers into the US without immigration reviews. [60] TPA agreements put overpopulated countries in a position to overrun the US. A TPA agreement cannot be repealed by the US Congress without the consent of the foreign country benefiting from the agreement. [60] The US media failed to keep US citizens informed of this broad reaching legislation that could cost millions of US citizens their jobs.

FOREIGN GRADUATES GRANTED 2 ½ YEARS TO FIND US JOBS!

High tech American workers will be aghast to learn that, in April 2008 months before our presidential election, Microsoft and other H-1B employers praised the US Department of Homeland Security for increasing the time foreigners graduating from US colleges can stay and search for a visa job from one year to almost two and a half years! [727] Our government knew there was no shortage when highly skilled Americans were being laid off in mass. Later in January of 2009, Microsoft announced that it planned to cut 5,000 jobs. [729] (When was US law changed from requiring foreign graduates to leave within 60 days of graduating to allowing a year?)

AUTOMATIC GREEN CARDS FOR FOREIGN GRADUATES!

After the H-1B visa quota increase was blocked in 2007, and facing a big backlog of H-1Bs wanting green cards, US Rep Zoe Lofgren a Democrat from California, had the audacity to introduce several bills that would allow foreign graduate students to get permanent residency green cards directly, instead of first getting H-1B visas. [731]

H-1B & OFFSHORING SUPPORTERS GET KEY POSTS

According to a February 2009, *ComputerWorld* article titled, "H-1B, Offshoring Supporters Get Key Obama Administration Posts," President Obama "filled some of his top White House posts with people who not only support expanding the H-1B visa program, but also see offshore outsourcing as a plus for the U.S. economy." One of his appointees, Diana Farrell selected to serve on the National Economic Council and as economic advisor to Obama, is the "former director of the McKinsey Global Institute, McKinsey & Co.'s economics research arm." McKinsey is the consulting firm behind many of the studies that claim H-1Bs and offshoring US jobs benefits the United States. Another appointee Judd Greg, Obama's Commerce Secretary, was quoted as saying, "We're actually creating jobs by bringing bright people into this country." Gregg acknowledged that the H-1B had been misused to transfer knowledge to India; however, he thought this could be fixed with "minor adjustments to the program." The TechNet lobby lauded Gregg's appointment. The most shocking admission in the article was: *Indian offshore firms are the largest users of the H-1B visas and consider it critical to their delivery model for moving IT functions offshore. It is a point they have made repeatedly in U.S. Security and Exchange Commission filings.*" [730] How can our government allow this program to continue with this admission that H-1Bs enabled the offshoring of high tech American jobs? This violates Obama's campaign promise to Americans that he would stop the offshoring of our jobs.

The article mentioned two objectors to Obama's appointees. Senator Chuck Grassley (R-Iowa) believed that H-1Bs were taking jobs from Americans. And, assistant professor Ron Hira from the Rochester Institute of Technology, warned that Obama, "is either ignorant or naïve about the real job market for American IT workers. He is doing his level best, with these appointments, to undermine American workers and their livelihoods." [730]

INCREASING H-1BS DURING A RECESSION?

In 2007, then Senator Obama supported the Senate's efforts to increase H-1B quotas from 85,000 to 180,000—the House refused to approve the increase. [731] Obama's campaign promise "to stop giving tax breaks to companies that ship jobs overseas" did not tell Americans his solution was to bring the foreign workers here: "We should allow immigrants who earn their degrees in the U.S. to stay, work and become Americans over time. And we should examine our ability to increase the number of permanent visas we issue to foreign-skilled workers." [731] Note that Obama refers to foreign students as "immigrants" when they are not—they are granted "non-immigrant" student visas. Apparently Obama cares more for foreign students, perhaps because his father was a foreign student, than he does for American citizens.

Granting citizenship to the foreigners taking their jobs is not the change Americans were sold. Moreover, President Obama plans to double basic research spending—a significant amount of this money will go to fund US university research done by graduate students. Foreign students currently take about half of this research. So, *his plans may double the number of foreign graduate students who seek the H-1B and other visas.* [731] If Obama's plan is implemented he will devastate American programmers, engineers, and other high tech workers; and, make it impossible for them to support their families. Increased immigration on such a massive scale will enable foreigners who made no sacrifices to build and defend our country, and have demonstrated no loyalty to our country, to take over our country.

According to a March 2009 article titled, "H-1B: Indian CEOs Meet Obama Team" foreign corporate leaders from India had already met with the Obama team, and were reassured that unless US employment became much more severe the H-1B program would continue as would offshoring of American jobs to India. [735]

Chapter 8

Outsourcing & Offshoring Deceptions

Executives use outsourcing firms to cover up transferring jobs from US citizens to foreign workers.

Outsourcing occurs when a corporation contracts with another company (an outsourcing/consulting company) to do work that otherwise would have been done internally by full time employees. Outsourcing was originally used to help companies with tasks that were outside the scope of their primary business. For example, a manufacturing company may outsource creating and maintaining employee handbooks to a company that specializes in writing handbooks. This type of limited outsourcing may be very beneficial. Most importantly it does not require the company to disclose any confidential information.

Some companies abused outsourcing and hired programmers and engineers as independent contractors, who because of the amount of time they were working should have been hired as full time employees with full benefits. So, Congress passed the Tax Reform Act of 1986 which required that high tech workers such as engineers and programmers who had been working as independent contractors be classified as employees. Instead of the desired results, large consulting companies sprang up that hired these high tech workers as their employees. In turn they contracted their employees back to the corporations receiving the services.

Through outsourcing contacts these consulting companies controlled the hiring for many American high tech jobs. [63] This created a situation that was far worse for Americans than being independent contractors. The consulting/outsourcing companies paid lower wages and cut costs by requiring longer work hours and providing fewer benefits. Worst of all, once American programmers and engineers became employees of an outsourcing company, the outsourcing company could then force them to train cheaper foreign workers such as H-1Bs. Americans were required to write step-by-step process instructions the lesser skilled H-1Bs could follow and use to appear highly knowledgeable and skilled. Once the H-1Bs had work experience the outsourcing companies laid off the Americans.

OUTSOURCING USED TO COVER-UP HIRING FOREIGN WORKERS

The passage of the H-1B visa legislation in 1990 laid the foundation for an outsourcing boom. When American corporations hired H-1B visa workers, and laid off Americans they were met with public protests and lawsuits. So instead of hiring H-1Bs directly, corporate executives used outsourcing/consulting firms to cover up how many jobs they are transferring from US citizens to foreign workers. For example, when American employees laid off by Siemens were replaced with L-1 visa workers supplied by Tata Consultancy, Americans protested. Siemens management responded that, "They don't work for us. They work for Tata." [63] The H-1B visa legislation was a windfall for outsourcing companies in the US who made big business out of replacing Americans with foreign visa workers.

Outsourcing led to the mass transfer of high tech US jobs from citizens to foreign workers. In turn, foreign visa workers in the United States were used by foreign nations to promote transferring high tech US jobs to foreign countries.

The "thought leaders" behind the transfer of Americans jobs to foreign workers make fun of Americans who confuse outsourcing with hiring foreign workers directly. Americans do not know the difference because our media has failed to educate them. It is very simple. When a US company hires foreign workers directly, either in America or in a foreign country, the foreign workers become employees of the company, and therefore the work is not outsourced. When American citizens lost their jobs to foreign visa workers hired directly by a US company, then the Americans did not lose their job because of outsourcing. They lost their jobs because company executives hired foreign employees

to replace them.

Outsourcing occurs when a US corporation contracts with an outsourcing company to supply workers. The outsourcing company may employ Americans, however, many outsourcing companies are major employers of foreign visa workers in the US, and many outsourcing companies own offshore facilities. The outsourced work may be done on the client's site, or at the outsourcing company's site. The key difference is that the workers provided by the outsourcing company are employees of the outsourcing company, not employees of the US Corporation where they work under contract. Either way Americans are displaced by foreign workers.

To clear up another misconception, outsourcing is not synonymous with sending American jobs overseas. In the 1990's, the majority of outsourcing was done inside the United States. In 2004, over 70% of outsourcing was still being done inside the US. [80] When outsourced work is done in a foreign country, such as China or India, it is offshore outsourcing. It is common for offshore outsourcing to just be called outsourcing, thus the misconception that outsourcing is synonymous with sending work overseas. It is important to understand that the two are linked, because outsourcing in America was the first step towards offshoring American jobs.

OUTSOURCING DIRTY SECRETS

The whole concept of outsourcing jobs to foreign workers was conflicted. Both the buyer (US executives getting bonuses) and the seller (outsourcing company executives) had strong personal financial motivations that worked against US employees and US investors. Although outsourcing is sold as a cost savings strategy, the outsourcing company's business strategy is to maximize billable hours. They have developed a plethora of methods for increasing the hours they can bill after a contract is signed. Anything not spelled out in the contract is an additional cost.

Outsourcing companies used polished presentations claiming they cut costs up to 40% because of their methodologies; however, the truth was that many outsourcing companies, American owned and foreign owned, underhandedly cut costs by displacing American workers with foreign workers. Moreover, outsourcing companies became adept at making unqualified H-1Bs look highly skilled. They created an arsenal of professional looking templates the H-1Bs could use to appear to be expert analysts, programmers, and project managers. If an H-1B lacked work experience, skills, and/or ideas, they have the whole consulting firm of employees from which to draw. It is like having a whole network of people and resources secretly helping you take a test. In school submitting work done by others, and then representing it as your own would be called cheating. After the US citizen loses his/her job; the American company is at the mercy of the outsourcing company. The outsourcing company can begin jacking up billable hours, for often unqualified visa workers, and then making excuses for project errors and delays. Even worse, the outsourcing company can secretly sell the same work to a customer's competitor. Imagine how impressed the next US company will be when a lesser skilled H-1B simply keys in the same code, which may have been written mostly by an American programmer, piece by piece to make it look like he/she is creating the software—and another US citizen loses his/her job from deceptive, unfair competition.

OUTSOURCING MEGA DEALS

The IT outsourcing contracts signed by American companies were huge. In 2001, nine mega deals totaled $15.1 billion. In 2002 there were 14 mega deals that totaled $23.4 billion plus four more mega deals were pending that were estimated to be worth $15.3 billion. IBM won seven out of the 14 mega deals in 2002. [104] The amount spent on large outsourcing projects grew by 44% during 2003, and reached $119 billion. [80] Large consulting firms found a lucrative business model transferring US citizens' jobs to foreign workers. A 2005 ranking of outsourcing companies listed IBM first with a market valuation of $140 billion, ADP second with a value of $26 billion, and Accenture at $23 billion. The next two slots went to Indian outsourcing companies—Infosys at $19.9 billion, and Wipro at $14.6 billion. [80]

OUTSOURCING FAILED TO DELIVER COST SAVINGS

Year after year of investigations found outsourcing companies repeatedly failed to deliver the cost savings promised. One 1998 investigation found that 46% of the outsourcing contracts never provided any savings. [523] According to a 2003 investigation, 50% of outsourcing deals failed to deliver the value promised. Another study that year found that 30% of companies did not receive any cost savings, and some actually paid more than if they had kept the work in-house. [80] A 2004 study reported that less than one fourth of the companies saved more than 25%, and 10% of the companies had no cost savings. [398] Another 2004 study reported that 80% of the companies responding had outsourcing experiences fraught with problems such as failures to meet time commitments, failures to meet performance requirements, and cost overruns. [80] A different 2004 survey reported that 21% of the companies that had outsourced were compelled to prematurely terminate the outsourcing contract. Reasons for the terminations included the financial instability of the outsourcing firm and the failure to deliver on promised commitments. By 2005, an investigation found the number of companies that cancelled outsourcing contracts midstream jumped to an incredible 51%. The number one reason for contract cancellations was failure of the outsourcing firm to deliver on commitments. The survey also found that an additional 13% of the companies that tried outsourcing terminated the relationship at the end of the contract. [510] Another 2005 survey of 25 major corporations that had outsourced $50 billion in contract work found that 70% were dissatisfied. Almost 50% did not receive the promised cost savings. In 25% of the corporations responding to the survey, the outsourcing work was so inferior the work was brought back in-house. [80] [122]

OUTSOURCING CUSTOMER SUPPORT CAUSED LOST REVENUES

Outsourcers should be required to disclose to US companies that an estimated 80% of companies that have tried outsourcing customer support did not achieve the cost savings promised. And, they should also be required to advise potential clients that an estimated 60% of companies that tried outsourcing customer support lost customers. [503] Outsourcing customer service could cost a company 30% more than maintaining the services in-house. Outsourcing customer service resulted in a high customer defection rates and other hidden costs that far outweighed the purported savings. [83] For example, Dell, a large computer manufacturer, had to stop sending corporate customer technical support calls to Bangalore, India due to a flood of complaints. Despite complaints, Dell continued to offshore customer support for American consumers. A November 25, 2003, *earthlink.net* Technology News release reported that more than half of Dell's 44,300 employees are overseas foreign workers. [126]

OUTSOURCING LAWSUITS

Problems with outsourcing were so frequent and severe that law firms began to specialize in outsourcing lawsuits. As early as 2000, lawsuits from failed outsourcing projects were a growing field for litigation. Outsourcing clients were so dissatisfied that 53% of outsourcing customers renegotiated their contract. In 25% of the renegotiation cases the outsourcing company lost the contract due to customer dissatisfaction. [132]

OUTSOURCING "HOLLOWS OUT" AMERICAN COMPANIES

Outsourcing companies pitch their outsourcing contracts to high level CEO's not to the corporate IT experts. Outsourcing companies target executives who are not tech savvy enough to know how to evaluate the outsourcing proposal, but who can be lured when shown how to extract a large bonus on projected savings by signing outsourcing deals. [132] After outsourcing companies convinced US executives to layoff the highest paid Americans, the executives became pawns of the outsourcing company. An October 2005 Electronic Design article titled, "The Shifting Design Cycle," quoted Walter Shawlee, president of Sphere Research Corp. as saying: "While layoffs seem to make companies look good on the balance sheet and in the stock market, they irretrievably hollow out businesses in terms of real ability and product quality." Shawlee observed that it was "the worst kind of duplicity" when executives lay off massive numbers of highly skilled Americans then turn around and claim the US has a high tech labor shortage. [451]

DID OUTSOURCING CAUSE US COMPANY FAILURES?

Outsourcing rarely produced the cost savings promised. A group that surveyed several outsourcing firms discovered that while in 2004 outsourcing companies claimed only 7% of their customers prematurely terminated; by 2005 they admitted that 49% terminated their outsourcing contracts early. *The number one reason the outsourcing firms gave for the contract terminations was that their customer went out of business.* [510] Was outsourcing causing US companies to fail? Companies that no longer exist cannot give feedback on outsourcing experiences. [510] Was outsourcing allowing foreign competitors to steal intellectual property, business plans, customers, and more? *While outsourcing often fails to deliver cost savings, it always results in "knowledge transfer" because the outsourcing company's employees gain access to proprietary strategic business and technical data.* [523]

EXECUTIVES TAKE BIG BONUSES AND COVER-UP LOSSES

Despite all the problems, outsourcing continued as executives covered up the losses from cost overruns, customer defections, foreign knowledge transfers, and national security risks. The most logical explanation of why outsourcing and offshoring continued to grow is the linkage to shady accounting tricks used to take huge executive bonuses. Moreover, executives who elected to outsource, and then discovered it was a big mistake were understandably reluctant to share the lessons they learned with their peers. Especially they are reluctant to report the failure of an initiative they promoted and received a bonus for. However, slowly but surely the truth begins to emerge.

FOREIGN GOVERNMENTS OFFER OFFSHORE ENTICEMENTS

US politicians may be surprised to learn that cheaper foreign workers were not the main reason for offshoring. Foreign governments provided incentives to American corporations that cut the cost of capital to attract strategic US high tech industries. The main reasons high tech and other US companies went offshore were foreign government enticements in the form of lower taxes and other incentives. [615]

OFFSHORE TO AVOID HEALTHCARE COSTS

Cutting healthcare costs has also been a major factor in American companies deciding to outsource and/or offshore to foreign workers. Outsourcing allows American Corporations to evade paying for expensive health insurance. For example, in 2004, due to rising health care costs, GM spent more on health insurance than on steel to build vehicles. Retirees and their families were responsible for 69% of GM's massive health insurance costs. [271]

US GOVERNMENT TAX INCENTIVES FUELED OFFSHORING

Our government gave tax breaks to US corporations that moved operations offshore, and compounded the offense by giving incentives to keep profits outside of the United States. If corporations produced products in the US they had to pay 35% of profits in taxes. However, if US corporations go offshore they pay no US taxes as long as they keep the money outside of the US. Tax deferment incentives encouraged companies to reinvest profits in foreign countries rather than invest in improving operations in the US. This is destroying our country. US multinational corporations kept billions of dollars of income outside of the United States, so that they could cut the amount of US taxes they paid.

Executives taking advantage of the tax breaks looked like they were brilliant managers earning fantastic returns, when what they were really doing was inflating profits by avoiding paying US taxes. Consider for example that Hewlett Packard was reported to have kept $14.4 billion of foreign earnings in tax deferment. Not only did this deprive the US government of important taxes, it accelerated the cutting of US jobs. To keep from paying US taxes, companies like Intel and HP reinvested their profits in foreign countries creating jobs in other countries. *The big winner profiting from the tax deferment on the offshore outsourcing was India.* [134] To avoid paying US taxes some American companies even set up offshore shell divisions that consisted of a PO box. According to an April 13, 2009 report titled "Are You Paying for Corporate Fat Cats?" in 2004, 61% of US corporations "paid no corporate income taxes between 1996 and 2000." American companies used offshore loopholes to avoid paying taxes, including "24 of the largest federal contractors." American citizens are stuck with the bill. [689]

In March 2004, the Institute of Electrical and Electronic Engineering (IEEE) requested that the US government stop providing companies financial incentives for offshoring, and begin enforcing intellectual property export controls. The IEEE emphasized that protecting American jobs and technology was vital to our economy and national security. [88] In May 2004, the IEEE-USA had 235,000 engineers as members who were concerned about job losses to offshore outsourcing. The IEEE-USA sent several proposals to the US Congress trying to stop the destructive mass movement of high-tech jobs to foreign countries. [129]

SECRET US GOVERNMENT ROLE IN CAUSING ECONOMIC CRISIS

The 2009 US economic crisis should have come as no surprise to our politicians. Our government had plenty of advance warnings to know that outsourcing and offshoring were causing enormous harm to Americans and our economy. Yet, both federal and state government computer jobs were channeled to foreign workers—violating the public trust and harming our economy.

You are Good Enough to Tax but Too Expensive to Hire!

One of the biggest secrets is that our federal government's role goes far beyond passing legislation they knew Americans opposed, and failure to prosecute executives who provided false testimony to get H-1B legislation passed, and illegally replaced Americans with foreigners. One of the largest employers outsourcing jobs away from US citizens is our own government. Politicians, like executives, wanted to keep the H-1B program and outsourcing out of the public eye. You are good enough to tax, but too expensive to hire! *The large amount of taxpayer-paid computer work performed by non-citizens for at least 12 state governments and 9 federal agencies is a scandal crying out for investigation.*" [63] The government has been taxing Americans then spending many of those tax dollars to pay foreign workers. Each time this is done it depletes the US economically. [88]

The US Government has been especially lucrative for Information Technology (IT) outsourcing companies. Our government spending on IT services ran $37.1 billion in 2002, and was projected to reach $63.3 billion by 2007. This dependency on outsourcing companies' services ranged from global intelligence information needed for military defense, to personal communications between military personnel and their families, and more. [220] The transfer of government jobs to foreign workers and foreign countries played a major role in causing America's 2009 economic crisis. The US government has betrayed American workers, "U.S. governments are increasingly using India to manage everything from accounting to their food stamp programs. Even the U.S. Postal Service is sending work to India. Automobile engineering and drug research could be next." [300] The American public was misled by the political rhetoric of keeping the government smaller. Our government was replacing American employees by outsourcing, thus shifting defense jobs and other strategic jobs to foreign workers.

The US government has been called, "the biggest shopper on the planet." For example, in 2001 alone, the US government bought $235 billion worth of goods and services. The scope of US government spending ranged from nuclear research, to food, to military equipment, and much more. [135] Each year billions of dollars flows from US government spending into businesses that sell goods and services to the federal government. When these businesses began hiring foreign workers they were transferring money taken from US taxpayers to foreign workers and foreign governments. [205] In 2001, many of the corporations listed in the top 100 recipients of federal government contracts were hiring foreign H-1Bs directly or through outsourcing companies. To name just a few of the contractors and the dollar amount of government contracts they received: Lockheed ($3 billion), Northrop Grumman ($1 billion), Raytheon ($1 billion), Electronic Data Systems Corp. ($970 million), AT&T ($796 million), TRW ($922 million), Boeing ($788 million), Dell ($455 million), Unisys ($452 million), Motorola ($373 million), IBM ($359 million), Verizon ($209 million), WorldCom ($201 million), Oracle ($174 million), Lucent ($157 million), Honeywell ($156 million), KPMG ($150 million), PricewaterhouseCoopers($126 million), Carlyle Group ($112 million) ...[137]

The US government has the power to quickly remedy the dearth of research jobs available to US engineers, programmers, and other high tech fields. The National Science Foundation (NSF) spent $5.6 billion in 2006, and proposed an increase to $6 billion in 2007. The Defense Advanced Research Project Agency spent $3 billion in 2006 and proposed an increase to $3.3 billion for 2007. The National Institute of Standards and Technology (NIST) proposed a budget of $581 million for 2007. [515] These technology contracts could put highly skilled US citizens, who were unfairly displaced by foreign workers, back to work. This money was budgeted to finance research in biology, computer science, engineering, nanotechnology, biological warfare defense, space programs, network-centric warfare technology, guidance technology, and much more. These jobs should be done by Americans.

States Were Also Hiring Foreign Workers

Outsourcing of technology contracts by state and local governments reached $10 billion in 2003, and was predicted to more than double reaching $23 billion by 2008. [140] For example, in 2002, the state of California had outsourced $76.6 million worth of work to technical services companies. These outsourcing companies had operations in the US and overseas. State officials signing these contracts did not

know how much of this money was going to pay for work done by foreign workers.
[105]

In 2003, the state of New Mexico signed an offshore contract with a company in India for $6 million to program an online unemployment claims system. That same year the Pennsylvania Department of Corrections contracted for an overseas company to program critical systems. New Jersey had contracted with an offshore company in India to answer calls from people on welfare. [144] In 2003, taxpayers in New Mexico were outraged when they discovered that foreigners were programming software for the Taxation and Revenue Department, and the state even used private attorneys to help these foreign workers get green cards. Taxpayers in New Jersey were also outraged when they discovered that the state had hired contractors who then subcontracted welfare service support calls to Bombay, India. [63]

By 2005, forty or more states were offshoring the administration of electronic cards for food stamps. Many states outsourced public sector jobs to consulting companies. *Most government officials signing these contracts do not know how much of this work is being done by foreign workers in the US, and how much is being sent overseas.* An audit of the state of Washington exposed that 36 out of 41 state agencies were contracting with outsourcers to do work offshore. Offshoring of state government work was rapidly accelerating. In 2004, $10 billion was spent on outsourcing contracts and this was projected to jump to $23 billion by 2008. [141]

INSOURCING MYTH

When a foreign company has operations in America it is called "insourcing." A growing US backlash was building in response to US citizens' job losses to foreign workers. Executives and foreign countries hyped the insourcing myth to diffuse outsourcing protests. For example, in a May 10, 2004, *Electronic Design* article, "Outsourcing: How Safe is Your Job," by Ron Schneiderman, the VP of Marketing Intelligence for the research firm iSuppli Corp. claimed that sales to Asia were "keeping American workers employed in semiconductor manufacturing and design jobs." [129] They cleverly fail to mention that the primary reason Asia is a big consumer of semiconductors is because executives in US corporations offshored production of computers and other electronic devices. The computer chip technology was created in the US not Asia.

The most frequently used insourcing examples are Japanese automakers that employee US citizens who produce cars in America for sale in America. [95] But really this only helped prevent job losses, because Americans were already producing automobiles to sell in the US market. This caused less economic damage than importing foreign cars, because at least many American workers were employed.

However, the corporate profits belonged to a foreign company, not a US company. Are any of the Japanese cars produced in America exported to Japan or other nations?

A 2004 article in the *economictimes.indiatimes.com* claimed that foreign companies created almost 6.4 million jobs in America during the recession, and paid wages to workers in America of about $350 billion. It further claimed foreign investment helped lessen the impact of the 2001 economic slump in the United States. [95] While this sounds good, it is very deceptive according to a September 13, 2004, *Economic Recovery Review* article by Dean Baker titled, "Outsourcing". According to his investigation of "insourcing" the claims of foreign investment creating jobs for Americans were false: *"The vast majority of jobs at foreign owned firms were not created by foreign investment, but rather are the result of the decision of foreign companies to buy up existing U.S. companies."* [68] When a US Corporation was acquired by a foreign company; the US employees were then considered insourced. This created a clever way to deceptively claim that foreign companies created jobs for Americans. In reality no jobs were created. In fact, many Americans lost their jobs when buyers brought in foreign visa workers and pressed for offshoring.

From 1998 to 2000, foreign companies spent $900 billion acquiring US companies, while US companies only spent $419 billion buying foreign companies. [488] Even more significant was the big difference in what was being bought and sold. American citizens were getting the short end of the stick in both types of deals. Buying American companies allowed foreign nations to acquire advanced US technology that they then used to challenge America's technology leadership. [488] US companies in stark contrast often bought foreign companies to acquire cheap foreign workers to cloak how American jobs were being transferred to foreign workers. Mergers almost always cause layoffs. A 2000 engineering survey, found that 97% of the respondents had been impacted by a merger. [229] How many of the foreign acquisitions were bought using money obtained because executives in American companies hired foreign visa workers, and/or outsourced and offshored American jobs to foreign countries?

To gain a better understanding of what has been going on, imagine executives in a US corporation being approached by a foreign outsourcing company with branches inside the US. The outsourcing company shows executives how they can get paid huge bonuses by outsourcing information technology (IT) jobs. The US executives sign the outsourcing contract with the agreement that the outsourcing company hires 900 out of their current 1,000 American information technology workers. At this point the outsourcing company may claim it created 900 jobs for Americans when in fact it cut 100 jobs. Next the outsourcing company may import 200 low paid H-1B visa workers, and then claim that it created another 200 jobs in the US job market even though none of these jobs went to Americans. The acquired American employees are forced to train the H-1Bs. After about a year the 200 H-1Bs have enough on the job training that the foreign outsourcing company lays off 200 Americans, and imports 300 more visa workers. After another year, 300 more American workers are laid off. And, so the pattern goes. Despite causing hundreds of Americans to lose their jobs, the outsourcing company claims to be creating jobs in America.

Another insourcing deception relates to the difference in how US offshore and foreign insourcing companies were staffed. For example, a US corporate subsidiary in China would hire mostly Chinese employees. A US corporate subsidiary in India would hire mostly Indian employees. In stark contrast some foreign owned firms operating subsidiaries inside the United States hire many H-1B and L-1 visa workers from their country of origin. Americans lost jobs when foreign companies insourced, and Americans lost jobs when American corporations offshored work to foreign countries.

Another insourcing deception involved studies that produced misleading data. For example, insourcing analysts used the Bureau of Economic Analysis (BEA) data that tracks foreign businesses owned or controlled by US corporations, and it tracks US businesses owned or controlled by foreign corporations. The BEA data does not track how many American jobs are lost due to offshore outsourcing to foreign owned companies located in foreign countries. Additionally, the BEA does not track who is being hired to fill these jobs. It only considers "the number of jobs" available in each country. US-owned businesses located in India provide jobs to Indians. Unfortunately, many Indian-owned businesses located in the US actually hire a large percentage of H-1Bs. And finally, the data in the BEA report fails to acknowledge how many of the jobs in the US "created" by foreign ownership were actually replacing jobs previously filled by Americans with H-1Bs. The massive American job losses resulting from US corporations contracting with outsourcing companies for jobs such as software development or for call center support were not included. [69]

Another insourcing claim was that the US made money selling computers, software, and telecom equipment to foreign outsourcing companies. It is absurd to compare selling a $2000 computer to a foreign programmer in exchange for an $80,000 per year programming job. With regard to insourcing generating income for Americans, foreign outsourcing companies did spend a lot paying American PR companies to develop propaganda, buying US politicians, paying American law firms for assistance with immigration and contracts, buying US media, and they spent money to get US accounting firms to claim cost savings from outsourcing. So, a few Americans did make a lot of money at the expense of the millions of Americans harmed. The net impact of "insourcing" from foreign acquisitions and foreign outsourcing contracts to America is highly destructive.

Our own government promoted the insourcing myth. For example, in 2004, the US Labor Secretary Elaine L. Chao was quoted as saying that the number of US jobs lost to foreign countries "was far outweighed by the number of jobs in the United States at foreign owned companies." [68] If outsourcing, insourcing, and offshoring were in fact benefiting America it would be reflected in our trade deficit. In 2004, when she made this claim the US trade deficit was already almost $600 billion annually. [68]

FOREIGN OUTSOURCING FIRMS ALLOWED TO "IMPORT" H-1BS

Our government allowed foreign owned outsourcing businesses to staff up their US offices hiring foreign visa workers. [516] This violated the premise that the H-1B was approved to help American companies be globally competitive. Foreign outsourcing companies knew that US corporations were leery of the risks from offshoring, so they set up outsourcing offices inside the US. Outsourcing then became an easy sell when they showed US executives they could get huge bonuses based on "projected cost savings". These foreign outsourcing firms cunningly claimed that America is an importer of high tech jobs even though these jobs did not exist in a foreign country. It was deceptive propaganda to claim that hiring foreign visa workers is importing jobs. This is not importing jobs for Americans; it is invading America with foreign workers taking American's jobs. There is a significant difference.

OUTSOURCING AND OFFSHORING FINANCIAL INDUSTRY CRISIS

The 2009-2010 economic crisis should be no surprise to executives in US industries who were rapidly transferring jobs to foreign countries. In October 2004 it was reported that there were several foreign owned offshore businesses raking in over $1 billion a year from selling outsourcing. The offshoring market had already exceeded $10 billion. Offshoring was growing around 20% per year, and was expected to continue to grow at this rapid rate through 2008. [80] Our government received warnings from the beginning of the H-1B visa program that this legislation was harming Americans and was economically destructive. It has taken twenty years for foreign countries to ravage the US economy.

The US government sat on the sidelines and did nothing to protect America as executives in large American corporations offshored strategic industries. The 2009-2010 US financial industry crisis was largely a product of transferring American jobs to foreign workers. For example, a 2004 research report claimed that 100 of the world's biggest financial services companies planned to transfer around 2 million jobs to low wage countries within five years. *Researchers found that one-third of the largest financial companies had already offshored work, and that over the next two years this number would grow to 75%.* [140]

Chapter 9

India Dominates Outsourcing & Offshoring

While India took about 50% of H-1B visas per year, its domination of US high tech jobs that were offshored was even greater. For example, in 2002, India took 85% of the software outsourcing market. [774] Although India got the jobs by offering cheap labor, once it had the jobs, India rapidly increased the wages billed for its programmers. Nonetheless in 2004, India still had 80% of the offshore market. [301]

A June 14, 2003, *Times of India* report titled, "US Gives India Assurance on Outsourcing," by Chidanand Rajghatta estimated that India's outsourcing revenues would reach $20 billion by 2008. Most of this outsourcing money would come from the US. [86] Even American movie studios outsourced animation for movies to India. [586]

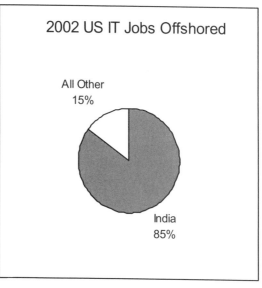

Another 2003 study estimated that more than one out of every 10 American technology jobs would be offshored. [73] An August 2004 report claimed that multinational (i.e. US) companies planned to cut jobs in America as they set up subsidiaries in India. [80]

H-1BS AND L-1S IMPORTED BY INDIA'S OUTSOURCING FIRMS

India's outsourcing companies targeted America's IT services—a $240 billion a year industry. India's major outsourcing companies, Tata, Infosys, and Wipro exploited the Y2K scare to gain access to this US industry. [300]

India's outsourcing companies set up subsidiaries inside the United States where they obtained big outsourcing contracts with American corporations. India's outsourcing companies then channeled in massive numbers of H-1B and L-1 visa workers from India.

> Note because there are many more American employers than Indian outsourcing companies in the United States, most H-1Bs are employed by US owned entities including US businesses, US federal and state government agencies, and US universities.

These outsourcing company owners created an illusion of entrepreneurial superiority, by using the H-1B visa program to exploit their own people. [33] These consulting firms *bill US corporations as much as four times what they are paying the visa workers.* [338]

From the beginning of the passage of the H-1B visa legislation in 1990 to present (this "temporary" visa program turned 20 years old in 2010), Indian owned outsourcing companies were some of the biggest employers of H-1Bs. For example, a list of companies with the most H-1B visa workers in 2002 was dominated by Indian owned outsourcing companies including: Mastech, Tata Consultancy, Syntel, Wipro, Tata Infotech/Tata Unisys, HCL America ... [338] In 2006, the top ten companies that hired H-1Bs were: Infosys (India), Wipro (India), Microsoft (USA), Tata (India), Satyam (India), Cognizant Technology Solutions (India), Patni Computer Systems (India), IBM (USA), Oracle (USA), and Larsen & Toubro Infotech (India). Moreover, from 2007 to 2012 Infosy planned to hire 29,448 H-1Bs, and Wipro planned to hire 24,012 H-1Bs. [665] India outsourcing companies such as TCS, Infosys, and Cognizant used H-1Bs in America to help facilitate offshoring US high tech jobs to India. [115]

India-based outsourcing companies also dominate the L-1 visa hiring. For example, Tata, Infosys, and Wipro obtained major outsourcing contracts with American corporations then used L-1 visas to bring people from India into their US-based operations to perform the work. *In 2003, it was estimated that 50% of Tata's 5,000 US workers were L-1s, 33% of Infosys's 3,000 US workers were L-1s, and 32% of Wipro's US workers were L-1s.* [63]

Tata

Some critics claimed that foreign owned outsourcing companies operating in the US were breaking US laws by their hiring practices. For example, in 2004, the zazona.com website reported that Tata hired young upper caste males from India to work in the US. [153] Did Tata discriminate against hiring Americans in its American based offices?

Infosys

"The Infosys Financial Model" by T.V. Mohandas Pai, Director/Chief Financial Officer, at *www.infosys.com/investor/transcript/theinfosysfianancialmodel.pdf* explained that clients in the US have to report if they laid off workers within 90 days of hiring H-1Bs. *So as part of Infosys' financial model it expects to pay about $6,000 per American they displace. The model notes that it is much more expensive in Germany where the cost is 100,000 Deutsch Marks for each work permit.* [540] Attempts by Congress to extend the 90 day rule to 6 months to protect Americans from being displaced were repeatedly blocked.

In January 2007, Infosys reported that its quarterly net profit for October through December skyrocketed up 52.4% to $218 million compared to the same quarter sales of $143 million the previous year. The company added 43 new outsourcing customers. Infosys writes software for American companies including Goldman Sachs, and J. C. Penny Co. Infosys also claimed to be negotiating several huge outsourcing deals, but refused to disclose the company names. While American programmers were being laid off, Infosys hired 3,282 new workers bringing its total number of employees to 69,432. The company also said that the competitive pressure to keep billing low was easing and billing rates were stable and moving upward, and that companies in China were eager to outsource to Infosys.

Wipro

Wipro was ranked 23rd in *BusinessWeek*'s top 100 technology companies for 2004. Wipro sales jumped 43% in 2004. Wipro got most of its money from the U.S. It was planning to acquire some companies in Europe to expand its market. Wipro claimed to be the *"world's largest third-party R&D provider."* In 2004, Wipro expanded its market reach from software development and maintenance to add infrastructure management, financial services and product testing. [597]

According to a May 2, 2005, *US News and World Report* article, "Bangalore's Big Dreams," Azim Premji the Chairman of Wipro became the "richest man in India." Premji, a Muslim, owns 84% of Wipro. He attended college in America where he received a BS degree in electrical engineering from Stanford University. [122]

INDIAN FOUNDED US OWNED OUTSOURCING COMPANIES

Sometimes Syntel and Mastech are mistakenly referred to as Indian outsourcing companies. However, they are US companies founded by immigrants from India.

Syntel—Indian Founded Headquartered in Troy, Michigan

Syntel co-founded in 1980 by Bharat Desai and Neerja Sethi is headquartered in Michigan. Syntel was certified as a Minority Business Enterprise by several organizations. Its list of business partners included: IBM, Sun Microsystems, TIBCO, Oracle, and others. [724] In 1992, Syntel set up development centers in India and became one of the first US companies to provide onsite project management consultations for American corporations, and then offshore the software development to India. In 1998, with revenues of $160 million, *Syntel admitted that H-1Bs made up 66%* of its workforce. Syntel supplied contract workers to Ford, DaimlerChrysler, Kmart, an insurance company, and a state government. [468] According to a February 21, 2000 *Baltimore Sun* article "Indentured Servants for High-Tech Trade Labor", by Gary Cohn and Walter F. Roche, when Syntel convinced a major US insurance company to outsource its data processing, 250 US workers lost their jobs and insurance they needed to provide for their families. [468]

Mastech—Indian Founded Headquartered in Pittsburgh, PA

Mastech was co-founded by Sunil Wadhwai and Ashok Trivedi, both immigrants from India. Mastech, recognized as a Minority Business, is a US company headquartered in Pittsburgh, Pennsylvania. It has operations in five cities in India: Bangalore, Chennai, Noida, and Pune. According to Mastech's website, Tripti Noorani its VP of Immigration and Compliance helped get 20,000 H-1B Visas and 2,000 Green Cards for Mastech employees. [725]

According to a February 21, 2000 *Baltimore Sun* article "Indentured Servants for High-Tech Trade Labor", by Gary Cohn and Walter F. Roche, around 1998, when Mastech executives contributed to Senator Spencer Abraham's campaign funds (Abraham was the sponsor of the 1998 H-1B visa legislation that increased the number of H-1B visas that were granted per year from 65,000 to 115,000.), Mastech had revenues of almost $400 million and *admitted that H-1Bs made up nearly 35% of its workers*. Mastech supplied contract workers to large US corporations such as GE and even had a contract to work on White House computers. [468] They also wrote that, GE in August 1999 disclosed that it planned to acquire a $30 million share in Mastech; and then, GE also disclosed that within a three year period it planned to purchase $122 million in outsourcing services from Mastech. [468]

Cognizant

In 2003, Cognizant Technology Solutions based in New Jersey, paid its CEO Kumar Mahadeva $27 million which was an 80% increase over his 2002 compensation. This made Mahadeva one of the highest paid executives in the world. This IT company *employed 70% of its workforce in India*—almost 12,000 workers. Moreover, Cognizant planned to open a software development center in China. [6]

H-1B VISA RECRUITMENT "BODY SHOPS"

Because of the volume of people, the low pay, and the long work hours, India's IT outsourcing firms are frequently called "body shops." [96] The February 21, 2000, Baltimore Sun article, "Indentured Servants for High-Tech Trade Labor," exposed how funneling visa workers from India into the US had become a multimillion dollar industry. [468] "Body shop" recruitment firms get the H-1B visas approved and pay INS and legal fees. In return these firms bind foreign workers to contracts that exact severe penalties if they attempt to leave early or take jobs with clients. [31] H-1Bs' contracts may bind them to reimburse the "body shop" $10,000 to $30,000 if they leave early. Two Indian founded outsourcing companies, Mastech and Tata, have sued dozens of H-1B workers who left their companies to take jobs with US companies prior to completing their contracts. Despite all these abuses, millions of workers in India still seek these H-1B jobs. [479] Body shops "take advantage of the well-meaning visa applicants as the latter, *mostly unqualified, are funneled into the US by middlemen who help them with fake academic degrees and pad their resumes in order to secure the H-1B visas*" [32] "*It's a well-known fact that people in India will take two or three classes in Java programming then the body shop will create a resume for them.*" [24] When H-1Bs discovered that middlemen had falsified their credentials on the visa application they were told not to worry, that it was necessary to get them into the United States. [24] Once H-1Bs discovered their resumes were doctored, were they still innocent victims if they knowingly took Americans' jobs using fake credentials? This seems similar to buying goods that you know were stolen from someone else.

Most visa workers will not pursue legal actions for abuses due to costs and fears of being deported. However, an H-1B from India filed a lawsuit against a body shop when it attempted to exact a $77,085 finder's fee after the H-1B accepted a job with its client. In April 2001, the H-1B was awarded $215,050 by a California judge. This could lead to many more lawsuits against body shops. [56] Ironically, the reason these foreign workers were hired in the first place were the profits to be made from exploitation. The US citizens whose jobs H-1Bs took are the ones most deserving of a legal remedy.

BUSINESS PROCESS OUTSOURCING (BPO)

An April 28, 2004 article, "Indian BPO Guy: Hero or Villain?" described how immigrants from India were making a fortune selling offshore Business Process Outsourcing (BPO) in the US. They were persuading American corporations to offshore "accounting, auditing, telemarketing, research, tax preparation, and technical writing jobs" to India. They call it "efficient employment" when a US citizen is replaced by a worker in India for "one third the cost." Of course they cleverly do not include increased security costs from risks. The article was concerned that the American "brouhaha over outsourcing gains" may effect the 2004 presidential election. How much of the "moolah" in the "cyclical wheel of wealth creation" did the companies "helped" by these "modest," "leading practitioners", "apostles", "deft administrators" actually realize? Was offshoring as "dazzling" and "dynamic" as American managers were led to believe? It is amazing that the "internet and new-age telecom arrived"; Americans thought these technologies were developed as a result of our investing billions of dollars and decades of work in research. [98]

Many "offshoring specialists" operate in Silicon Valley. One of these specialists, Atul Vashistha, used his consulting company, neoIT to ship about 50,000 US jobs to India. Think of the harm to American families, communities, and our nation. [98] And, Vashistha is not the only one. The article says scores are "emerging from the shadows."

> Atul Vashistha came to the US on a student visa in 1989 to pursue an MBA at Arizona State University. He stayed in the US and was granted citizenship. In 1999, he founded neoIT. In 2003 neoIT facilitated contracts valued at a billion dollars. He estimated that 70% of this money went to overseas companies. In 2004, under a rising protest by US citizens, he defended outsourcing saying, "I feel that somebody has to speak up for it, and you know I have made a career out of globalization." [379]

While young Americans were risking their lives in war and our nation was struggling to revive our economy, these immigrants from India were plotting to increase India's BPO industry to $12 billion. Americans who object to this raiding of US jobs are personally attacked and labeled protectionists. Outsourcing promoters complained that the "world harps on globalization and free trade policies," but they are "modestly" working to help millions of people in their native land get jobs and dream big. [98] What about the millions of Americans they are harming? If they were granted US citizenship, their allegiance should be to America and fellow Americans.

Chapter 10

Dotcom Attack on US Stock Market

Foreign investors increase US stock market volatility and risks.

While the dotcom crash happened in April 2000, it set the stage for the 2009-2010 economic crisis. Once you begin digging deeply into how America got into the current economic crisis you will discover that the H-1B, dotcom crash, outsourcing, and offshoring are all closely interconnected and at the root of the crisis.

During the dotcom boom the US media was saturated with buzzwords and empty doubletalk. Terms like "New Economy" also referred to as the "New Paradigm" were used to lure the American public into thinking that earnings were irrelevant when picking stocks. Catchy buzzwords that had little meaning were hyped to encourage US investors to put their money into companies that were internet based—if it was a dotcom, it was supposed to be a good investment. However, most of the dotcoms in reality had no solid business foundation. It was deceptive nonsense that were it not for the magnitude of harm, it would be almost funny how people were misled by the pied piper media playing the buzzwords. [294] [295] [296]

Why did the media hype the dotcom stocks? Major US news networks including ABC, NBC, and CBS received a lot of revenue from dotcom advertising. These networks rode the dotcom wave. The more US citizens invested in dotcom stock, the more money they received in advertising. There appears to be a conflict of interest risk in the media reporting news on its advertising sponsors. [299]

FALSE PROPHETS OF FALSE PROFITS

Many American companies with offshore operations manipulated accounting records to charge overseas costs against US operations. This allowed them to falsely understate their US earnings to cut or eliminate taxes paid to the US government and to justify laying off Americans. This practice also allowed them to make offshore operations look much more attractive to investors than they actually were. [33] The conflict of interest of accounting firms providing consulting services to clients was brought to light by the Enron/Arthur Andersen disaster. Although Enron's accounting deceptions to manipulate stock values received media attention, there has been little in the news about how dotcoms scammed US investors. The dotcom bust did not "just happen" anymore than the Enron debacle "just happened". Many accounting deceptions proliferated that were used to artificially inflate earnings. One expert surmised: "The New Economy was a farce, and traditional economic principles still hold." [294]

US investors relied on accounting firms to audit corporate accounts and to ensure that financial statements and analysis were independent and objective. The Big 5 accounting firms included: Arthur Andersen, Price Waterhouse Coopers, Deloitte & Touche, Ernest & Young, and KPMG. *Unbeknownst to most Americans our Big 5 accounting firms were employing foreign H-1B visa workers and offshore foreign workers.* [387] These were the firms creating financial statements claiming major cost savings for high tech US firms if they replaced American scientists and programmers with H-1B scientists and programmers. Therefore, a conflict of interest not only existed at the management level it permeated down to the accountants and consultants. The Big 5 were selling consulting services, creating financial documents, and conducting audits using foreign workers that lured US executives to replace Americans with H-1Bs and offshore jobs to their country of origin. [778] In 2000, at the peak of the dotcom boom, a list of the top 20 employers of H-1Bs included: Mastech Corp,

H-1Bs may have played a big role in the 2009-2010 US economic crisis. In the midst of the banking crisis, it was reported that New York's financial area employed thousands of H-1Bs. [728]

Tata Consultancy Services, Computer People, Oracle Corp., PricewaterhouseCoopers LLP, Lucent Technologies, Motorola Inc., Syntel Inc., Intelligroup, Comsys Technical Services, Deloitte & Touche LLP, KPMG Peat Marwick LLP, Cisco Systems Inc., Keane Inc., Ernest & Young LLP, Intel Corp, SAI Software Consultants Inc., Indotronix International, Complete Business Solutions Inc., Computer Horizons Corp. [400] H-1Bs may well be responsible for much of the dotcom accounting fraud.

While dotcoms were hyped as "New Economy" companies, they were using old accounting tricks to inflate revenues. Accounting reports were misused to extract billions in IPO underwriting fees. Venture capitalists cashed in with some taking returns in the *"thousands of percent,"* [296] and many dotcom founders along with their officers and directors and advisors became instant millionaires. All at the expense of the American public that was misled and kept in the dark about what was really going on.

Arthur Levitt a former SEC Chairman woefully observed: "Managing may be giving way to manipulation. Integrity may be losing out to illusion." [296] The American public suffered as the inflated stocks they purchased fell like a rock. Many hardworking Americans lost their life savings, their kids' college money, and more. *Renowned economist John Kenneth Galbraith found the lack of honesty troubling: "I've been looking at auditors' signatures all my life, but I will never again do so without some doubts as to their validity. There must be the strongest public and legal pressure to get honest competent accounting."* [1]

Recording Revenues that Weren't There

One of the accounting tricks used was "aggressively" recording revenues before they happened. In December 1999, new SEC guidelines required companies using questionable accounting tricks to restate their financial results. In particular the new guidelines were targeting dotcoms that were suspected of not accurately reporting revenues. Over 30 dotcom companies had to restate their earnings claims under the new guidelines. With more accurate financial reports, many no longer looked like stellar performers. [296]

Bartering Ads to Deceive Investors

Another accounting trick, widely used to grossly overstate dotcom profits, was the bartering of advertising. Dotcom companies would display banner ads on each others' websites, and then the companies doing the swap would each record a million in revenues from advertising and a million in expenses. In reality, no revenues were generated. It was a deceptive scheme to create counterfeit dotcom profits to make the companies look like good investments. [296]

Shady Reversing

Another accounting trick used to deceive the American public was the use of reversing—i.e. claiming pure profits on inventory that had been written down to zero value in prior quarters. Reverses were also done on restructuring fees such as severance costs, and litigation charges. Reversing was widely used by high tech companies during the boom to make financial statements look impressive. Following the dotcom bust the use of reversals continued to increase. The American public was being deceived as accounting tricks were used to inflate financials, so that insiders and early stockholders could take a second swipe at the US economy. Reversing was a slick scheme because the accounting rules left too much room for interpretation. It was hard to pin down as a crime. However, reverses that were not properly disclosed mislead investors when the reverses significantly inflated income. [344]

Ponzi Scheme (Pyramid)

An article titled, "Up, Up and Away: CEO Compensation" by Holly Sklar written in 2000, likened the dotcom market manipulations to a Ponzi (pyramid) scheme. CEOs quietly cashed out early while at the same time they were using the media to hype the stocks to the American public. This allowed executives to take outrageous fortunes, cushioning themselves before the pyramid crashed and devastated American workers and shareholders. *Sklar found that the tax cuts passed by the Bush Administration that were supposed to help the Americans harmed, instead provided the biggest benefits to these executives who had wrongly enriched themselves at the expense of employees and American shareholders.* [2]

Pump and Dump

A "pump and dump" scheme is evidenced by a quick spike in the price of the stock followed by a sudden and dramatic drop in the stock value. Informed people who know the price is highly overvalued cash out dumping the stock when the price peaks. The dotcom boom and bust fit this pattern. It is illegal to manipulate the US stock market using a "pump and dump" scheme. This is an old method of swindling investors that does not require a great deal of skill. First the swindler buys stock, and then he pumps up the stock price by hyping it in the media. While the stock is highly overvalued, he dumps (i.e. sells) the stock. A 16 year old American was caught by federal authorities when he made several hundred thousand dollars using a pump and dump scheme. He bought stocks, and then he hyped it on the internet sending messages under different names recommending people buy the stocks. The messages claimed the stocks were highly undervalued and predicted the value of the stocks would jump to several times the current prices. When investors bought into the hype, he sold his stocks. He crossed the line legally because financial analysts are not allowed to personally profit from the stock predictions they make. [290] It's interesting that this 16 year old was prosecuted, but most of the insiders involved in the dotcom pump and dump schemes were never investigated — much less prosecuted.

During the dotcom boom, online bulletin boards were loaded with "hot" stock tips predicting big contracts, and exciting new products. The tips were posted by people claiming to be objective observers. However, many may have been company insiders, large stockholders or even paid fraudsters. After the dotcom crash, there was a big drop in stock tips on internet bulletin boards.

Investment e-newsletters were also used to pump and dump stocks predicting big jumps in stock values. After the newsletter's recommendations inflated the stock prices, officials quickly sold their stocks. Some companies paid people to write newsletter articles promoting their stocks. This is legal as long as the newsletter fully disclosed the relationship and payment. However, in most cases they did not disclose the payments, and instead lied claiming they were independent. They made a lot of money writing recommendations that misled American investors. [292]

Stock Market Scam Theory

How did so many people become rich—here is a dotcom scam theory:

Dotcom Startups Stock Market Scam Theory		
Scam Phases	**Inside Investors**	**US Citizen Investors**
Phase I: Startup	Insiders pay $1 per share for 5 million shares = **Invested $5 million**	
Phase II: Use media hype, accounting tricks and bribes to drive up stock price.	Stock skyrockets = Founders became multimillionaires based on stock valuations. So they claim to be "genius" entrepreneurs.	Americans hear about skyrocketing stocks and "genius" entrepreneurs and IPO.
Phase III: Insiders take company public and sell overvalued stock at peak.	Stocks peak at $100 per share. Insiders do a "planned" sell of 2 million shares = **Take $200 million**. Still own 3 Million shares	The American public buys 2 million shares at peak for $100 per share = **Invested $200 million**.
Phase IV: Market correction. Stock plummets.	Stock plummets to $1 per share. Still hold 3 million shares at $1 = $3 Million.	Stock **plummets to $1** per share. US citizens lose $197 Million

This is where the "genius" lies, when the stock corrects, the insiders are still "invested" in the company. They complain that their remaining investment dropped from $300 million to just $3 Million. In reality they never lost anything, they took the US stock market for $200 million on their initial investment of $5 million.

DOTCOM NOT A NORMAL BUBBLE

Startups with no real business model or plan were given millions of dollars in venture capital. [295] Many venture capitalists spinning off these wobbly ill-conceived companies extracted a fortune from our stock market.

The US stock market dotcom wild climb and devastating fall do not fit normal patterns. The magnitude of the dotcom boom to bust is hard to fathom. The growth was unprecedented with the NASDAQ exploding from 600 companies in 1996 to 5,000 companies in 2000. [294] This steep climb set the stage for the plunge. While the dotcom crash started in early April 2000, it continued downward to 800 companies by 2002. Investors in the US stock market lost trillions of dollars. [294] In 2000 alone the NASDAQ dropped by $3.33 trillion—a loss so huge one analyst estimated that it would pay for the value of over 1/3 of the houses in the US. Of course many people bought the stock before it peaked, so this was a paper loss. [355] The true loss was the amount invested in buying highly overvalued stock minus the amount the investors received when they sold the stock after the market corrected.

The dotcom boom was fueled by the media, rife with propaganda, making bold claims about the "New Economy." It all sounds impressive until you discover that it is not true. For example, in his 2002 book, *Conquer the Crash*, Robert R. Prechter Jr. revealed that the US has not experienced anything even close to a "New Economy." He compared the US economic (dotcom boom) expansion of 1974 – 2000, to the US economic expansion that occurred from 1942 – 1966. Prechter found the dotcom economic expansion was weaker: The Gross Domestic Product average annual real growth rate was weaker, the industrial production average annual gain was weaker, the capacity utilization was lower, and the monthly average unemployment rate was worse. Logically you then would expect the Dow Jones Industrial Average (DJIA) gain to be less during the 1974 – 2000 expansion. Instead he discovered that the DJIA gain of 1930% during this time period was double the amount of 971% for the stronger bull market period from 1942 – 1966. (p. 6–9) Even more surprising is his "Year-End Stock Market Valuation" chart graphic (p. 56) which shows that the normal range for the stock price to book value ratio is between 1 to 2. The 1990's stock market skewed severely off this normal valuation pattern. By 1995, he showed stock overvaluations ran way above the normal range with a ratio of 4—i.e. overvalued by 2 to 4 times. His chart shows the most extreme stock overvaluation peak occurred in 2000 with the ratio at an astounding 10. [21] This means that when *millions of Americans lost money in the dotcom crash, stocks overvaluations were running 5 to 10 times the book value.* [21] From January 2001 through January 2002 Americans' stock investments continued to be ravaged as 435 Internet companies folded. [299]

FORBES LIST OUT-OF-WHACK

In March 10, 2000, *Forbes* magazine's Forbes 500 list of top companies was the largest in its 32 years of reporting with 892 making the list. The number of new companies making the list for the first time more than doubled over the previous year jumping from 76 in 1999 to 190 in 2000. The new companies on the list were dominated by dotcom and dotcom-related businesses—23% were Internet companies, 15% computers and electronics, 14% telecommunications, 11% computer software and services, and 6% banking and finance. To make the list based on sales revenues, a company had to meet the minimum sales requirement of $2.6 billion. However 172 of the companies making the list in March 2000 never even came close to $2.6 billion in sales. They made less than $250 million. Instead of sales revenues, market capitalization got them on the list. Market capitalization is calculated by taking the number of outstanding shares of stock times the current market price for one share. For example, if a company has 1 million shares outstanding and the current price for one share is $100 then the market capitalization of the company is $100 million. While the list was compiled March 10, 2000, within weeks the dotcoms began to fall like flies. Market values of the new companies added to the list plummeted in early April. Almost 50 of the new companies would not have been included in the Forbes 500 list had the data been gathered four weeks later. Many of these new companies were teetering on going out of business. [367]

Two years later, in 2002, *Fortune* magazine published, "The Greedy Bunch", listing 25 companies where executives greedily cashed in by selling highly overvalued stock while US citizens were being hyped into buying the stock. The list used two criteria—first it selected corporations that had stock valuations plummet by 76% or more, secondly from these corporations it identified the corporate officers and directors that took the most money out by selling stock from January 1999 through May 2002. The 25 companies were ranked by greediness, with Qwest Communications at the top of the list: a Director, sold $1.57 billion, and a former CEO sold $230 million. [369]

Qwest Lawsuits

Qwest, a Denver-based telecom company incorporated in Delaware, was the subject of multiple lawsuits. According to February 18, 2004, Denver Business Journal article titled, "Qwest Lawsuits Settled," three lawsuits were filed against Qwest Communications International Inc. Shareholders sued several directors and officers for "breach of fiduciary duty." In response to the lawsuits the company produced over six million pages of documents. *Shareholders were advised that Delaware law would make it difficult to win an insider trading case against the company officers and directors.* The $25 million settlement was to be paid to the company as if it were revenue by a company indemnity insurance fund "established to indemnify its directors and officers." [373] Two years later, according to a September 30, 2006, Salt Lake City *Desert News* article, "Settlement is Approved in Qwest Lawsuit," a $400 million settlement was reached on a consolidated lawsuit that "accused Qwest Communications of civil fraud in connection with a multibillion-dollar accounting scandal." Qwest agreed to compensate shareholders. The settlement covered Qwest and several executives with the exception of a former CEO and a former CFO. [756]

TECHNET LOBBY—CEO'S BUY US POLITICIANS

John Doerr organized TechNet as a political network of CEOs in high tech industries including "dotcom titans." *TechNet was founded in 1997, when Silicon Valley executives banned together in opposition to a California initiative that would have made it easier for shareholders to sue companies that mismanaged their investments.* Notice how the timing relates to the big dotcom boom. TechNet's founding members included executives from Kleiner Perkins, Cisco, Netscape, CNET, and more. At the time *Doerr who was a co-founder of the Silicon Valley venture capital firm Kleiner Perkins Caufield & Byers (KPCB) "had a stake in more than 250 technology ventures."* He was on the board of several high tech companies including Sun Microsystems, Amazon, and Google. Doerr "helped raise a record $40 million to oppose the shareholder proposition, ensuring its defeat." [559] (See also Vinod Khosla co-founder of Sun Microsystems and partner KPCB.)

TechNet later lobbied for offshoring and increased H-1B visa quotas. TechNet's lobbying paid off: "TechNet scored victories on both of its top two legislative priorities." First TechNet got the US Senate to approve permanent normal trade relations with China. And, second, TechNet got the US Congress to pass legislation that increased the H-1B visa cap from 115,000 to 195,000. [559] [560] [22] [184]

By 1999 TechNet membership had grown to 140 executives from high tech companies. That year they made political contributions and pressured Congress to double federal spending on basic research. Remember university research was done by graduate students, and foreign students took about half or more of these positions. So, this would increase the number of foreign graduate students available to become H-1Bs. *From 1998 through 2000, during the peak of the dotcom boom, TechNet spent approximately $2 million lobbying the US Congress, and "contributed" $300,000 to elected officials in the US government, and in return TechNet got laws passed by the US Congress that benefited its membership.* [184] [194] TechNet's membership doubled by 2002. Its members included executives from the IT industry, biotech industry, venture capital companies, investment banks, and even law firms. It adopted the motto: "New Politics for a New Economy." TechNet lobbied hard for an "economic stimulus" package. [195] In November 2004, the president of TechNet, claimed that the US had a worker shortage and needed to hire people from other countries because half of the graduate students in our engineering, science, and math were foreign students. [196] The fallacy here was the assumption that a graduate degree is required to perform many of the jobs for which H-1Bs are hired including research. Bill Gates founder of Microsoft, Larry Ellison founder of Oracle, and Steve Jobs founder of Apple do not even hold bachelor degrees. Leaders of these companies know that a PhD is not necessary for most of the work. They have shown little interest in hiring US citizens with PhDs. [64]

A 2006 list of TechNet's corporate CEO members included executives from: IBM, Intel Corporation, Microsoft, Cisco Systems, Kleiner, Perkins, Caufield & Byers, Silicon Valley Bank, Texas Instruments, and more. [558] One of TechNet's "Accomplishments" from "giving senior executives a voice in national politics," was it: *"Maintained favorable accounting treatment for stock options granted to outside directors by defeating the Financial Standards Accounting Board's proposal that these options be expensed."* [558]

PROBLEMS AT THE SEC

The American public relies upon the Securities and Exchange Commission (SEC) to ensure a safe investment environment. This protection of public interest is essential for investor confidence. Our government and our legal system failed to protect Americans from stock fraud, and then compounded the offense when they failed to provide justice for victims of the dotcom/telecom/software stock market manipulation. Moreover, the government fumbled the process of cleaning up the corruption and conflicts of interest that enabled these stock market manipulations.

Following the dotcom crash, in August 2001, Bush made Harvey Pitt Chairman of the SEC. Pitt was criticized for meeting with executives of big corporations while the corporations were being investigated by the SEC for accounting fraud. [755] According to a July 20, 2002, article, "SEC Needs New Leader," by Jack Anderson and Douglas Cohn from the United Feature Syndicate posted on ljworld.com, Harvey Pitt *"fought proposals from his predecessor, Arthur Leavitt to end the practice whereby accounting firms could act both as auditors and consultants to the same corporation. This obvious conflict of interest for accounting firms is at the root of the current accounting scandals."* They note that this practice should have never been allowed in the first place. They said it was wrong for Bush to select Pitt, who had been "legal council for Arthur Andersen, LLP, the auditor and consultant of beleaguered Enron." The SEC Chairman "should have an incentive to serve the public interest." [778]

One critic claimed that Pitt hired McKinsey Management Consulting to analyze the SEC to help uncover crime and fraud in big business even though Enron's Jeff Skilling had previously been a high level executive at McKinsey, and McKinsey provided consulting services to big corporations. According to a November 6, 2002, New York Times article, "S.E.C.'s Embattled Chief Resigns in Wake of Latest Political Storm," by Stephen Labaton, the Bush White House "welcomed" Harvey Pitt's resignation. [755] Although Pitt was gone, McKinsey was allowed to continue the inside analysis of the SEC. December 9, 2003, *TheCorporateCouncil.net* editor Broc Romanek reported that a 270 page non-public report "prepared by SEC staffers and McKinsey consultants" claimed the SEC was short on resources. According to the findings only one third of SEC investigations were done internally; and, almost half of these internal investigations consisted of reading newspapers. [388] Apparently two thirds of SEC investigations were outsourced! How many of the newspapers relied on by SEC investigators were owned by the corporations or executives inflating the stock?

The continued failure of our government to reform the SEC was exposed by the Bernard Madoff scandal according to a *Fox News* story, "Madoff Tipster Blasts SEC, Says He Feared for His Safety." Harry Markopolos a securities fraud investigator told a House hearing that he had warned the SEC for a decade about Madoff's operations which caused investors to lose $50 billion in a Ponzi scheme. *He testified, "the SEC is busy protecting the big financial predators from investors."* Not only did the SEC take no action against Madoff, Markopolos said, "I became fearful for the safety of my family," and he worried that people like Madoff had so much power they were "in a position to end careers or worse." [719] Were the people gaining wealth and power through exploiting H-1Bs and outsourcing also eluding investigations by the SEC? Do they have people working in the SEC, or on SEC outsourcing contracts?

FOREIGN INVESTMENT DROVE DOTCOM BOOM

The overheating of the dotcom was driven by foreign venture capital and media hype: *"Foreign investment was a major contributor to the U.S. stock bubble."* [362] In mid 2001, a Canadian consultant astutely observed that the dotcom boom and crash resulted from what he called "venture capital disease." He said Canada was not "infected" and therefore the dotcom crash was primarily an American phenomenon. [296] From 1990 – 2000 foreigners "invested" 6 trillion dollars in the US. While Americans only had about 2.5 trillion invested in other countries. [355] This massive flow of capital appears to have primed the pump for the largest stock market pump and dump in history. The scale is difficult to comprehend. Silicon Valley was the epicenter of the dotcom boom where venture capital targeted US communications and US software. [305] In 1996, Silicon Valley dominated venture capital taking 36% with $2.1 billion invested in 492 startups. [462]

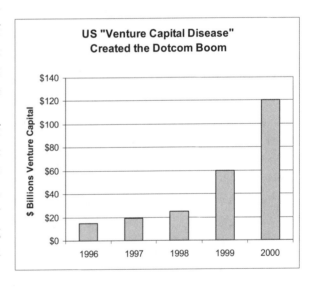

Total venture capital investments, foreign and domestic, in the US soared from about $15 billion in 1996, to an astounding peak of almost $120 billion dollars in 2000. [462] Foreign investments in the first quarter alone of 2000 hit $66 billion which is 55% of the $120 billion total for the entire year. Following the dotcom crash foreign investments in the US stock market declined. For example, in 2003 foreigners invested only $16.6 billion. [344]

Asian Venture Capital Sources

During the 1990's, much of the foreign investment in the US came from Asian sources, and the money was almost exclusively available to Asian born entrepreneurs. Massive amounts of venture capital were channeled from Taiwan to Silicon Valley in California. The amounts of foreign venture capital that flowed into the US were much greater than the numbers reported. While it is unknown how much they invested, it is known that the money invested by foreign individuals living in Asia radically increased during the dotcom boom. According to AnnaLee Saxenian's "Silicon Valley's New Immigrant Entrepreneurs," written in the year 2000, each network was prolific in raising venture capital for entrepreneurs from their ethnic group. For example, capital for Chinese startups in the United States came from Taiwan, Hong Kong, and Singapore. Alpine Technology Ventures funded Chinese immigrants' startups. The Draper International Fund financed startups formed by immigrants from India. InveStar Capital helped fund entrepreneurs from Taiwan. [372]

This Asian investment scheme created a business environment that favored Asian immigrants, not just in Asian sources of venture capital, but in American sources as well. To get in on the foreign "investment" deals, American venture capital firms hired Asian born partners who persuaded US firms to favor investments in immigrant startups over Americans. The venture capital deck was stacked against US citizens who were not of Asian ancestry.

Immigrant Founded Startups

Immigrant founded startups had excessive financial backing allowing them to outspend US citizen startups on marketing and supporting products. The main source of the dotcom boom came from startups in Silicon Valley. [294] Immigrant founded startups were by far overrepresented in the dotcom stock market boom. Dun and Bradstreet compiled a database of the 11,443 high tech companies started in Silicon Valley from 1980 to 1996. The study found that 17% of the CEOs for these startups had Chinese surnames, and 7% of the CEOs had Indian surnames. This makes it appear on the surface that Chinese and Indian founded companies totaled 24%, which is surprisingly high given that demographically they are about 3% of the American population. However, according to Saxenian's May 2000, "Silicon Valley's New Immigrant Entrepreneurs," this counting method "may understate the scale of immigrant entrepreneurship because firms that were started by Chinese or Indians but have hired non-Asian outsiders as CEO's are not counted." A precise count of immigrant founded companies is not available because of this stealth practice. She also notes that the "great majority" of these Asian entrepreneurs were foreign born. [372]

ASIAN MINORITY BUSINESS BENEFITS

To qualify as a minority owned business, a business must be 51% or more owned by minority persons. Our government classifies people from China and India as minorities.

According to federal statute, minority classification is supposed to help US citizens that are socially or economically disadvantaged. [473] Yet, clearly during the 1990's, with the influx of foreign money, immigrants from China and India were at no disadvantage in being able to get capital for business ventures. In fact, the white US citizen had a significant disadvantage. For ethnic groups that comprise 3% of the population to receive over 40% of some venture capital portfolios is clearly not a fair and equitable distribution of venture capital.

Organized According to Race

The Chinese and the Indian networks organized and operated separately with almost no membership overlap in their support networks. The networks established recruitment channels to quickly funnel cheap foreign labor from their home countries to staff startups in the United States. Networks provided mentoring to "co-ethnic entrepreneurs" (i.e. entrepreneurs of the same race and/or religion) These groups were exclusive and worked to advance their ethnic group. [372]

Does Collaboration = Collusion on Sales?

A Regional Advantage paper explained how Asian ethnic networks used their networks to form "very close relations with vendors in the Silicon Valley Area." They called this vendor collaboration. They meet with a network contact and agree to create an exclusive vendor relationship whereby only this vendor can meet the requirements. This collaboration would link startups to network contacts working in US corporations, and network contacts working in US federal, state, and local governments. They would develop technology that would "make use of the technology being developed by a friend of theirs." [128]

Chinese Networks Launched Startups

The Asian American Manufacturing Association (AAMA) helped launch Chinese startups in America. The group aggressively pursued US media PR to get publicity praising the achievements of Asian Americans. The AAMA linked engineers together with investment bankers for funding startups, consultants in advisory roles to American business leaders, lawyers for leveraging the US legal system to their advantage, and accountants dedicated to making offshoring to the Pacific Rim look financially appealing. [372]

Organization of Pakistani Entrepreneurs of North America

The Organization of Pakistani Entrepreneurs of North America (OPEN) was formed in Boston in 1998, and spread to Silicon Valley in 2001. (The same year as the September 11th attack.) They saw Silicon Valley as the place to launch global businesses run by Pakistani-Americans because it provides access to American high tech companies, access to American leading universities and research centers, and access to American venture capital. Specifically they targeted advanced technology companies including: HP, Sun Microsystems, Oracle, Google, Yahoo, Apple, and Cisco Systems. They also wanted access to UC Berkeley, Stanford, other labs and research centers. Finally, they wanted venture capital from Kleiner Perkins Caufield & Byers, Sequoia Capital, and other venture capital firms that had funded Indian startups. [644]

THREE PRONG STRATEGIC ATTACK

The synchronization of foreign born executives entering the upper echelons of major high tech US corporations, paralleled by the foreign born entrepreneurs starting dotcom companies, paralleled by the dramatic growth of foreign IT consulting/outsourcing firms entering the American job market was too coordinated to be just a coincidence. A closer look reveals that the dramatic overvaluation of the dotcom stocks, high tech stocks, and outsourcing stocks were interrelated. The number of immigrant founded dotcom startups was unprecedented and caused telecom and computer stocks to soar as dotcom companies bought equipment. The dotcom and telecom boom along with the Y2K hype ignited a burning demand for IT outsourcing. All three (dotcom/telecom/outsourcing) industries: 1) Created a artificial demand for H-1B workers. 2) Fueled offshoring of US jobs. 3) Engaged in media manipulation. 4) Led to highly overvalued stocks. 5) Were used to inflate executives' bonuses.

Dotcom Boom Created Artificial Demand for H-1Bs

At the peak of the dotcom boom in just a four month window from October 1999 to February 2000, 67,322 H-1B petitions were granted by the INS. At the top of the list for hiring these H-1Bs were US high tech and accounting companies and Indian outsourcing companies including: Motorola 618, Oracle 455, Cisco 398, Mastech 389, Intel 367, Microsoft 362, Rapidigm 357, Syntel 337, Wipro 327, Tata Consultancy Services 320, PriceWaterhouse Coopers 272, People Com Consultants 361, Lucent Technologies 255, Infosys 239, Nortel Networks 234, Tekedge Corp. 219, Data Conversion 195, Tata Infotech 185, Cotelligent 183, and Sun Microsystems 182.
[339]

Dotcoms Inflated US High Tech Stocks

The unprecedented number of dotcom startups manipulated the demand for internet computer servers and caused stock prices to soar for companies like Cisco, Sun Microsystems, and Intel. [299] During the boom from 1995 – 1999, the US stock market experienced bizarre growth rates. The NASDAQ jumped over 40% per year. The S&P echoed with a 26% per year jump. This crazy climb peaked in March 2000. Then the dotcom bust took the US stock market on a terrible dive. The "New Economy" telecom infrastructure companies soon followed in 2001. Cisco dropped 78%. Nortel dropped 90%, and JDS Uniphase dropped 91%. [364]

WHERE DID THE DOTCOM MONEY GO?

Most of the dotcom startups fueled by venture capital were poorly managed by inept entrepreneurs who did not have business plans or earnings to merit the soaring overvaluations of their stocks. [294] Dotcom companies, as other software companies, had very low startup and overhead expense. Unlike manufacturing companies that can lose millions in manufacturing facilities investments, high cost parts inventory, and expenses for overstocked product inventory, software's main expense is marketing. Software does not require expensive manufacturing facilities and requires minimal inventory costs. So how did US investors lose billions/trillions in the dotcom bust? It cannot be explained in inventory or in production facilities losses. Where did the money go? A large portion of the money went into the pockets of the founders of dotcom companies, their network of contacts, and into venture capital companies. These insiders sold stock at the peak, because they knew the stock was wildly overvalued since they had manipulated the media to drive up the price. Unsuspecting Americans were lured into buying, while they were selling.

Chapter 11

Indian "Mafia's" Dotcom Role

They arrived "nearly broke" as students, and US citizens were taxed to educate them.

They got rich selling dotcom startups, outsourcing, and offshoring.

A January 24, 2000 article, "The Curry Network," posted on tiecarolinas.org stated, *"TiE represents only a fraction of what some Silicon Valley executives call the Indian Mafia, a gang that voraciously seeks IPO opportunities. A veritable international hydra, the group's tentacles reach from California to Boston to Bombay to London, always in search of new ideas and serendipitous connections."* [312] As a group, none compares to the Indian "Mafia" operating in the US during the dotcom boom. In 1998, a report estimated 40% of Silicon Valley startups were "Indian-spawned." How much wealth this network created is questionable. However, how much it was able to extract from US corporations and the US stock market is astounding.

As mentioned earlier India dominated IT outsourcing. This outsourcing played a major role during the dotcom boom. It is important to note that "India had barely 6,800" software professionals in 1985. [335] Yet, twelve short years later in 1997, India was "quietly but quickly emerging as a leader in the field of software engineering and web-based services." This would have been impossible if our universities had not been used to educate our competition, and to persuade American software companies that they must outsource to "retain competitive advantage." [335] Management thinkers from India advised Corporate American executives that offshoring to India was essential because programmers in India were paid "only 15%-20%" of what US programmers were paid. By 1997, India had geared up to produce "about 80,000-85,000 software professionals per year." [335] Common sense would tell you that transferring strategic US high tech jobs to India would jeopardize our competitive advantage, not help us retain it. Note that this was done "quietly" so that the American public would not know. The Indian "Mafia's" role in the dotcom boom went well beyond outsourcing. Most members kept a low profile so Americans do not know who they are and what role they played.

OVER 100,000 INDIANS BECAME MILLIONAIRES!

A list published in 2000, on multiple websites claimed that by the year 2000 at the peak of the dotcom boom, more than 100,000 Indians in Silicon Valley had become millionaires. [192] [350] [359] [310] Did the US corporations who bought their startups, and the US citizens who bought their stock get a good deal, or did Americans get scammed on a scale that is hard to fathom?

Ten of the new companies on the out-of-whack Forbes 500 list published in March of 2000 (list discussed in the previous chapter), were owned or operated by Americans who immigrated to the US from India. Their companies, i2 Technologies (ITWO), Juniper Networks (JNPR), Sycamore (SCMR), Aspect Development (bought by i2), Exodus (bought out), InfoSpace (INSP), MicroStrategy, Redback Networks, and Tibco Software (TIBX), made the list mainly because of soaring stock prices. [367] Using Google Finance to compare stock performance histories for five of these startups shows a pattern strikingly similar to a pump and dump scheme where the stock skyrockets to a wildly overvalued peak then plummets sharply. (Given that Google was in a list of top 100 employers of H-1Bs, the fair use legal protection is invoked for the vital public interest of US citizens. Also, Google states that it is not liable for any errors or omissions and expressly disclaims the accuracy, adequacy or completeness of the data. Therefore, the data must be verified.) Even just one company following the pattern computed would be highly suspect. However, multiple companies following this same pattern, all during the same time frame, indicate a high probability of a US stock market manipulation. This pattern in combination with any substantial insider sales merits investigation.

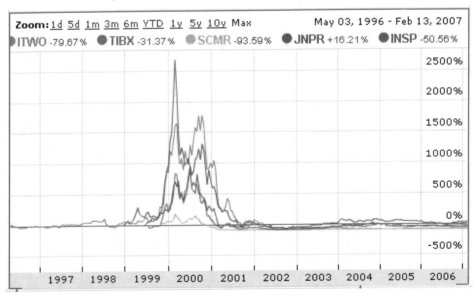

In 2000, the Indian network pointed to the number of people from India listed in the "Forbes Richest 400 Americans" as starting companies claimed to be worth over a billion dollars. The list included entrepreneurs Sanjiv Sidhu (i2 Technologies), Gururaj Desh Deshpande (Sycamore Networks), Pradeep Sidhu (Juniper Networks), Naveen Jain (InfoSpace), Rajendra Singh (Teligent), Romesh Wadhwani (Aspect Development). [309] By 2001 Forbes published a new list—a list of dropoffs who are billionaires no more. Included in this list were: Gururaj E. Deshpande, Naveen Jain, Pradeep Sindhu, Rajendra Singh, Romesh T. Wadhwani. [371] [395]

INDIAN "MAFIA" NETWORK TAKES ROOT IN THE UNITED STATES

The seeds for the Indian "Mafia" in the US were planted after WWII when US Aid helped fund and build the Indian Institute of Technology (IIT). In the 1970's graduates of IIT entered US university graduate schools. They arrived in the United States "nearly broke" [312] which means that Americans picked up the tab for their education. Their temporary student visas legally required them to return to India after completing their studies, but instead they stayed in America and looked for jobs in the heart of America's high tech research and development region—Silicon Valley. They got jobs in US corporations such as Cisco, Intel, and HP. [463] [312]

In 1987, Prakash Chandra founded the Silicon Valley Indian Professionals Association (SIPA). In the early 1990's, *delegates from the government of India traveled to the United States, and persuaded SIPA to promote US business relations with India, and to "fill the information gap" for India.* [372]

Passage of the 1990 H-1B visa program legislation positioned India to gain insider access to closely guarded US technology secrets. SIPA provided strategic information of interest to, and worked closely with the government of India and Indian businesses. In 1992 Chandra returned to India, and the mantle for India was picked up by The IndUS Entrepreneurs (TiE) organization. [372]

Multiple sources tell the story of how the Indian "Mafia" took root in America. For example, a November 27, 2000, article titled, "The TiE that Binds," tells the progression. First, they got a degree at IIT or some other technical school in India. Second, they obtained a student visa to attend graduate school in the United States. Third, they got jobs in Corporate America. Fourth, they founded startups that, with the help of the "Mafia" network, they sold to American corporations and/or sold stock in the US stock market to become multi-millionaires. [463]

THE INDUS ENTREPRENEURS (TIE) AKA THE INDIAN "MAFIA"

There are a couple of stories of how TiE was started. According to one story, in 1992, twenty people who had entered the US as students from India and settled in Silicon Valley were invited to India to tell about how they became wealthy entrepreneurs in America. On this trip they met and decided to launch The IndUS Entrepreneurs (TiE) network. "IndUS" was used to signify that they were people from India living and working in the US. [512] [333] According to another story, TiE was spawned in 1992, when India's Secretary of Electronics traveled to Silicon Valley to meet with Kanwal Rekhi, Suhas Patil, and Prabhu Goel. While waiting on the Minister to arrive, they decided to form the TiE network. [372]

TiE Political Connections

TiE claims to not engage in political activities, yet it traces its origins back to a meeting with a government official from India. And, TiE acknowledges that the Indian Government sought its help to advance India economically. [653] Additionally, TiE has connections to high level US government officials that most Americans do not know about. For example, an article published in 2000 titled, "TiE has Helped Create Businesses Worth More Than 200 Billion," claimed that: "A 200 person TiE delegation was invited to accompany President Bill Clinton to India to meet with the Indian PM earlier this year." [653] This was the year of the dotcom crash.

Executives in US Corporations TiE Connections

TiE is a network of entrepreneurs, professionals, and *executives in US corporations.* TiE's members are strategically positioned in US Universities, the US software industry, the US IT industry, the US biotechnology industry, and US services industries including legal, financial, and more. According to the TiE website it is the place to come for contacts if looking for money, or advice. [592]

Exclusive Organization

When TiE started in Silicon Valley, its members were 80% first generation immigrants, and 20% second generation immigrants. TiE spread to "Boston, New York, Dallas, Atlanta, Chicago, Los Angeles, and Washington, D.C." as well as to London and multiple cities in India. [653]

TiE claims to be an open and inclusive organization, yet TiE began as an exclusive invitation only organization. TiE is comprised primarily of immigrants from India and Pakistan. Charter members included entrepreneurs who founded startups, *executives in Corporate America*, and senior professionals. The majority were from India. [345] TiE is a tight knit group. They rub elbows with other Indians at work. Many live in neighborhood clusters in multi-million dollar houses. [331]

In 2007, TiE's website claimed that TiE welcomed all entrepreneurs and was not based on race. That contradicted earlier claims such as the "TiE Rockies Speakers 2000-2001" agenda which claimed, "TiE, a network organization based in Silicon Valley that promotes entrepreneurship among the Indus people." [310] Indus refers to people originating from South Asia.

INDIAN "MAFIA" DOTCOM STARTUPS

Many immigrants from India living in Silicon Valley were hyped by the media as "genius entrepreneurs." [121] For example, an article, "Those Magnificent Indians in Forbes List," published in 2000, by *http://www.indiaexpress.com* proclaimed that immigrants from India have a "Midas touch," that they "weave magic" in the US, and that people from India have a superior genius for creating wealth. [304] The H-1B legislation, venture capital funding, and media coverage created an illusion of genius. It does not take a genius to start a company when there are pre-established channels for hiring visa workers, and obtaining venture funds designated for immigrant startups. Nor does it take a genius to generate revenues when the network has people in US corporations to guarantee customer sales.

Connections Give Advantage in Hiring H-1Bs

In 2002, when there were an estimated 2,000 startups in Silicon Valley, the network again claimed that "*40% are Indian spawned.*" [331] IIT graduates founded half of these Indian startups. Indian entrepreneurs said that they can hire technical people faster than other American startups because of their connections to a "pool of Indian engineers" [331] A January 22, 2002 article, "H-1B Visas Jump in 2001," on *CNET News.com* by Rachel Konrad substantiated this claim: "*By the mid 1990s, when technology surrounding the Internet caused an unprecedented economic boom, the H-1B program became a conduit for computer programmers and engineers, mainly from India and Taiwan.*" She noted that this continued despite "massive layoffs of Americans." [42]

TiE Non-Profit? TiE = "Deals, Deals, Deals"

TiE is called a non-profit organization, yet TiE's primary function is a place to make deals: "*Every other month, The Indus Entrepreneurs (aka TiE) holds its meeting ... The main course is deals, deals, deals. The organization has emerged as a premier deal generator in Silicon Valley.*" Large venture capital firms had many connections to TiE. For example, in 2000, one partner in the New Enterprise Associates venture capital firm revealed that almost all of the venture deals in his company's portfolio had some connection to TiE. And, almost half of the companies in its venture capital portfolio had a CEO who was involved in TiE.

Moreover, TiE's annual conference was funded by "big-name sponsors" such as Goldman Sachs and Kleiner Perkins Caufield & Byers. [312] According to an article titled, "TiE has helped Create Businesses worth more than $200 billion." ... "Since its inception TiE has managed to IPO over 50 start-ups—making it more prolific than many venture capital funds." Members joined TiE for access to business connections, financial strategies, and access to venture capital. [345] *In 1999, TiE claimed that "the leaders of TiE had become multimillionaires.* [467]

Misleading Financial Statements

In December 1999, new SEC guidelines required companies to restate misleading financial statements. For example, MicroStrategy was also one of the dotcom companies forced to restate financials under the new guidelines. In March 2000, MicroStrategy restated its 1998 and 1999 financial results. Instead of the $12.9 million profit claimed in 1999, MicroStrategy had to admit instead that it lost between $33.6 million and $39.9 million. [296]

Another example, TranSwitch was one of the many technology companies that used reverses to inflate financial statements according to a 2003 article in *BusinessWeek* titled "The Secret Behind Those Profit Jumps." In October 2003, TranSwitch

> Were sales channeled to companies in the network? Cisco had Indians rise to executive positions, and Cisco bought products from TranSwitch whose founder Santanu Das was a charter member of TiE New York. [346]

reported a net income of $2.6 million on sales of $5.7 million making the company look like its profit margin was 50%. However, 23% of TransSwitch's reported net income resulted from reversing i.e. selling inventory it had previously written down to zero value. [344]

"Amazing Web" = Collaboration or Collusion?

The TiE network members became rich largely through outsourcing and dotcom startups. By 1998, there were 788 high tech startups ran by people from India. [604] The "Mafia" created an "amazing web" that gave a whole new meaning to insider collaboration and connections: *Indians invest in one another's companies, sit on one another's boards, and hire each other in key jobs.*" [289] In just a 10 year period—that correlates with both the H-1B visa boom and dotcom boom. Members of this network had started companies whose combined stock valuations reached an astounding $235 billion. [289]

In AnnaLee Saxenian's May 2000, "Silicon Valley's New Immigrant Entrepreneurs" Working Paper published on the web, she lauds how ethnic networks opened doors for immigrant entrepreneurs. Major American corporations such as Sun, Oracle, HP, and others had large numbers of people from India employed. Saxenian included a quote from Moham Trika, CEO of inXight a venture startup within Xerox that gave an eye-opening revelation into how immigrant entrepreneurs got wealthy.

> *"Your ability to manage risk is improved by these networks. ... I can approach literally any big company, or any company in the Bay Area, and find two or three contacts ... through the TiE network I know so-and-so in Oracle, etc. ... every major software company or any software company must have at least two or three Indians or Chinese in there ... And because they are there, it is very easy for me, or my technical officer, to create that bond, to pick up the phone and say: Swaminathan, can you help me, can you tell me what's going on ... he'll say don't quote me but the decisions is because of this, this and this. Based on this you can reformulate your strategy, your pricing, or your offer ... Such contacts are critical for startups."* [372]

TARGET "UPPER ECHELONS" IN CORPORATE AMERICA

The prime target of the Indian "Mafia" was Corporate America: "The Indian network works well, especially because the larger companies like Sun, Oracle, and HP have a large number of Indians." [372]

Indian "Mafia" used US Media to Promote Agenda

The Indian network got a surprising amount of US news media promotion. For example, in November 25, 1998, *BusinessWeek*'s cover pictured IIT students, and was titled, "WHIZ KIDS, The Indian Institute of Technology is Breeding American Business Leaders from Silicon Valley to Wall St." (Does America need India to "breed" our leaders? Imagine the reaction in India if they were taxed to educate American youth, and we claimed that Americans were breeding the future leaders of India.) Taking American jobs made them *"highly prized in India's contractual marriage market."* [303] The story reads like a PR piece calling IIT a "star factory" with "impossibly high standards" that graduated "Whiz Kids", the "hottest export India has ever produced." It claimed IIT graduates had "technical brilliance" and "great management skills" with a "leg up on American students." All their claims were then contradicted when the article told how IIT graduates anxiously seek acceptance into US universities because IIT *students "know that an advanced degree from a U.S. institution is the entry ticket to an American or global corporation"*—it failed to mention that it was illegal to misuse non-immigrant student visas to seek employment in America. The article said US universities offered IIT graduates financial aid—it failed to mention they were taking taxpayer aid that should have gone to young Americans.

According to this *BusinessWeek* story, "IIT grads in the U.S. have been formalizing their powerful network." They surpassed all other Asians in obtaining jobs in the "upper echelons" of Corporate America. India expected IIT graduates to follow the example of Taiwan which had "exported" engineers to the US. *Once in executive positions in American Corporations IIT graduates were expected to channel investment money and global trade to India. They were expected to "set up ventures in their native country" and to "play a key role in the resurgence of India."* [303] The story estimated 40% of Silicon Valley startups were "Indian-spawned" and IIT graduates accounted for about half of these startups. It lauded "the rise of the IITians": Suhas Patil founded Cirrus Logic, Kanwal Rekhi founded Excelan, Vinod Khosla co-founded Sun Microsystems and became a Partner in venture capital firm Kleiner Perkins, Rajat Gupta became Managing Partner of McKinsey & Company, Victor J. Menezes became Co-CEO Corporate & Investment Banking for Citigroup, Rakesh Gangwal became CEO and President of US Airways, Desh Deshpande founded Cascade Communications ... [303]

Disturbingly, this *BusinessWeek* story ran just six months after India's May 25, 1998, nuclear bomb test that caught our government off guard and resulted in US sanctions against India. Did Vasant Prabhu, an IIT graduate, who was President of the Information and Media Services for The McGraw-Hill Companies from June 1998 to August 2000, the parent company of *BusinessWeek*, play a role in getting this IIT media coverage? [366]

"Mafia" Penetrated Upper Echelons of American Corporations

In 2000, multiple websites posted an article under the heading, "Proud to be an Indian" that said immigrants from India had obtained high level management positions in big American corporations including: Arthur Anderson, United Airlines, US Air, CitiBank, Providian, and Bell Labs. [192] It also claimed Rajat Gupta head of McKinsey was advising major multinationals "on how to run their business." [192]

In 2002, the "Proud to be an Indian" article was updated and claimed that by 2025, India planned to emerge as a "superpower in IT & Medical research." [377] It stated: *"We are known as the Indian Mafia. We are the wealthiest among all ethnic groups in America, even faring better than the whites and the natives."* [377] It stated that Indians had reached upper management in Corporate America including: *major US government contractors:* The Carlyle Group, General Dynamics Corporation, Litton PRC, Lucent Technologies, Motorola, Raytheon System Corporation ..., *mortgage companies:* Fannie Mae, Freddie Mac ... , *financial investment companies:* Venture Fund, Columbia Capital, ..., *internet companies:* Network Solutions, America Online, Cybercash, The Motley Fool, ..., *telecom companies:* MCI WorldCom, Nextel Communications, Bell Atlantic, ..., *high tech companies:* Hughes Network Systems, MicroStrategy, Teligent, MindBank, DynCorp, Consumer Elec. Association, Draper Atlantic, Spacevest ..., *airline companies:* US Airways, United Airlines CIENA Corp, *consulting companies:* Computer Associates, SAIC, ..., *medical healthcare companies:* INOVA Health System, and more ...[377]

"Ousted" Indian CEO's

According to a 2001 article, some US CEOs who were born in India were "ousted" from the US corporations where they had risen to power. Rana Talwar CEO left Standard Chartered plc. And, Rakesh Ganwal left US Airways following a third quarter loss of $766 million. However, Rono Dutta remained as president and COO at US Airways despite the huge losses. [366]

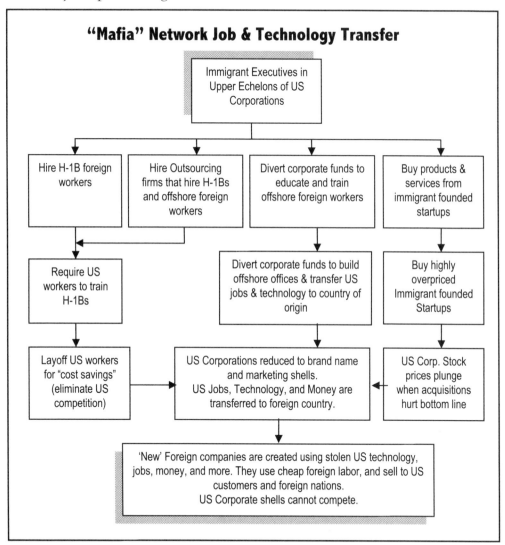

INDIAN IMMIGRANTS SOLD STARTUPS TO US CORPORATIONS

Acquisitions and mergers create an opportunity for executives to manipulate financial statements to take bonuses. The companies rarely benefit. "More than two-thirds of all mergers fail." [354] Acquisitions and mergers cost executives nothing. They are gambling with stockholders' investments, and employees' jobs.

A July 2000, article claimed dozens of people from the India network penetrated the executive ranks of US telecom blue chip corporations including AT&T, Bell, Lucent, Cisco, and Qualcomm. The article then said that in the 1990's people from India started several network and telecom companies that at the peak of the dotcom boom had stock valued at over $100 billion. A few of the startups listed included: Nexabit Networks, Stratumone, Tachion, Qlogic, Juniper Networks, Cerent, Sycamore Networks, Exodus Communications, Brocade Communications, Cobalt Networks InteliNet Technologies, and Accelerated Networks. Many immigrants from India became rich by selling their startups to US corporations: *"In at least half a dozen cases, the Indian founders have sold their companies to giant conglomerates for fortunes in excess of $500 million."* [244] Did US companies pay grossly inflated prices for acquisitions that had little or no real value? For example, in 1996, Lucent paid an astounding $900 million for Nexabit even though the company had no revenues. Nextabit was founded by Mukesh Chatter. Another example, the VP of distribution channels for Cisco was from India. He and his friends *keep a low profile preferring to remain anonymous.* He claimed all his friends worked in high tech jobs and *almost all have sold a startup to a large American corporation.* [289] Interestingly, Juniper networks, an Indian startup, was said to be "the greatest threat to Cisco." [331]

Raj Singh Sold Three Startups for More than $11 Billion

In 1999, Raj Singh sold three startups to US companies for more than $11 billion. He sold a chip startup named StratumOne to Cisco for about $435 million. This was a record setting price—two to four times the amount normally paid for a communications chip company. He also sold an optical transport startup named Cerent to Cisco for $6.2 billion. This deal caused quite a stir and shock in the industry at the amount paid. He sold Siara Networks to Redback Networks for $4.3 billion. [357] To put the size of these three acquisitions in perspective the reported US trade with India ran $11 billion. By 2000, he had accumulated $540 million from his telephony business. Yet despite all this wealth, Singh *kept a low profile.* To most Americans he was "virtually unknown." [330]

Who is Singh? He grew up in Meerut, India. He graduated from an engineering school in India in the 1960's. He struggled and found little success in India. Singh entered the US in 1980 using a student visa to attend the University of Minnesota. He got a Master's degree in computer science, and then moved to Silicon Valley where he got an entry level job at National Semiconductor. For the next fifteen years he jumped from job to job working at different US corporations. Then he met Suhas Patil, a charter member of TiE while working for Cirrus Logic a company Patil founded. Patil became one of his mentors. Vinod Khosla, also a charter member of TiE, helped Singh get the seed money for his first startup named Fiberlane. Khosla was on the board of directors at Fiberlane. Cerent and Siara were spun off from Fiberlane then sold. [357]

Once Singh sold his three startups he partnered with Raj Parekh, a charter member of TiE, to create the venture capital firm Redwood Ventures Partners. In 1999, Redwood funded over 40 startups. He began to travel around the world "fixing business deals." In 1999, Singh was on the board of 23 companies. Most were in Silicon Valley, however, others were overseas. In addition to funding startups, Singh planned to make financial contributions to fund education in India. [357]

KANWAL REKHI—"GODFATHER OF INDIAN DOTCOMMERS"

While most members of the "Mafia" kept a low profile, Kanwal Rekhi sought publicity. Rekhi is often referred to as the "godfather" of the India "Mafia"—

"godfather to a generation of immigrant entrepreneurs." At the peak of the dotcom boom immigrant entrepreneurs from India were lauded in US media as "hidden geniuses of the tech revolution." [289]

Kanwal Rekhi, a Sikh from Kanpur India, entered the US in 1971 on a student visa to pursue a Masters degree in electrical engineering at Michigan Tech University. He was a graduate of IIT Bombay in his early 20s and arrived in the United States with only $10, which means American taxpayers and/or American businesses must have paid for his education. The YMCA provided him a subsidized place to live for only $4 per night. Rekhi married an American, and worked in the United States as an engineer. [350] [351] [289]

A November 23, 2001, article, "Upstarts: how India's dotcom pioneers staked their claim in Silicon Valley your space," by Ajay Singh in Asiaweek.com dubbed Rekhi the "godfather of Indian dotcommers." [359] Prior to the dotcom crash the combined value of 19 of the startups Rekhi helped launch were hyped to have a $235 billion stock market valuation. In December 2000, following the horrific dotcom crash, Rekhi is quoted in the Hindustan Times stating, "The whole dotcom world was not a robust set-up ... I said in January (2000), that 99 per cent of the companies would fail. There is no value here." Rekhi believed that the dotcoms were not doing anything new. [358] American investors should have been told this instead of all the hype about dotcom stocks.

How Rekhi Got the Money to Fund Startups

In the early 1980's Rekhi along with two Indian partners founded Excelan, a computer networking company. Rekhi was CEO. In 1987, they approached a venture capital company to help them launch an IPO. Rekhi was offended when the venture capital firm asked him to step aside and make a former HP executive CEO. They warned Rekhi that if the stock did not sell his investment was at risk. Profiles on

Rekhi recall how he resented that Americans viewed people from India as poor managers and may not invest in stock IPOs of companies founded by someone from India. Rekhi agreed to allow a former HP executive to act as CEO to take Excelan public. [350] [351] [289] Excelan became the first Indian startup to receive venture capital funding. The maneuver worked and the American public bought into the IPO. A year after the IPO Rekhi reclaimed his CEO title. In 1989, Excelan was sold to Novell for $210 million making Rekhi a millionaire. *Thus began the pattern of the Indian "Mafia" spawned startups, often with token CEO "whiteys", to launch IPOs and/or to sell these startups to major American corporations in multimillion dollar deals.* Rekhi then went to work for Novell.

"Godfather" Rekhi Said TiE Founded out of Anger

Rekhi co-founded TiE in 1992, while he was chief technology officer at Novell. A TiE "Organizational Profile" published in the web by larta.org, quoted Rekhi, "The genesis of TiE was based in fundamental anger..." [332] One article wrote that Rekhi, said, "he was passed over for the chief executive job twice in favor of non-immigrants who Rekhi believed were less capable than he was." [463] In another article Rekhi also claimed that he was passed over for a promotion and a white guy who was "only half as good as me" got promoted. Rekhi asserted that TiE was formed to help South Asians "our people" become entrepreneurs. [467] TiE became a powerful network to benefit people from India and Pakistan. [463] In 1994, Kanwal Rekhi joined the Board of Advisors to the President of Michigan Technological University, and later was awarded an honorary doctorate degree in Business and Engineering. [310] In 1995, Rekhi quit his Chief Technology Officer job at Novell, and shifted his focus to TiE where he *"cultivated his Godfather image."* [463]

Rekhi Funded Immigrant Startups

By 1998, Rekhi had funded 15 startups. [350] [312] In June 1999, Rekhi claimed that Indian owned American business startups had stock valuations of "about $5 billion." Two of the companies he talked about were CyberMedia and Infospace. [467]

A May 15, 2000, article in *Fortune*, "The Indians of Silicon Valley," Melanie Warner wrote about Kanwal Rekhi: "The hidden geniuses of the tech revolution are Indian engineers—here's how one bucked stereotypes, got rich, and has become the godfather to a generation of immigrant entrepreneurs." The article claimed all the startups Rekhi funded were founded by people from India, and that *Rekhi made most of his money financing these startups.* During the dotcom boom his personal wealth was estimated to be $500 million. Despite all these investments, few people from India were CEO's. Many of their startups were *sold to large American corporations.* Rekhi's biggest payoff came from helping K.B. Chandrasklar launch Exodus. Rekhi put in $1 million for a 2% stake that was hyped as valued at $130 million at the peak of the dotcom boom. [289]

A September 22, 2000 article "Networking Godfather to Visit Triangle" by David Mildenberg in the *Triangle Business Journal* claimed Rekhi had invested millions in almost 48 startups and just about every one was run by someone from India. Mildenberg asked Rekhi, "Isn't there something sinister about what could be perceived as a cliquish nationalist approach?" to his investments and business dealings. Rekhi claimed that TiE was diverse because it had members from both India and Pakistan. [351] A "TiE Rockies Speakers 2000-2001" list on http://tie-rockies.org pictured Rekhi as the September 2001 speaker, and said he was connected to over 50 startups in Silicon Valley. [310]

TiE Reciprocity

In 2001 Rekhi claimed TiE had helped entrepreneurs obtain $75 billion in venture capital. [332] While it appears the American public largely got a raw deal from investing in these companies, TiE founders and early investors got rich on deals. According to a May 15, 2000, *Fortune* article, "The Indians of Silicon Valley," by Melanie Warner, she wrote, "As in all good networks, reciprocity keeps the wheels turning." K.B. Chandrasekhar (Chandra) explained, *"I always make sure Kanwal gets a good deal."*

The article also mentions another investment deal for a web service company named Impresse: "Chandra got to do something virtually every investor in the Valley would kill to do–he invested alongside Kleiner Perkins and Benchmark. Rekhi, because he's the godfather and everyone wants him to invest, also got in on the deal." And Satish Gupta, CEO of Cradle Technologies got in on the deal because the CEO of Impresse was an angel investor in his company. [289]

"MAFIA" RECEIVED UNJUSTIFIED VENTURE CAPITAL FUNDING

Immigrants from India received unprecedented venture capital financing to fuel dotcom startups. This is surprising because there was no history of entrepreneurship in India that would justify this favoritism. And, as recently as 1993, India's software piracy rate ran 89%. [374]

A December 14, 1999, redherring.com/insider article, "The 'Indian Mafia' Muscles onto the Web," by Vanessa Richardson, reported that many of the startups founded by immigrants from India received their funding with the assistance of TiE. The article says Rekhi is a Pakistani educated in India and the US; and, refers to Rekhi as the ""*Godfather*" of TiE." Rekhi is quoted as saying that *Indians seeking venture capital get preferential treatment, "even over whites."* [333]

Vinod Khosla Link Sun Microsystems & KPCB Venture Capital

In 1992, Vinod Khosla, along with Rekhi, was a founding member of TiE. [323] Also, like Rekhi, Khosla sought publicity, unlike most members who preferred to remain anonymous. Khosla, an IIT graduate entered the US by attending graduate school at Stanford. In 1982, Khosla co-founded Sun Microsystems along with Scott McNealy, Andy Bechtolsheim, and Bill Joy.

While the "Mafia" network hypes his role in founding Sun, Khosla was only with Sun until 1985, not during the time the company became "wildly successful." In 1986, Khosla joined venture capital firm Kleiner, Perkins, Caufield & Byers (KPCB) where he became a managing partner. [312] [188] KPCB has sponsored TiE's annual conference.

Through KPCB Khosla obtained positions on the boards of many high-tech startups such as: QWEST Communications, Corvis Corporation, Juniper Networks, Siara Systems, Asera, Concentric Network, Corio Inc., Doublebill.com, Coreon Inc, Broadband Office Surmodics. [188]

According to an August 7, 2000, IndoLink article titled, "Silicon Spice Acquired by Broadcom for $1.2 Billion," Khosla was also involved in very big acquisition deals such as Cisco's $6.9 billion acquisition of Cerent, and Redback Networks' $4.3 billion acquisition of Siara. KPCB provided venture capital to Silicon Spice led by Vinod Dham. Cisco also provided funding to Silicon Spice, and Cisco was a customer of Silicon Spice. [390]

Investing in a company and then buying from that company guarantees sales. In fact, buying from the company invested in could be done to manipulate financial statements to make a company appear more valuable to the public than it really is.

KPCB where Khosla was a managing partner was said to be one of the biggest venture capital firms in Silicon Valley. In March 2001, KPCB revealed that *"40% of its portfolio consists of companies founded or managed by people of Indian origin."* [187] They claim India Diaspora living in the US are intellectually elite. [187] It is to be noted that people originating from India represented less than 1% of the US population, but obtained 40% of the KPCB deals.

According to the May 15, 2000, *Fortune* article, "The Indians of Silicon Valley," Khosla was the "wealthiest Indian in the Valley." [289]

Major American Corporations Funded Dotcom Startups

The level of venture capital investment linked to Java, Sun Microsystems's software for creating internet programs and other applications, was surprising.

In August 1996, KPCB announced a $100 million Java Fund for dotcom startups. The ten corporations that partnered with KPCB to form the fund were: *Sun Microsystems (Vinod Khosla co-founded)*, Cisco, Comcast, Compaq, IBM, Itochu, Netscape, Oracle, Tele-Communications, and US West Media Group. The contributions were approximately: KPCB $30 million, Sun $15 million and the other companies' ranged from $4 million to $7 million each. [432] [431]

In June 2000, a VP for Sun Microsystems estimated that 70% of the company's growth the prior year came from the dotcom boom. [117] Did the Java Fund play a key role in manipulating Sun Microsystems stock to make the company appear "wildly successful"? A failing Sun Microsystems was acquired by Oracle in 2009. How many insiders got rich during the wild dotcom ride?

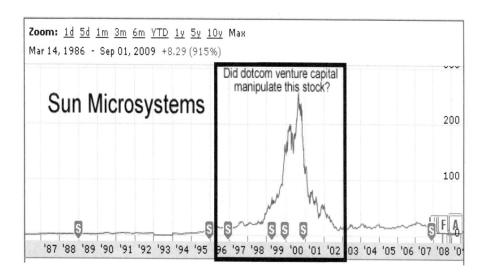

Did immigrants from India in the upper management of US corporations misdirect corporate funds to provide venture capital to Indian startups? Were American stockholders in these US corporations aware that their money was used as a source of venture capital? Did both executives in the US corporations providing the venture capital and executives in the startups conspire to inflate sales through reciprocal purchasing? Were any Java Fund startups later bought by the ten partners? Did the executives get bonuses tied to these deals?

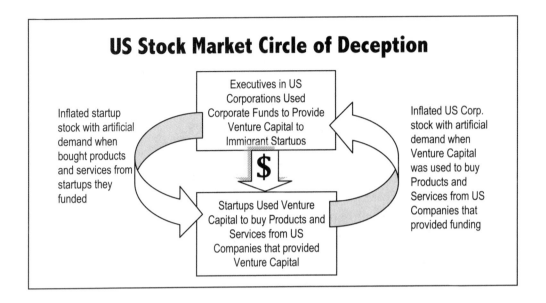

US Stock Market Circle of Deception

Executives in US Corporations Used Corporate Funds to Provide Venture Capital to Immigrant Startups

Inflated startup stock with artificial demand when bought products and services from startups they funded

Inflated US Corp. stock with artificial demand when Venture Capital was used to buy Products and Services from US Companies that provided funding

$

Startups Used Venture Capital to buy Products and Services from US Companies that provided Venture Capital

In 2001, the managing director for Sun Microsystems India, explained how the networking works. *You put money in their bank accounts so they have money to buy from your company.* His comments were summarized: "We give preference to companies that we do business with for everything." "Sun is

The year 1996, when the Java Fund was formed, was a pivotal year in setting the stage for India's run on high tech US visas and the US dotcom stock market. In the first two quarters of 1996, more venture capital money flowed into the US software industry than to any other industry sector. And, there were other Java funds fueling the dotcom boom. For example, in 1996, another venture capital firm, Bessemer Venture Partners became involved in funding Java startups.

one of Citibank's top clients ... and Citibank happens to be Sun India's largest customer." [118]

Indian "Mafia" Secret Money Source the Middle East?

Was money from the Middle East channeled into the United States to fund Indian immigrant founded startups? A Saudi Prince who bought shares of US media also invested in InfoSpace founded by an immigrant from India. [267] The Carlyle Group reported to have upper level management connections to India, [377] was also reported to have Saudi investors; and, Carlyle invested in Silicon Valley startups. [341]

Furthermore, recall that Senator Spencer Abraham was the sponsor of the massive increase in H-1B visas in 1998. This is peculiar for a couple of reasons. First he was the Republican Senator from Michigan (1995 to 2001), yet it was Silicon Valley in California where the push for the H-1B visa originated, not Michigan. [518] Secondly, the H-1B legislation primarily benefited India and people of Indian ancestry, but

Spencer Abraham was not Indian, he was the only Arab American in the US Senate. In 1998, two big outsourcing companies founded by immigrants from India, Syntel and Mastech, were listed as top employers of H-1Bs, and "contributed" towards Abraham's 2000 reelection campaign. Abraham raised $14.5 million for his 2000 campaign, yet constituents decided not to reelect him. [518]

SHAREHOLDER LAWSUITS

Americans who worked hard all their lives and lost their savings, their retirement, their kids' college money, and more deserve a just legal resolution to dotcom stock manipulations. The following lawsuits are just a few samples. How many more lawsuits were there? Why did the media not provide more coverage?

InfoSpace Lawsuit

There were multiple lawsuits filed against Infospace an Internet startup founded in 1996, by Naveen Jain. InfoSpace was hyped by *Wall Street*, *Forbes*, other business journals, and on television. In a March 2005 article, "Dot Conned and the American Way," at dvorak.org, the writer claimed he was not impressed when he interviewed Jain on "Big Thinkers", a show owned by TechTV. During the dotcom boom, InfoSpace's market value peaked at $31 billion (supposedly worth more than Boeing). Jain's shares soared to $8 billion allowing him to buy an extravagant house on the waterfront and two yachts. In March 2000, InfoSpace stock plummeted from its peak price of $260 a share to less than a dollar a share. A federal judge in Seattle ruled that Jain had broken insider-trading laws. *The author was astounded when the SEC instead of pursing Jain came to his defense. He asks "What's going on here?"* [293] Infospace denied all allegations of wrongdoing. According to a March 9, 2009, Associate Press article, "Supreme Court Turns Down Appeal From InfoSpace Founder," in the *Seattle Times*, the Court refused to hear Naveen Jain's appeal to sue his former lawyers who he claimed bungled an insider trading case resulting in a $247 million judgment against Jain. According to the article, "Jain claimed InfoSpace would become the first company worth a trillion dollars, but it lost more than $30 billion in shareholder value during the dotcom bust and Jain was fired in 2002." [753]

Computer Associates Lawsuit

A September 2004, article titled "Ex-Computer Associates CEO Kumar Indicted," claimed that: "Three executives, including Kumar, split stock bonuses worth $1.1 billion in 1998." And, "The SEC said that during the company's 2000 fiscal year, Computer Associates "prematurely recognized" more than $1.4 billion in revenue from at least 116 contracts that had not yet been signed." The software company was accused of a multibillion dollar accounting scandal. Sanjay Kumar denied the charges. Three former lower level executives "entered guilty pleas" and cooperated with prosecutors which helped with moving "toward indicting other high-ranking company executives." According to the article, "the company agreed to pay $225 million to shareholders in a settlement that allows it to defer criminal prosecution." [297]

I2 Technologies Lawsuit

On May 10, 2004, an article titled, "i2 Settles Class Action and Derivative Lawsuits," posted by *Yahoo Financial News* reported that shareholders filed a class action lawsuit against Indian founded i2 Technologies. An $84 million settlement was reached for the lawsuit and other derivative lawsuits that were pending. Company insurance paid $43 million of the settlement. Another portion was paid by Sanjiv Sidhu, i2's CEO and chairman who agreed to buy $20 million in common stock, and the remainder of the settlement was paid by i2. Once again the Defendants, i2 and its directors and officers, admitted no wrongdoing. [421] An interesting note—in October 2002, Enron's Ken Lay resigned from the board of i2 Technologies. [298]

DOTCOM MONEY USED TO ACQUIRE US BUSINESSES & ASSETS

March 7, 2001, a Time Magazine article, "The Golden Diaspora," by Anthony Spaeth/New Delhi, posted on www.indianembassy.org claimed, "the Indian diaspora in the U.S. tends to be the intellectual and commercial elite." This article, written almost a year after the US dotcom crash, quoted AnnaLee Saxenian, and claimed, "The number of Indian American New Economy millionaires is in the thousands." Not all the millionaires were in Silicon Valley. For example, Gururaj Despande who lived on the east cost in Massachusetts was a co-founder of multiple network technology companies and was estimated to have accumulated over $4 billion from his startups. [187] This diaspora used money gained from outsourcing and startups to acquired US businesses and assets. For example, in 2007 a Wikipedia post, "Non-Resident Indian and Person of Indian Origin," displayed fourteen pages of data. (A non-resident Indian (NRI)—is a term used by India to refer to people originating from India who live in the United States and other countries.) According to this posting, *NRIs acquired 35% of US hotels and 50% of US economy lodges worth a combined estimated real estate value of $40 billion.* [618] Why would they aggressively acquire billions in US hotels? Were US hotels bought by Indians used to house foreign students from India, H-1Bs from India, and illegal aliens from India living in our country? If so, even money foreign students and foreign workers circulated in the United States was intentionally channeled specifically to benefit their ethnic group.

DOTCOM FUNDED SCHOOLS IN INDIA TO ENABLE OFFSHORING

According to a May 2000 article, "India Schools Cash In on Silicon Valley Wealth," much of the money taken from the US during the dotcom boom went to fund schools in India. [360] These schools are essential to NRIs offshoring US jobs to India. By 2003, TiE membership in Silicon Valley had grown to 2,500. These Silicon Valley members were a branch of the global TiE network comprised of 800 Charter members plus 8,000 regular members. [512] [333] On its web site, TiE wrote about giving back to the community which sounds good until you realize by "community" they mean people from India and the Indus region. In 2003, the India diaspora who had become wealthy as entrepreneurs in America, were working with institutes of higher education in India to help *their country* to "scout, mentor and incubate talent in India to create entrepreneurs." [319]

Kanwal Rekhi School of Information Technology

In July 1999, the Kanwal Rekhi School of Information Technology (KReSIT) was opened in Bombay India. Funding for starting KReSIT came from Kanwal Rekhi and Nandan Nilekhani. They were preparing the IT industry in India to experience a major boom in growth. The school was created to train IT leaders in India. [349]

Rekhi—Raising Money for India's IIT

In 1999, Kanwal Rekhi and Mr. Nandan, the president of Infosys, raised money to turn India's IIT into a world class university and research center for bio-sciences, bio-engineering, nanotechnology, and more. They claimed they were paying back their debt for having gotten a free education at IIT. In their own words: "The IIT is generating funds by working on technology transfer and consultancy projects." [315] This quote links consulting with US technology transfer.

In December 1999, Kanwal Rekhi led a group of thirteen Indian immigrant Silicon Valley CEOs, all IIT graduates who became rich during the US dotcom boom, on a trip back to India to meet with the Prime Minister. The group planned to raise $1 billion for IIT; under the condition they replace India's government role as IIT overseer with business and academic leaders. Although they represented their "contributions" as philanthropic, some were concerned that they had ulterior motives to take control of India's state assets. [360]

Dotcom Money Built Education Centers in India

Another group of Indian immigrants living on the East coast of the US, raised money to pay for high level advanced degree educational centers in India. This group was led by Purnendu Chatterjee who was the managing director of the Chatterjee Group based in New York. Their long term goal was to create a Silicon Valley type technology environment that would make India a superpower. One of these immigrants, K.B. Chandrasekhar felt that instead of rising to power through a military war, that India could accomplish a superpower status by intellectual competition. [360]

Dotcom Money Built Indian School of Business (ISB)

An August 2002 article, "Hyderabad's Harvard: A University Built on an Arid Plain with Funds from Overseas Indians ...," revealed that $75 million of overseas money was spent to build the Indian School of Business (ISB) that opened in Hyderabad, India in July 2001. The school admitted that the dotcom crash in the US stock market dried up much of its funding. ISB has ambitious goals of competing head to head with schools such as Harvard and Wharton. Major contributors included Kanwal Rekhi, K.B. Chandrasekhar, B.V. Jagadeesh, and Romesh Wadhwani. The idea to build *ISB was conceived by Rajat Gupta, a managing partner of McKinsey* based in New York. Another McKinsey employee, a consultant named Pramath Sinha, also a native of India, was the school's dean until June 2002.

McKinsey along with Citibank and HSBC provided student scholarships for ISB. And McKinsey along with Lehman Brothers and others recruited from ISB's first graduating class of 128 students. ISB graduates able to get jobs in the US were paid about $80,000 a year while those who stayed in India only got about $17,000, quite a pay difference. The curriculum was developed with the help of Northwestern University's Kellogg School of Management, Wharton, and London Business School. India diaspora in top US business schools are helping India compete against the US schools where they were employed. Some took teaching stints at ISB then returned to their jobs at US universities. ISB sent letters to US universities to recruit PhD graduates for its faculty. [492]

Heritage Fund to Finance Education and Research

TiE was building a global network of "IIT-ians." As part of this strategy, in 2002, The Heritage Fund was created to help finance student research and education at IIT Bombay. [361]

Chapter 12

"Mafia" Exploits US Economic Downturn

In his farewell address George Washington warned that "corrupt" citizens who favor a foreign nation may "betray or sacrifice the interests of their own country."

The suffering from the dotcom crash in 2000 should have been a time when loyal Americans joined together to help revive our economy. While America was reeling from the devastation of our stock market dotcom crash, the US was attacked on September 11th, and once again loyal Americans should have rallied together to help fellow Americans strengthen our country during war. However, some groups exploited the war to get rich. The timing of the terrorist attack was extremely fortuitous for executives at risk of being investigated for dotcom, telecommunications, and other stock fraud. If not for attention diverted by the attack and subsequent war, many more executives beyond those at Enron and WorldCom may have been investigated.

India used the economic downturn caused by the dotcom crash and the war to push for US corporations to dramatically accelerate offshoring. Not only was India going after more programming jobs, India wanted US corporations to finance setting up research centers in India, and for US venture capital money to fund startups based in India. [6] Recall that the Economic Circulation Model™ shown earlier disproved the cost savings from outsourcing and offshoring US jobs to foreign workers. American companies, in preparation for offshoring more jobs and services paid huge amounts of money for IT to become "Internet-centric." [299]

Pressuring American companies to offshore under the guise that it would help them survive the destructive impact of the dotcom crash was taking American corporations down a self destructive path. To revive US corporations, and the US economy, the strategy needed was to cut outsourcing and offshoring, not accelerate and expand it.

200,000 INDIANS BECAME MILLIONAIRES IN THE US BY 2007!

A "Non-resident Indian and Person of Indian Origin," topic published on Wikipedia in 2007, said, "One in every nine Indians in the US is a millionaire, comprising 10% of US millionaires. Source: 2003 Merrill Lynch SA Marketing Study." [618] If this is true, given that NRIs were less than 1% of the US population, they were demographically 900% overrepresented in the millionaires' category. Either NRIs were 900% superior to other Americans or something very disturbing has been going on under the radar in America.

In April 2007, USINPAC's website claimed that the United States had 200,000 millionaires with roots to India. [625] How did so many Indians (Sikhs, Hindus, and Muslims), who arrived in America broke, become millionaires? *It appears highly suspect and sinister that during the war in Iraq where many young Americans are risking their lives, the Indian "Mafia" network doubled its number of millionaires in America from 100,000 to 200,000. Were they making money off the war?*

In 2007, according to an AT&T (att.net) report "Engineers Learning People Skills," the University of California's Berkeley's director of Entrepreneurship & Technology was Professor Ikhlaq Sidhu, and its dean of engineering was S. Shankkar Sastry. Students in the school of engineering were taught to be entrepreneurs. Students were laughingly taught that independent investors were the three "Fs", meaning friends, family, and fools. [662]

SECRET MONEY SOURCE—US DEPARTMENT OF DEFENSE!

A January 4, 2007, article, "Skilled Indian Immigrants Create Wealth for America," by Francis C. Assisi on *http//:www.indolink.com* (*INDOLink.com, Inc. trademark– "Linking Indians Worldwide"*), pictured Vivek Wadhwa and was written about his Duke study "released today." The article had a "Related Findings" section where the author and Elizabeth Pothen "concluded that Indian immigrants in America account for less than 0.75% of the US population, but their contribution to the U.S. Department of Defense (DoD) research is more than *20 times the population base.*" The article claimed this was the first time the magnitude of US defense research jobs occupied by Indian workers had been quantified. Most of these jobs were in academics, i.e. university professors who had business startups on the side. They employed "younger post-doctoral fellows and graduate students, *also of Indian origin*, for their research efforts." *The research foreign students were doing* "ranged from homeland security to missile technology, advanced ceramics and munitions ..." The stated goal was to "maintain America's superiority in military technology." [685] How many people originating from India have risked their lives fighting to defend America? Americans have a right to know how much of our tax money has gone to fund Indian startups doing US government research.

TIE ROLLING IN DOUGH AND DEALS AFTER DOTCOM CRASH

While America was reeling from the April 2000 dotcom crash, TiE members were ready to spin-off more startups and IPOs made possible by the Internet. [312] They were holding meetings and conferences and talking about the money they made from the dotcom, telecom, and outsourcing.

TiE Meeting in California Following the Dotcom Crash

A SiliconValley.com: Special Report article titled, "The TiE That Binds," was posted November 27, 2000, by Ben Stocking of the *Mercury Times*. The article featured a picture of Rekhi being "treated like a movie star by aspiring young entrepreneurs." At this meeting in October 2000, just months after the dotcom crash where US citizens lost trillions, *TiE members hobnobbing at the Santa Clara Marriott were referred to as a "room full of billionaires."* It was noted that Indian owned American companies in Silicon Valley were important to "the home country" because *they recruited visa workers from India and brought business to India.* [463] TiE members had lots of money to invest: "The recent dot-com implosions and falling tech stocks notwithstanding, this bland conference room is burning with entrepreneurial spirit."

The article talked about how members had gotten rich selling startups. For example, in 1996, Suhas Patil got $12 million, over a 400% return on his $2.8 million investment in Vani Kola's internet software company RightWorks. (Note: Patil was on the faculty at MIT before he started Cirrus Logic a semiconductor company.) Then there is Sabeer Bhatia who sold Hotmail to Microsoft for over $400 million. By far, the most revered TiE network member was Kanwal Rekhi who they said had $250 million. And in turn, Rekhi claimed that he knew about 30 more Indians that had as much or more money than he did. [463]

At this meeting, Rekhi was approached by a wannabe Indian entrepreneur, and was "horrified" that the individual put in his own money when according to Rekhi he should get "other people's money." The wannabe also confided to Rekhi that "several of his Indian friends were on board ... but they have visa problems." Rekhi told him: "Those are not the kind of people you need! You need mainline, quality people! You need whiteys!" [463] If you look at startups connected to TiE many of the people getting rich helping launch these companies were "whiteys." For example a My 15, 2000, *Fortune* article, "The Indians of Silicon Valley," wrote that, "construction executive Ed Shay and venture capitalist John Doughery, who have since (1995 to 2000) invested in almost every one of Rekhi's deals." [289] How many of the "whiteys" investing in these startups were executives in big American corporations who also used corporate funds to buy products and services from these startups, and/or to acquire these startups?

2000 TiE Meeting in Bangalore India IT Conference Speakers

Kanwal Rekhi was the first of 20 speakers on the list for a 2000 TiE Conference held in Bangalore India some time after the dotcom crash. The conference brochure tells about the speakers' dotcom startups, how they used the media to promote Indian outsourcing, and how they were helping India. According to the conference brochure Rekhi was President of TiE, on the Board of Advisors for Michigan Tech, on the Board of several startups, *promoting recognition for India's universities, and he gave $2 million to IIT for a new Information Technology school.* [469] (Recall that a few years later in 2005, US Congressman Bobby Jindal cosponsored the special recognition bill for IIT.) Also speaking was Poornima Jairaj, a Charter member of TiE, and a partner with Global Technology Ventures (GTV) started in May 2000 (a month after the US dotcom crash) by the Sivan Group & Banc of America for accelerating the creation of Indian founded technology startups by providing everything from money, to management teams, to legal advice to even preparing a 59 acre business incubator park in Bangalore. Although GTV preferred to help entrepreneurs create startups in India, it was willing to help Indian entrepreneurs in Silicon Valley if they created startups with "strong business linkages to Bangalore." [469]

Other speakers at this 2000 TiE Bangalore IT conference in India included: AnnaLee Saxenian the author of studies used to promote hiring H-1Bs and outsourcing to US business and US government agencies. Subroto Bagchi the Cofounder and CEO of Mindtree Consulting who helped get India's software industry started by setting up Wipro's US operations in Silicon Valley and *getting over 100 articles published.* Dewang Mehta, the President of NASSCOM, who had organized 100 international seminars *to lobby the US government,* and other governments to promote outsourcing software and dotcom work to India. Atul Vashistha the co-founder and CEO of neoIT selling offshore business process outsourcing to US companies. Nandan Nilekani, a TiE member, cofounder of NASSCOM, and on India's Securities and Exchange Board. Alex Lightman, whose book *America Inc. "addresses the feasibility of running the United States as a publicly owned company."* Raj Popli a TiE Charter member who managed a Silicon Valley fund that helped launch 40 technology startups including Internet and telecom startups, many of which had IPOs. Rhul Singh, a Charter member of TiE California & Boston, Managing Partner Dhunn-Carr in Boston, invested in and was a Director for several companies including telecom, software, and hardware companies. Sridhar Mitta who set up Wipro's R&D division that sold outsourced R&D services to Cisco, Lucent, Sun Microsystems, Alltel, ... set up a Wipro subsidiary that licensed semiconductor intellectual property, and who co-founded the Technology Holding Company to help Indian entrepreneurs in India and America startup global companies that sell Internet services for managing Utility Infrastructure. Sridhar Iyengar, a Charter member of TiE and partner with KPMG since 1968, who led its India operations for three years increasing business in India by 400%. [469] How many of the speakers were US citizens?

The list of conference attendees also included a speaker from the SiliconIndia magazine, additional venture capitalists, and more. [469]

2001 SILICONINDIA INVESTOR ENTREPRENEUR FORUM

The Siliconindia website claimed to be "a very exclusive club" that brings together the "Asian Indian community." In 2001, Siliconindia held an Investor Entrepreneur Forum at its Annual Conference where technology workers, entrepreneurs, venture capitalists, and academics from around the world meet to "exchange ideas, network, and cut deals." At the conference, "selected companies" gained an audience with high profile Silicon Valley venture capitalists. In addition to money, the selected companies were meeting key business contacts, recruiting employees for the startups (H-1Bs?), and finding customers. This exclusive club stated that Siliconindia provided members with advantages that gave them "greater traction in the market from all perspectives." [306] While they came to Silicon Valley, USA, their website was titled Siliconindia.com. They published a siliconindia magazine that had a circulation of 60,000 readers. [312]

TIE "INVISIBLE HAND"—"THE BEST KEPT SECRET"

TiE's website stated in September 2004 that within a 30 day period four of its members sold companies. Matrix (CEO Piyush Sodha) was sold to Symbol Technologies for $230 million in cash. Intelsat (COO Ramu Potarazu) was sold to Zeus Holdings for about $3 billion. AC Technologies (CEO Satya Akulawas) sold to PEC Solutions for $50 million in cash. And, DigitalNet Holdings (CEO Ken Bajaj) was sold to BAE Systems North America for about $595 million cash. [592]

Forbes composes a list of the top 100 venture capitalists. In 2005 three Indians in the top 10 of this list included Ram Shriram, Vinod Khosla, and Pramod Haque. [189] According to a 2005 article, "TiE—The Secrets of Success", by Kim Gerard on http://www.tie-asia.org, TiE was described as "the best kept secret" because of how it is the "invisible hand behind" 300 or more startups at any point in time. The typical India entrepreneur startup model in 2005 was to have a split workforce in Silicon Valley and in India. Membership in TiE was expanded to include not just people with Indus ancestry, but also people with business interests in India, Bangladesh,

Nepal and Sri Lanka. By 2005, two percent of TiE's charter members were non-IndUS people. TiE's "charter" memberships are by invitation only. TiE connects entrepreneurs from India with TiE members who are executives in large US corporations, US banks, and US venture capital firms. [604] The article credits TiE for the "technological emergence" of India. And, tells how since 1998 "India's economy has skyrocketed" and that *"TiE and India are feeding off each other."* The article talks about the US dotcom fiasco and the devastating US economic downturn that followed over the next five years as just the beginning, *"We've not even begun to see the results of what these folks have begun to put in place over these past several years."* [604] When this article was written TiE was over 12 years old, still most Americans did not even know this network was operating in the United States. From its "California hub" TiE's tentacles extended to nine countries including Pakistan. In the article a TiE member explained that the connection went beyond business ties to "your mother, your grandmother" and ties to India. Contacts for "deals and recruitment" provided an edge, "The Rolodex is more important than what you know." [604]

Interestingly, the same article that lauds giving ethnic preferences to Indians claims that Rekhi was an "outspoken critic of discrimination against Indian entrepreneurs since the 1980's." [604] Recall Rekhi came to America as a foreign student with $10 in his pocket, yet he thought Americans discriminated against people from India. Some American minorities did not agree with Rekhi.

American Minority Exploitation

H-1Bs took minority benefits that should have gone to American minorities. In a June 4, 1999, article, "Jessie Jackson is Blowing Smoke, Says TiE's Rekhi," Kanwal Rekhi challenged Jessie Jackson's claim that Silicon Valley discriminated against minorities. Rekhi said that people from India were discriminated against because of the color of their skin. Yet Kekhi claimed Silicon Valley jobs went to people from India because they were well educated in math and science. Rekhi wanted Jessie Jackson to know that, "In Silicon Valley especially, it is all merit driven. It is how smart you are." [467]

> In May 2006, doctors in India went on strike to protest affirmative action allowing lower caste Indians which account for 80% of India's population to increase their representation in government run hospital jobs from 22.5% to 49.5%. Students at seven medical colleges in India went on hunger strikes. Although India has laws against discrimination the lower castes are at the bottom socially from education opportunities, to jobs, to property ownership. Police had to use water cannons and batons to subdue protestors. [581]

However, Tony Brown saw it differently, in September 7, 2001, he wrote a paper titled, "Why Indian H-1Bs Are Not Superior and Aframericans Are Not Cry Babies." Brown challenged the "best and brightest" claims made by promoters of the H-1B visas, pointing to research that uncovered a lucrative illegal industry based in India that was falsifying resumes and flooding unqualified H-1Bs to staff immigrant founded outsourcing "body shops." [720]

TiE Member Tracking US College Students & US Alumni

On TiE's website it said that in May 2005, a startup named Intelliworks raised $6 million in venture capital. Intelliworks planned to sell software to US Universities that would track potential students, current students, and alumni like businesses track customers. The plan was to compile a massive database that linked data from student transcripts, to scheduling interviews, to soliciting donations, and more. Intelliworks customers were said to include The Wharton School, Duke University, Northwestern University's Kellogg School of Management, MIT, and more. [592] Will this system be used to screen out American student applicants, and to influence hiring? How is privacy protected?

THEY ARE "RESHAPING CORPORATE AMERICA"

In December 8, 2003, *BusinessWeek* published a twelve page cover story article titled; "The Rise of India: Growth is just starting, but the country's brainpower is already *reshaping Corporate America*." The story reads like a Public Relations piece promoting offshore outsourcing of US corporate R&D to India. Manjeet Kripalani in Bombay India co-authored the story with Pete Engardio. According to the cover story, the economic damage caused by the dotcom crash had American companies scrambling to cut costs by offshoring R&D to India. *It proclaimed the chief architects behind the offshoring business model transfer of US R&D to India were 30,000 Indian diaspora who worked in Silicon Valley at major US chip and software companies.* The Indian diaspora were persuading high tech American Corporations where they worked, such as Intel, Cisco, and Oracle, to build offshore research labs in India. They claimed the cutbacks in foreign worker visa quotas caused American companies to speed up offshoring. The article also claimed that by the year 2000 (i.e. the peak of the dotcom boom), people from India had founded or were executives in 972 companies. Many of the companies they founded were outsourcing companies, dotcom companies, or dotcom related. The very companies that appear to have played a major role in causing the US economic downturn that they were exploiting. One subtitled segment named, "Brainpower India and Silicon Valley: Now the R&D Flows both Ways", featured Kanwal Rekhi who credited offshore outsourcing to India with saving US companies from "oblivion" after the dotcom crash. [300]

According to a 2003 *EETimes* article, when the dotcom crash caused the US economy to plummet, 40,000 H-1B visa workers left the US and returned to India. [123] This created an enormous pool of high tech workers in India that had received on-the-job training in the US. These workers were all in need of jobs when they returned to India. The US high tech industry created its own competition.

Advising US Companies "Vital for Profits" to Offshore

American corporations were "advised" they must offshore to survive the economic downturn caused by the dotcom crash. For example, in June 2003, The Sand Hill Group sponsored an Enterprise Offshoring Conference in California, where it *decreed that offshoring of US software development was "vital for profits" because of the downturn in the US economy.* The Sand Hill Group, a combination investment firm and a research firm, released a study that reported, "more than 8 in 10 software companies are now shipping work overseas or plan to do so in the next year." (Was Sand Hill making forecasts that profited companies it invested in?) It noted this was a controversial topic in the US where *offshoring caused high tech unemployment and jeopardized US technological leadership.* [113] This conference held in the United States advised US companies to transfer strategic software jobs to foreign nations while our nation was at war.

Offshoring gives foreign access to strategic US technology and databases. Madhavan Rangaswami, a co-founder of The Sand Hill Group, asserted that US executives were not concerned about intellectual property risks inherent in offshoring. [84] In 2005, Rangaswami and his fellow "strategists" continued to advise that US software companies "must take development offshore" to generate margin for investors. Surprisingly, in 2005 his

> Was Rangaswami on both sides of the deal in 2000 when Aspect Development was acquired by i2 Technologies in what was touted as the biggest software acquisition ever at $9 billion? Soon afterwards, i2 stock fell like a rock causing one of the worst dotcom crashes—US citizens lost billions of dollars. Both of these US corporations were founded by immigrants from India.

dual role as an advisor to Aspect Development and i2 Technologies was still listed in his expert advisor credentials in spite of how these two companies devastated American investors. [455]

9 OUT OF 10 IT JOBS WENT TO H-1BS IN 2001

According to a 2002 analysis, the dotcom crash triggered the downturn in the US economy for American IT workers, but acted as a windfall for foreign IT workers. In 2001, *over 500,000 American IT workers were laid off, while the number of foreign H-1B visas issued by our government increased by 70% hitting record levels.* American IT workers vital to our economy and national security were devastated in a job market that denied them jobs [29] Another 2002 analysis found that *H-1Bs took, "9 out of every 10 new IT jobs in 2001"* [43] Young Americans graduating with a degree in IT had little chance of obtaining employment in their field of study.

REKHI ADVISED H-1BS ON EXPIRED VISAS TO STAY ILLEGALLY

According to a May 4, 2001, *India West* report on isn.org titled, "Kanwal Rekhi Joins ISN Advisory Borad," by Viji Sundaram, Rekhi announced that he would join the advisory board for the Immigrants Support Network (ISN) which represented H-1B visa holders. Almost all the members of ISN were from India. US citizens deserve an explanation of how there can be an Immigrant Support Network for H-1Bs who were awarded temporary "non-immigrant" visas. At the April 29, 2001, meeting Rekhi promised ISN members to utilize his political clout to influence US politicians. *ISN's members "knew that when Rekhi speaks, people, especially politicians listen."* [347] According to another April 29, 2001 ISN report by Murali Krishna Devarakonda titled, "Kanwal Rekhi Advises Laid-off H-1B Workers Not to Leave," acting in his new advisory role, Rekhi spoke to a group of about 50 H-1B visa holders. He advised laid-off H-1Bs to stay in the US illegally because *based on his 35 years of experience; people who stayed illegally had a better chance of immigrating to the United States than those who returned to India.* [348] Who were the people Rekhi knew that stayed illegally that were granted US citizenship? Were members of the Indian "Mafia" among the illegal aliens granted amnesty in 1986? Do the dotcom, outsourcing and offshoring all trace back to this amnesty?

REKHI—PROMOTED OFFSHORING TO INDIA

In 2003, with the United States economy struggling to overcome the devastation of the dotcom crash, a backlash was brewing in America to the offshoring of work to India. When a New Jersey Senator discovered that the processing of welfare and food stamps had been outsourced to India, she tried to get a bill passed requiring that state government work had to be done inside the US. According to a August 4, 2003, article, "Growing Partnership: Major US Companies are Setting Up Offices in India for Software Development," by Sandip Roy-Chowdhury on *http://indiacurrents.com* Rekhi accused politicians who attempted to stop offshoring of US government jobs as grandstanding. He saw outsourced government jobs as "problematic" but saw no such problems with offshoring by the private sector. Rekhi thought offshoring to India had progressed to a point that trying to stop it was like trying to stop the tide. Despite much evidence to the contrary, *Rekhi claimed that offshoring American jobs to India would cut costs more than 50%. And, he claimed the US had a high tech worker shortage and needed H-1Bs and offshoring because: "America was not producing enough software engineers to start with."*

Rekhi argued that it was more economical to send the work to India (offshore) than to hire H-1Bs, because imported workers in America had to be paid more. He is even quoted as saying, "Outsourcing to India will enable *us* to do the jobs that no American will do at the wages Indians are paid." [586] Notice that Rekhi used "*us*" referring to himself not as an American, but as an Indian. This also establishes that the source of the cost savings claims and high tech American worker shortage claims track back to the Indian "Mafia".

US DOTCOM CRASH = WINDFALL FOR INDIA OUTSOURCING

December 11, 2002, a CNET News.com report titled "U.S. Firms Move IT Overseas," by Ed Frauenheim, reported that American IT service providers were compelled to send service jobs overseas because of Indian outsourcing firms operating in the US such as Wipro and Infosys. The Indian companies were doing much better during the "tech-downturn" than American outsourcing companies. Over a six month period both Wipro and Infosys increased sales revenues by 26%. This contrasted dramatically with US companies such as EDS which only experienced a 4% increase over a 9 month period. [102] The report explained that the Indian firms, while doing IT service projects for American clients, may send *90% to 95% of the work offshore to India.* As a result the article estimated that in 5 to 10 years, 40% to 50% of American IT service jobs could be lost to overseas competition. [102]

Indian outsourcing companies "compete head-on with IBM, Accenture, computer Sciences, EDS, and others." An October 2004 article titled, "India's Outsourcers Gain Traction" touted the growth of Infosys, Wipro, and Satyam. All three companies had "attractive valuations" as they competed against American companies for software infrastructure-process, and business-process outsourcing. Most of the growth came from the US: 70% of Infosys' sales, 53% of Wipro sales and 73% of Satyam sales came from North America. They set up a network in America with onsite customer contacts, and then channeled most of the work offshore to India. All three raised wages by double digits, 15% to 20%. [587] Another source listed the following Indian outsourcing firms: HCL America, Information Management Resources, Mastech Systems, Overseas Technologies, Syntel, Tata Consultancy Services (TCS), and Wipro. [138]

Software exports from India ran $17 billion in 2004, up from $13 billion in 2003. [80] In 2004, an article was published titled "India to See R&D Outsourcing Boom." According to the report India had $1.3 billion of information technology R&D in 2003, and was forecasted to jump to $9.1 billion by 2010. In 2003 India's telecom R&D was $0.7 billion and was forecasted to jump to $4.1 billion by 2010. India was launching a national initiative targeting strategic US technologies for outsourcing ranging from semiconductors, to micro-electronics, to nanotechnology. The article acknowledges that *there is some resistance to India taking over this R&D through outsourcing contracts due to low levels of expertise, risks of intellectual property theft, and the risk of instability in the R&D facilities.* [119]

US Corporations Persuaded to Offshore High Level Jobs to India

By 2004, the IIT-ians claimed that large numbers of IIT graduates had jobs working for *NASA, Microsoft, and IBM.* They had strategically penetrated the executive ranks of Corporate America. One example is Arun Netravali, the former president of Lucent Technologies' Bell Labs. They had people in the financial arena including: Vinod Khosla as a venture capitalist with Kleiner Perkins, Victor Menezes as senior VP at Citigroup, and Raghuram Rajan was the chief economist for the International Money Fund. In the consulting arena they had people *advising Executives in Corporate America* such as Rajat Gupta former managing director of McKinsey. And, they had people prepared to launch startups such as Gururaj Deshpande who had founded Sycamore Networks. Their penetration of US media is so pervasive they even used comic strips for PR propaganda, for example, they said that Asok in the Dilbert comic strip was an IIT graduate. [190]

World Bank Outsourcing

In June 2001, Prabhat Garg hired an America company to develop prototype software that would provide business links to United Nations and World Bank contracts. Garg then had the software development done in his native India by a company that accepted stock in his company as payment. He claimed the Indian company was better and cheaper than the American company. [101]

In 2003, the World Bank outsourced work to Satyam computer Services including developing software for operations, transitioning to the Internet, document management and message communications. [586] The World Bank moved its back office work, previously done in the West, to developing countries. [776]

In 2004, a *World Bank study claimed that India was the ideal location for software companies because it provided quality and low costs.* The World Bank planned to provide India $3 billion over a four year period. How much of this World Bank money came from the US? The US was already providing taxpayer money

Vinod Khosla's sister Meera Khosla worked at the World Bank. [188] None of the articles used as reference sources mentioned whether she played any role in directing World Bank deals to Indian owned companies. However, it is interesting to note that she and Vinod were both working for organizations in charge of distributing massive amounts of money supplied by US sources to fund startups.

to finance about \$130.2 million to fund development in India. [124] Who did this study for the World Bank?

India BPO Outsourcing 2006

In July 2006, India got 90% of its software services and BPO revenues from exports. Infosys had continued to benefit from the economic downturn in the United States which was used to justify offshoring jobs. Infosys customers included Goldman Sachs and Airbus. Infosys outperformed forecasts when it reached a 50% jump in quarterly profits. *This growth resulted from increased outsourcing by Western companies.* [588]

US FUNDS OFFSHORING GROWTH IN INDIA

This offshoring did not just happen. It was carefully planned and initiated. How did funding startups in India impact the US financially? How much of the 2009 banking crisis in the US resulted from US banks providing venture capital to India?

Rekhi's Offshore "vision" Funding Startups in India

The Indian "Mafia" in the United States launched a new trend of channeling money from the US to fund technical incubator companies connected to IIT in India. The incubators were spawning startups for: "routing technology, information security, robotics, business activity monitoring, electronic design automation, and decision support systems for financial institutions." These were the same technologies as found in many of the American corporations where they had accessed proprietary and confidential computer systems to provide IT and business process outsourcing (BPO) service and support. This incubator plan was part of the charter founding "vision" for the Kanwal Rekhi School of Information Technology (KReSIT) which was opened in Bombay India in July 1999. Recall that Rekhi used dotcom money to fund KReSIT. Prior to the dotcom crash in America, he was positioning India to exploit the crash. *He planned to spin off incubators in India to compete against American businesses.* [190] In 2001, Kanwal Rekhi began traveling to India every other month. [350]

In 2006, Rekhi Raising Special Fund for Offshoring to India

In February 2006, an announcement titled, "Kanwal Rekhi Raising \$150-\$175 Million India-specific Fund," on *VC Circle* tells how Rekhi's organization, Inventus Capital Partners, was raising money to invest in *Indian startups* in Bangalore and Silicon Valley. [602]

Corporations Channeled Investment to India

People from India obtained upper management positions in high tech US companies. [118] By 2002, American technology companies, including: Oracle, IBM, Sun Microsystems, Cisco, and Microsoft, had pumped about $10 billion expanding offshore operations in India claiming it would cut costs. [175] This drained money out of the US economy already suffering from the dotcom crash and the war. For example, in June 2000, two months after the dotcom plunge, a Hindu news article reported that *Sun Microsystems was expanding operations in India as it had promised to do when India's IT Minister visited the United States.* [117] The Sun center in Bangalore claimed to be its largest engineering center outside the US and that "28 percent of Sun Microsystems employees are either Indians or people of India origin." Many Indians working in the US "want to come back home," to India. [117] This transfer of US technology to India started quietly in 1995, when Sun set up the first 100% multinational subsidiary in India. In 1999, Sun launched its India Engineering Center (IEC) employing about 30 people. IEC expanded after the US dotcom crash to employ 500 people in India. [118] Oracle also began shifting resources to India in 1991. In 2002, Oracle expanded its Oracle Technology Park in Bangalore, India building a 213,000 square foot facility complete with an 11 story parking garage, recreation center, onsite cafeteria, and a fully stocked library. [175]

"India-centric" Plan Required to Get Funding for US Startups

A September 2002 article published online by the CIOL Cybertimes, titled, "TECH START-UPS: Indus Valley, Circa 2002", claimed "A global telecom civilization is taking shape. ... a new Valley is coming up. Call it the New Indus Valley ..." by Shyamanuja Das. It claimed Indians were "the most talented engineers in the valley ..." (i.e. Silicon Valley USA), and talks about TiE. Yet, the article attributes the emergence of India to the following three factors that all trace back to access to American education and technology: Indian founded startups in Silicon Valley, Indian IT outsourcing companies, and the big win for India the recent trend for multinationals i.e. US corporations to fully outsource product development to India either by building development centers in India, or by outsourcing development to Wipro, HCL or other Indian companies. [378]

While the American economy was suffering a severe downturn, members of the Indian "Mafia" had millions to invest to spawn a "new breed of startups." "That Indian-promoted companies account for the biggest chunk of Silicon Valley start-ups is not new." (Unbelievably, they are talking about their role in the US dotcom.) The new "India-US model" startups were incorporated in America like the dotcoms; however, now *venture capital funding was contingent on an "India-centric" business plan that required high tech product development work be offshored to India.* [378]

Because US corporations had replaced Americans with visa workers during the 1980's and 1990's, India had a lot of 30-45 year olds living in America trained in product development and ready to become entrepreneurs and start companies. These workers maintained close contacts with India. Many had jobs that allowed them to go on frequent trips to India where they developed business contacts. In September 2002, it was reported that Silicon Valley "is today full with start-ups which have at least one Indian member in the core team." Indian entrepreneurs accounted for an estimated *two-thirds of startups* targeting the network equipment. [378]

TiE Channeling Investment Money to India 2007

By 2007, TiE's website claimed that in addition to its 1,000 Charter members it now had 10,000 members spread over 5 continents. TiE is funded by membership dues and sponsors ranging "from venture capital investors, law firms, accounting firms, banks, ..." *TiE says that it was at "the forefront of promoting venture capital in India."* TiE's goal was "to bring the cult of wealth creation and entrepreneurship to South Asia and provide global networking opportunities." [659]

Indians in Silicon Valley Fund New India Based Startups

The most significant change of all in 2002, was that *Silicon Valley venture capital firms favored funding startups headquartered in India instead of the United States. The intent here was to position India to create a "Silicon Valley" in India.* [378] Because US corporations transferred US jobs to India, there were many people in India with product development experience ready to work for new Indian startups that would compete against American companies in US markets and globally. These *startups were to be used to help India create its own intellectual property.* By creating their own products they could require customers buy service and support from India, not the United States. This "new breed" of startups would target not only the United States market but global markets in Asia, Africa, and more. Deals were already being made with China and Hong Kong. [378] (i.e. prior to this time their startups were based mostly on US intellectual property)

American Corporations Outsource R&D

As a result of the economic downturn, many American corporations began a dangerous new trend of offshoring higher level product development jobs to India persuaded this would cut costs. Some of the American corporations that offshored high tech development to India included: Cisco, Siemens, Lucent, TI, and Alcatel. These American companies made it possible for India to move up the telecom "value chain." They provided the money, the technology, and the training to create a huge supply of workers in India with high level product development skills. [378] This was a big change because previously offshored jobs were the lower skill jobs. Another big change was that India no longer felt a need to keep a low profile cloaking US offshoring *with secrecy and working anonymously.* [378]

US "PRIVATE EQUITY POURS INTO INDIA" 2005

According to a 2005 *BusinessWeek* article, "Private Equity Pours Into India," by Manjeet Kripalani, *large US equity companies such as Carlyle (a US military contractor) and the Blackstone Group were channeling money to India funding startups in high tech outsourcing, one prime target was the US pharmaceutical industry.* According to the article, after hiring McKinsey & Co. for consulting advice, Blackstone decided to invest $1 billion in India. [721] Most of this funding was done while America has been distracted by the war. What role did offshore private equity funding play in creating the 2009 US financial crisis?

GREEN CARDS TO ENABLE MORE INDIAN STARTUPS IN 2009

Recall in August 2007, Vivek Wadhwa a professor at Duke produced a study that claimed Immigrant entrepreneurs benefited America. He wanted the US to grant H-1Bs more green cards. A backlog of 500,000 H-1Bs were trying to get green cards. According to Wadhwa's study from 1995-2005 immigrants "contributed disproportionately" to the US economy. For example, immigrants founded 52% of the companies started in Silicon Valley—sounds like California's economy is doing great. He claimed that during this time period immigrant founded companies employed 450,000 people. However, if over one million H-1Bs were brought into the US, and they only created 450,000 jobs that is a huge net job loss to US citizens. Moreover, he neglects to acknowledge that many of their startups hired visa workers and offshored American jobs.

Two years later, in August 2009, he posted a blog: "Free H-1Bs, Free the Economy." He wanted our government to grant green cards to over a million H-1Bs including: "doctors, engineers, scientists, researchers and other skilled workers." [742] (Note that in just two years the number waiting in line for green cards doubled!) US law requires that companies must attempt to hire US citizens before they can sponsor foreign workers for permanent residence green cards. [709] Wadhwa wrote H-1Bs are "stuck in the same old jobs they had maybe a decade ago when they entered this country." (A decade for temporary jobs? Many unemployed Americans would be more than happy to take these jobs.). He warns that unless we grant the green cards, which will also let their spouses apply for jobs, H-1Bs might return to their "home countries" and compete against the US. He says that H-1Bs were discriminated against even though in 2001 they took nine out of ten IT jobs, which shows

Americans were the ones discriminated against. He called US citizens "Xenophobes" if they objected to granting more green cards. And he mocks the "silly patents filed with the U.S. Patent Office" claiming that 25% of US global patents were filed by non-citizens. [742] How many patents does he think that displaced unemployed American engineers and scientists can file with no job and no access to many of our research labs? And, what good is a global patent to the United States when foreign countries flagrantly violate the patent protections?

Wadhwa's blog claimed that granting H-1Bs green cards would "boost" the US economy. *He lamented that H-1Bs cannot start companies; but, if granted green cards they could form "tens of thousands of startups."* [742] The following is a longer term look at the US stock market performance of five of the startups they talk about. It appears they did not "boost" the US economy, but rather played a role in the dotcom boom and bust that triggered accelerated offshoring primarily to India. Do we want more of this?

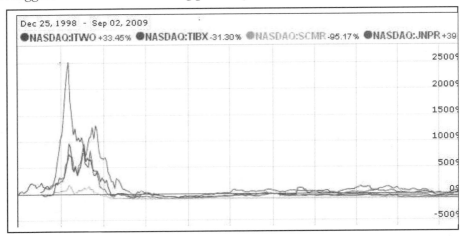

What if over a million more H-1Bs get green cards, work here ten more years, and then return to their "home country"—where will that leave America? While if they leave now, we have enough unemployed high tech Americans to fill the jobs, ten years from now we will not be able to rebound. We need Americans with no divided loyalties whose "home country" is the United States to fill these medical and high tech jobs. According to a September 20, 2009, article, "More of World's Talented Workers Opt to Leave USA", by Emily Bazar, *USA Today.* Wadhwa projects that 100,000 people living in the United States will return to India, and 100,000 will return to China. He surveyed some of the people leaving who have worked in strategic US high tech jobs and found they were lured by financial incentives including *foreign government enticements,* better job opportunities (created by offshoring US IT jobs), and the lower cost of living. Moreover, he found that *they wanted to return to their culture and families.* [744]

Chapter 13

US Media Manipulation

"To bury the truth, buy the media." (Unknown)

Where were the news stories of compassion for hardworking well educated US citizens forced to train foreign workers taking their jobs? Where were the stories of compassion for American children whose families were torn apart by job losses? Our media was manipulated to evoke sympathy for illegal aliens, visa workers, and workers in foreign countries who "just want a better life for their families," and to deny media coverage for hardworking Americans who lost their jobs, their health insurance, their homes, their children's' college funds, their life savings …

The H-1B program received hardly any media coverage despite the fact that millions of Americans were harmed by the fraud, not to mention the national security risks surrounding the H-1B visa program. [568] Executives controlled the media and managed to keep the H-1B program under the radar of the majority of US citizens: "The national media treat H-1B as a non-issue …" [63]

Had the "desperate shortage" of American high tech workers been true, then executives would have wanted to toot their horn with media coverage. However, the media was glaringly silent while millions of Americans lost critical high tech jobs, and while billions of dollars of US technology was transferred into foreign hands. *"One of the most shocking things about the H-1B program is how little anyone appears to know about it."* Even the Citizenship and Immigration Services that is charged to oversee the H-1B program does not know how many H-1Bs are working in the US nor does it know how many applied for green cards. [661]

A 1998 Harris Poll taken while Congress was working on legislation to increase H-1B visa quotas revealed that most Americans, 86% had little or no knowledge of the H-1B proposed increase before Congress. When US citizens were made aware of the H-1B visa program they were overwhelmingly 82% opposed. [36]

On rare occasions some of the hidden offshoring agendas were leaked to the press. For example, a December 23, 2003, article titled, "US Companies Quietly Moving More Jobs Overseas," by David Zielenziger for Reuters, reported that the companies did not want to attract attention, and were concerned that it was not "politically correct to talk about it." According to the story, when an internal IBM memo was leaked to the Wall Street Journal about plans to offshore 4,700 US high tech jobs to India and China in 2004, IBM executives "declined to comment." [100] Another internal corporate memo leaked to the press instructed managers to conceal offshoring plans from Americans employed in the jobs targeted for offshoring. [95]

According to a "Executive Excess 2004," report by the *Institute for Public Studies* and *United for a Fair Economy*, in 2003, a Sprint CEO was cited as telling the US media that the company planned to offshore "several hundred" jobs, however a memo leaked to the press told a different story—Sprint was planning to offshore over 3,000 US jobs. By 2004, Sprint had contracted with IBM to outsource 5,000 to 6,000 jobs. It was believed that IBM would offshore these jobs to *a call center in India that IBM had just acquired.* [6] These types of leaks should have been investigated as major news stories because of the impact on America. However, even when offshoring secrets are leaked to the news media the US public cannot expect to be well informed. Why? Because according to a 2003 Reuters article, "U.S. Companies Quietly Moving more Jobs Overseas," *our major US media companies are also involved in outsourcing and offshoring including: Walt Disney Co, Time Warner, CNN, and Fox News* **"none of which want public disclosure."** [100]

BusinessWeek Blasts American Offshoring Paranoia

In the December 8, 2003 issue of *BusinessWeek*, cover story heralding "The Rise of India", included a commentary by Michael J. Mandel titled, "Meeting the Asian Challenge" which claimed, "there's no evidence of a major flight of educated jobs from the U.S." The article laments that, "Rather than embracing innovation, Americans seem to be concerned with adopting protectionist measures and trying to hold on to existing jobs. Rather than worrying about IT positions going offshore, the U.S. should focus on generating new jobs—in new industries—at home." [300]

InformationWeek Attacked H-1B & L-1 Critics

InformationWeek is owned by CMP Media. In February 2004, Dr. Matloff, a critic of the H-1B and L-1 visas and offshoring, noted a "rank conflict of interest" [464] in an InformationWeek article that attacked H-1B and L-1 visa critics. The article, like most of the H-1B propaganda, was reporting a new study about how curbing any of these visas would harm the US economy. The study was done by the Carnegie Mellon University's Software Industry Center (SIC). Lobbyists for these visas like to use US university "studies" to gain congressional approval for their agendas. Matloff laments that InformationWeek "was not aware" [464] that Tata Consultancy Services (TCS), an Indian company heavily involved in using H-1B and L-1 visa workers, is also a founding partner of and holds a seat on SIC's board. TCS influences what research is done, and then gets access to research results. TCS also has access to SIC researchers and graduate students. Either InformationWeek failed to adequately research its sources, or perhaps, it did know. Matloff found that this study was written by a "codirector of SIC not by a researcher." [464] Just a few days after the report was released it was cited in the Washington Post praising the H-1B program. [464]

CBS FLIP FLOP FROM INVESTIGATION TO PROPAGANDA

60 Minutes is owned by CBS, and the CBS Television Network is owned by Viacom, a multi-national corporation. What happened to 60 Minutes' ownership or sponsorship from 1993 to 2003 that so dramatically changed it from an investigative reporting program into what appears to be a PR tool promoting transferring Americans' jobs to foreign workers?

60 Minutes Exposed H-1B Visa Fraud in 1993

In October 1993, a 60 Minutes segment titled "North of the Border" Leslie Stahl did an excellent report exposing H-1B fraud. Stahl reported that executives in major American corporations who replaced American programmers with cheaper visa workers refused to be interviewed. Stahl exposed that even small businesses operating out of garages were abusing the visa to bring in cheap foreign programmers. She reported that "thousands of unemployed American programmers turn up at every computer job fair in Silicon Valley, and most of them leave disappointed." The reason, *companies were not willing to hire an American when they could hire two or more visa workers for the same price.*

Stahl exposed that the visa law was based on fraud, because the foreign programmers did not fill a labor shortage as represented to Congress, nor did these foreign programmers have unique talent and skills—a prerequisite for obtaining their visas. She reported that our government failed to enact penalties against companies that blatantly lied on government forms to get foreign programmers' visa applications approved. Stahl reported, "The firms lying on their forms are often those foreign suppliers. They're commonly called body shops." The Indian body shops "pick the programmers, then get them their visas and assign them to the American companies."

She scoffed at the absurdity of a six year temporary classification: "That's a joke. Everyone's going to laugh." Stahl exposed the "biggest joke of all" was that these workers were paid the prevailing wage as required by law. For example, she reported that one Indian outsourcing body shop had about 600 applications for special visas, yet these special foreign programmers were all paid $26,500, well below the prevailing wage as required by law, and definitely not indicative of being anything near special in skill and talent.

Stahl also exposed how these body shops evaded paying US taxes. For example, a foreign programmer working at HP was employed by an Indian outsourcing firm that paid her $250 a month salary in India, plus a monthly living allowance of $1,300 to cover expenses in the US. Her total pay was less than $20,000 a year. [568] So this foreign worker lived in the US tax free, benefiting from technology and infrastructure built and paid for by Americans.

Stahl exposed how business lobbies pressured the government not to stop this visa scam. The report also faulted the US government for failing to check the validity of the qualifications on visa applications and for failing to track how many foreign programmers are inside the United States. She reported that the Clinton administration had asked the US Congress to change the law and require that Americans be hired first. The report ended that Congress was considering the Clinton Administration proposal. [568]

60 Minutes Visa Flip Flop in 2003—What Happened?

After exposing the H-1B visa fraud in 1993, ten years later 60 Minutes did a flip flop when it broadcasted, "Imported from India" in 2003. This show was more of a political propaganda piece promoting the import of visa workers from India than a critical news story. It began with incredulous voiceovers spoken by Lesley Stahl. Were these her own words or were they scripted? She elevated the Indian Institute of Technology (IIT) as being better than Harvard, MIT, and Princeton all combined. She even stated that US Ivy league schools are "safety schools" for students in India who cannot get into IIT. The story said: "IIT undergraduates leave

> Only one IIT university made it to the list of Top 500 Research Institutes. IIT Kharagpur was 403 on the list out of 502. The top ranking research institutes were Harvard, Stanford, Cambridge, UC Berkeley and MIT. The US had 170 universities in the list of 502. [523] This means that 60 Minutes was providing misinformation to the US public with regard to our universities and the qualifications of foreigners taking Americans' jobs.

their American counterparts in the dust." [323] If these statements were true, the software industry would have been invented in India, however, it was invented in America by Americans.

Stahl asked why India would spend so much money to send people to the US. The show said that IIT graduates were "India's most valuable export." This is where 60 Minutes should have gone deeper. The government of India subsidizes 80% of the costs including room, board and IIT tuition. IIT is cheap compared to the cost of US universities. A student's family pays only $700 per year while the government pays $2,800. So to produce a four year IIT graduate the India government spends about $11,200 each. [323] The math of why India would do this is simple. If India can "export" a programmer to take a high tech visa job for $50,000 a year, and the programmer transfers 40% back home to India, then India would get $20,000 per year—almost double India's investment in the first year. After that it is all gravy for India's economy. So, for every 100,000 graduates India can place in the US, about $2 billion flows directly out of the US economy and into India's economy.

Vinod Khosla was introduced in this 60 Minutes news segment as "one of Silicon Valley's most important venture capitalists." Khosla told Stahl that entrepreneurs from India had created hundreds of thousands of jobs in Silicon Valley. [323] Khosla should have been asked how many of these "created jobs" were filled by hiring American citizens, and how many were filled by hiring foreign visa workers. And he should have been asked to clarify if the jobs were "created" or if the jobs were taken away from American citizens. When India used visas to displace US citizens, it did not benefit the US as he claimed. For our society it caused soaring unemployment costs, strained our infrastructure from excessive population growth, lowered the US standard of living, and reduced the taxes the US government collected. Khosla admitted, "India now is benefiting significantly from the cycling of knowledge." [323] This has been a one way transfer of knowledge and proprietary United States jobs.

Narayan Murthy, the founder of Infosys, an Indian outsourcing firm (i.e. body shop) was also interviewed. Infosys made Murthy rich. Murthy said that admissions to IIT were strictly based on merit. This is not credible given that earlier Ms. Stahl stated that 90% of the students are male. It is not believable that women in India are that intellectually inferior to the men. It is more likely that the women are comparable in intelligence and that admission is not strictly based on merit. [323]

A glimmer of the truth is finally revealed when Narayan Murthy explained to Stahl how India benefited by getting IIT

> Murthy received a lot of US media coverage. *BusinessWeek* named him in its list of "The Stars of Asia" in 1998, 1999, and 2000, and named him a 1999 entrepreneur of the year along with eight others. Ernst & Young named him 2003 World Entrepreneur of the Year. Fortune magazine named Murthy and one other person "2003 Asia's Businessmen of the Year." [601]

graduates inside major US corporations. *According to Murthy, IIT graduates' big goal is to penetrate the management ranks of Corporate America so they can "persuade" US corporations to "start operations in India." Murthy also said IIT's have succeeded in selling offshoring strategy to US corporations such as Texas Instruments, General Electric, and Citibank.* [323]

Rebuttals

In a rebuttal, Dr. Norman Matloff called "Imported From India" a "60 Minutes puff piece on the Indian Institutes of Technology (IIT)." According to Matloff "neither the curriculum nor the faculty can match any of the top universities in the U.S." He pointed out that the IIT faculty had not generated the level of research papers, patents and textbooks required to establish IIT as a top university.

Matloff suspected that the story was "deliberately set up by expensive PR firms" making a big push to promote India's "Brand IIT." He called the show: "a fawning, unbalanced advertisement under the guise of "news."" As a footnote, Matloff received a response from 60 Minutes which said the show was run at the request of an Indian doctor not a PR firm. [324]

> Murthy "is an IT advisor to several Asian countries." He is also on the Board of Overseers at the University of Pennsylvania's Wharton School, on the Board of Trustees at Cornell University, on the Board of Advisors for Global Leadership at Tuck School of Business. [601]

Later Dr. Matloff expanded his rebuttal. To assert the superiority of IIT, Murthy had referenced his own son as an example of how US universities were used as "safety schools." IIT rejected his son; however, his son was admitted to Cornell. Matloff did not believe the "safety school" argument. In his opinion Cornell provides a better education than IIT. Matloff suspected that Murthy's son got into Cornell because his rich father had donated money to Cornell. Matloff discovered that Murthy's son had an even greater advantage—Murthy was on the Cornell University Council. Even more disturbing, Matloff discovered Murthy contradicted what he said on 60 Minutes in an Indian magazine article, where Murthy chastised IIT students because even with a better student-teacher ratio, the Americans still repeatedly outperformed them. It appears that Murthy intentionally misrepresented the facts. [324]

Despite complaints by viewers, 60 Minutes failed to air letters of dissent as it had in the past. According to Matloff, even a cursory investigation by a high school student would have revealed that the claims of IIT being the "best in the world" were not true. He believed that the show was a PR piece to help India increase the H-1B visa caps and to promote offshoring to India. Matloff noted that the government of India saw the H-1B as a means to get ""their" people into the US corridors of power." He pointed out that US media was being manipulated by "corporate and political interests." [327]

It gets worse—November 2, 2004, this 60 Minutes "puff" piece was nominated for an Emmy by The National Television Academy for "Outstanding Coverage of a Current Business News Story." [328]

60 Minutes—2004 Offshoring Propaganda Piece!

The January 2004, CBS 60 Minutes story "Out of India" reported by Morley Safer was more of a promo for offshoring to India than critical news reporting. It included statements such as "India is Nirvana" for US companies because it cranks out a million college graduates a year they can hire much cheaper than American workers. And, "India epitomizes the new global economy." [308]

The people quoted in this 60 Minutes report were people profiting from the offshoring of American jobs; hardly the right people to pick for objective reporting. In the story, Raman Roy, the chairman of Wipro Spectramind one of India's biggest outsourcing companies, and the person who came up with the scheme to persuade US companies to offshore customer service calls to India, claimed that US companies saved 30 to 50% by offshoring calls to India. Had Safer done his homework, he would have questioned these savings. Raman Roy contradicts himself when he claims America should accept offshoring because the economy is global and geography is irrelevant; yet, he boasts getting these US jobs has given India "a terrific sense of national pride ... a huge amount of nationalistic pride." Safer never questioned the absurdity of switching from "globalization" propaganda for America to "national pride" for India. What about American national pride?

Safer did not even raise an eyebrow when workers in India told how they were trained to lie to Americans to make them think they were talking with someone in the United States. They used a "phone" (phony) name that sounded American such as Nancy or Sean when their real name might be Sangita or Tashar, and they practiced sounding American by watching and mimicking American movies. [308]

During this 60 minutes story, Partha Iyengar, an analyst in India that works for Gartner, an American research firm said, "The reason the (US) companies are coming here is to really be more competitive and that cannot be bad for the U.S. economy." And he talks about how the "outsourcing revolution" has benefited India's economy. Iyengar claimed that US offshoring to India is "the best example of globalization" because India has tapped into the US "knowledge industry." [308] Note that Ivengar's job was dependent on offshoring to India.

Also interviewed was Arjun Raina who taught workers in India how to pressure Americans for debt collections. He told them to be polite at first and use an American accent. However, he sees the good part as being when the bill collector in India can forget the fake accent and being polite, and can get aggressive with the Americans who are not able to pay their bills. [308]Again 60 Minutes never raised major issues. How ironic for US citizens, who lost their jobs to foreign workers, to then have foreign workers call and harass them to pay bills they cannot pay because they lost their job.

The story also included Dave Wyle, an American entrepreneur who set up an offshore company named Sureprep in Bombay India for processing US taxpayers' tax returns. He said that it was much cheaper to hire a worker in India than in the US. Offshoring US citizens' tax returns preparation began in 2003 when 1000 US tax returns were sent to India. By 2004, the number exploded to 25,000, and it was forecasted that by 2005 the number of US tax returns prepared in India would leap to 200,000. Wyle business depended on offshoring US citizens' tax returns to India. He claimed to already have over 150 US accounting firms as clients in 2004. To his credit Morley Safer did question offshoring tax returns saying, "But most people regard their tax returns as among the most private things they have. Is there any risk of that security being broken with tax returns flying though the ozone?" Wyle claimed the security was superior, because they do the work on computers and do not have paper and pencils or printers in the work areas. [308] What an absurd defense—the data was accessed via computer files that may be electronically copied and sent to multiple locations. The violations of privacy of US citizens were inadequately discussed.

MEDIA CONFLICT OF INTEREST DURING DOTCOM ERA

It was not just questionable accounting practices that deceived US investors during the dotcom boom. The media perpetuated deceptive stock investment data that misled investors.

Beginning in the early 1980's, our media started to rely on Information Technology (IT) analysts for quotes and recommendations on technology companies without investigating conflicts of interests. While financial analysts were required by law to disclose if they were helping to market a product, IT analysts were not required to disclose such conflicts of interest. IT analysts could work for a company or a company's competitor without disclosing these connections when making product recommendations and sales projections. [365]

In 1998, the conflicted and convoluted nature of some of the research and studies done to promote consulting and outsourcing business were being questioned. IT analysis and projections had become a big business for companies such as Gartner, IDC, Yankee Group, Forrester Research, and Giga. Gartner (which also owns Dataquest) made over $395 million in 1997. That same year, IDC generated over 200,000 studies. These firms were regularly quoted in IT publications. [365]

According to a September 1, 1998, *Computer Dealer News* story, "Scrutinizing the Scrutineers: How Accurate are High Technology's Pithy Pundits?" by Robert Thompson, computer analyst firms were on the one hand selling research advising technology companies on products and market trends, while at the same time they were submitting commentary to the media recommending products and predicting market trends. *"It's a tricky business, with technology firms, public relations organizations, computer analysts and the media all tangled in the same web. However, no one in the industry appears to doubt the impact analysts have on either the companies for which they work or the public that buys the product they comment on."* [365] US citizens were relying on the media for making objective independent investment and buying decisions while the people providing the advice were paid by the technology companies. This type of reliance on IT analysts was in full swing in 1998, and fed into the dotcom boom. Some technology companies may have hired analysts specifically to craft projections to manipulate our media and mislead US investors. Were H-1Bs among IT analysts making recommendations?

INDIAN "MAFIA" MEDIA MACHINE

It was surprising to discover that the Indian "Mafia", in addition to starting companies, created a media machine to hype these companies and Indian "geniuses". [312] In 2005, the Indian "Mafia" network actively pursued positions as writers and commentators in strategic "opinion-forming" US media such as the Wall Street Journal to influence US executives in business decision making. Several people originally from India became writers and reporters for CNN. [240]

Indian-express.com

In February 2000, indian-express.com published, "Where Integrated Chip Means Indians, Chinese," by Chidanand Rajghatta, *he refers to non-resident Indians (NRIs) living in the US as "dazzling achievers," and boasts about how they are frequently featured in major "American business and technology magazines."* He said that in 1998, five NRIs were in *Forbes* list of 100 richest people in the high tech industry, in 1999, one NRI made Forbes list of richest immigrants getting $540 million from his telephony business, and several NRIs' startups were in Forbes list of the 200 best small companies. Three NRIs made it to Forbes list of "the 40 richest Americans under the age of 40. The three named were Naveen Jain of Infospace with $861 million, Sanjay Kumar of Computer Associates with $335 million, and Mukesh Chatter of Nexabit Networks with $250 million. And it is not just Forbes. The "reputed tech magazine Red Herring" included 2 Indians, Mukesh Chatter of Nexabit and Desh Deshpande of Sycamore, on its list of top 10 entrepreneurs. The article also says Indians have created the SiliconIndia and TechMantra magazines for "the community" [330]

SiliconIndia Magazine

The Indian network is behind "*siliconindia*", a business and technology magazine. A list of the "*siliconindia*" Editorial Board members included: "Ashok Trivedi, Desh Deshpande, Jayshree Ullal, KB Chandrashekar, Kanwal Rekhi, Mohanbir Sawhney, NR Narayana Murthy, Radha Basu, Ramesh Jain, Sabeer Bhatia, Vijay Vashee, Vinod Dham, Vinod Khosla, Yogesh Gupta." [242] It is interesting that these business professionals are on an editorial board for a publication writing about their accomplishments. Not something most Americans would expect.

Hindustantimes.com

In November 2003, an article published by the *Hindustantimes.com* titled, "Eighteen Indian Companies in Forbes List," boasts that 18 companies based in India made it to Forbes magazine's 200 List of successful companies outside the US. According to this article, Forbes praised the success of the Indian companies given the worldwide economic conditions. At least three of the IT companies named became wealthy through targeting US jobs for outsourcing and offshoring—Wipro, Infosys Technologies, and Satyam Computers. It is also interesting to note that 4 Indian pharmaceutical companies and 3 Indian banks made the "coveted list." [320]

US Television Targeted

On the TiE website in 2006 the group complained, "Not Enough Asian Faces on the Telly?" TiE wanted to put more Asian faces on American television, especially Asian couples with kids at home for diversity PR. [592] Look for PR promoting India's goal of becoming an IT and medical superpower by showing people with roots to India as IT and medical experts.

INDIAN OUTSOURCING DEBARMENT COVER-UP EXPOSED

On rare occasions some critical reporting gets through. According to a *foxnews.com* "Exclusive: World Bank's Web of Ties to 'India's Enron'" on January 12, 2009, by Richard Behar, three Indian outsourcing companies, Satyam, Megasoft, and Wipro, were debarred by the World Bank. One of the most disturbing aspects of the report was that *World Bank officials concealed the corruption for over three years and pressured the Government Accountability Project to "keep the information under wraps."* World Bank officials "felt no obligation to the global corporate community to share that information publicly until late last month." Unaware of this corruption, American corporations "entrusted their most sensitive computer networks" to these outsourcing companies. For example by 2009, more than 150 Fortune 500 companies such as Citicorp, General Electric, Microsoft, Nestle, Dell, and Merrill Lynch were listed as Satyam clients when Satyam "imploded" in a $1 billion accounting fraud. [722]

According to Fox News the investigation uncovered that the outsourcing companies were awarded bank contracts soon after providing benefits such as preferential shares to bank staff. The Satyam and Megasoft debarments were linked professionally and personally—Satyam's cofounder Srini Raju was the younger brother of Satyam's chairman Ramalinga Raju. Srini "merged one of his Indian companies into Megasoft based in Virginia." Ben Hu, a technology official with the World Bank, "became a director of Megasoft," and he was credited with facilitating Megasoft's "relationship" with the World Bank. When bank officials became concerned that Satyam was getting too many deals, Megasoft was waiting in the wings to get the deals.

After the Bank discovered that Satyam gave "preferential Satyam shares" to the Bank's Chief Information Officer Mohamed Muhsin, Satyam was banned in 2007. However, two years earlier in 2005 Satyam had already begun converting its contract employees at the World Bank into Megasoft employees. When the Bank decided to debar Satyam it had a hard time extricating Satyam which had extensive involvement in the setup and control of the Bank's computer systems; and, because a Satyam contract employee had "implanted spyware in the bank's systems." The Bank's astounding solution was to keep Satyam's employees as contractors controlling its computer systems by converting them into employees of Tata (another Indian outsourcing company.) and EDS. [722]

The Fox News exclusive also reported that in 2005, Wipro sold "Friends and Family" shares to Muhsin. In 2005, the Bank awarded Wipro a $650,000 contract for "of all things" meeting compliance requirements for providing shareholders protection through financial transparency. In 2007 following an investigation, Wipro was banned from doing business with the Bank because of preferential stock deal with Muhsin. In 2005, the Bank "escorted Muhsin out of his office in Washington", and in 2007 Muhsin was banned from ever working for the Bank. [722]

Were these same tactics used to obtain outsourcing and offshoring contracts with American corporations, and even our government? Such collusive means to get contracts not based on the best quality and best cost, but rather based on bribes and ethnic networks is highly destructive.

Chapter 14

It is Time for the Sleeping Giant to

Wakeup

"Liberty cannot be preserved without a general knowledge among the people, who have a right ... and a desire to know ..." —*John Adams*

Time is of the essence. America is in the midst of a severe economic crisis. The purpose of this book is to help get America back on track economically by providing an economic recovery model—the Economic Circulation Model™. This model shows that it is essential to get Americans back to work and stop the transfer of their jobs to foreign workers. Based on the information uncovered, certain individuals and groups need to be investigated to determine if they have engaged in crimes against American citizens and against America. In particular executives should be investigated who took outrageous bonuses by replacing American workers with foreign workers through deception and buying legislation. And, ethnic network organizations need to be investigated to determine if they conspired to take US education opportunities from young Americans, to misuse our universities to obtain management consulting positions and to produce bogus studies to take jobs from skilled high tech Americans, if they engaged in racial discrimination, if they engaged in illegal activities such as stock market fraud, and if they acted as foreign agents against America to benefit foreign nations. Outsourcing firms need to be investigated to determine if they unduly influenced and mislead congress, and if they conspired to take American jobs. These investigations need to be conducted by officials who have not received money or benefits from any of these sources.

SEEKING JUSTICE

It is important that Americans focus on justice not revenge. Americans need to exercise our rights to peaceably join together and demand justice and accountability for the theft of our jobs, savings, and more. Foreign governments and corrupt executives aggressively lobbied our government for the H-1B, L1 and other visa legislation which was used to displace high tech American workers. Without regard or concern for the American lives they were destroying, families they were breaking apart, and the children they were harming, US executives laid off Americans, and US politicians passed legislation unjustly enriching executives at the expense of American workers and their families. They harmed the very people who had made our nation the leading technology power in the world.

We need people of discernment and wisdom. How can we find justice when influence money pressured Congress to pass laws that exploited American workers and taxpayers? What determines legal vs. illegal activity? Can criminals hide behind laws that they got passed by "bribing" our politicians, laws that deny justice as opposed to seeking justice? Our economy is dependent on trust in our stock market and financial institutions. Should executives who used corporate funds (i.e. stockholder money) to buy liability insurance, and then mismanaged companies to unjustly enrich themselves at stockholder expense escape legal justice? Has the SEC exposed and stopped crime or has it helped cover-up foreign manipulations of financial reports and more? Our nation needs strong leaders with integrity. We need to come up with a just way to identify the executives and lawmakers who have wronged Americans. However, in doing this we do not want to harm executives who created prosperity and are deserving of the money they earned. We cannot afford to allow the system to get bogged down with legal maneuvers and delays. We need a just and speedy resolution.

JOBS FOR AMERICANS VITAL TO US ECONOMIC RECOVERY

Americans are hurting. The first thing we need to do is stop the bleeding. The more layoffs companies do anticipating financial losses, the more losses we have. The number one priority needs to be keeping Americans working, and getting Americans back to work who lost their jobs through no fault of their own. *Recall from the Economic Circulation Model that employing Americans circulates money in the US and generates much more in taxes and business earnings than the job itself.* Additionally, there needs to be a moratorium on the home foreclosures for Americans who did not buy homes beyond their financial reach—but are in jeopardy of losing their homes because they lost their jobs through no fault of their own, or because they took out home equity loans to pay college expenses to educate their children. There needs to be a time extension that is adjusted according to the amount of equity in the home.

It is essential that in an orderly and timely manner the executives who have mismanaged our corporations be replaced by managers who will look out for the best interests of American workers and American investors. We need talented managers who can help revive failing companies. And the economic recovery also requires that politicians who sponsored harmful legislation be removed and replaced by politicians who will represent the American people and revive our economy by putting Americans back to work.

AVOIDING PITFALLS & PREJUDICE

It is important to note that Americans loyal to America come from many races. While the ethnic networks involved in H-1B visa fraud and outsourcing and stock market manipulations are predominantly Asian, it is important to remember that the American executives and politicians involved are predominantly white. Moreover, these executives in some cases were also responsible for exploiting workers in Asia. Key partners in sorting out this mess may well be Americans of Asian ancestry who love our country and who have no connections to the ethnic networks.

While we help fellow Americans recover from the damage, we need to minimize the harm to people in China and India, the majority of whom had nothing to do with these harmful visa programs and outsourcing. Most Americans have always wanted the people in Asia to enjoy prosperity and freedom. The people involved in these ethnic networks probably make up less than 1% of the population in China and in India. Moreover, it is not in the best interest of the majority of people in China or India for the US to collapse. Nor is it in our best interests that they be harmed.

COMPENSATION AND HEALING FOR AMERICANS HARMED

Many talented high tech Americans were laid off and forced to leave their profession when they were displaced by foreign workers. Executives who wronged these workers should be required to return the millions of dollars they took in undeserved bonuses to create a fund to finance re-educating these Americans and/or their children to restore what was wrongfully taken. If this money was well managed it would help strengthen our nation. The money should go to deserving Americans who have the academic ability to gain admission to a top ranked US university, and to maintain good grades. It could pay for four year undergraduate programs, or 2-4 year graduate research programs. Maximum claims per family should be limited to $80,000, and $40,000 per person.

Government funded research should be redirected to skilled Americans who were laid off, or to talented young Americans enrolled in undergraduate programs or graduate school. To make research jobs economically feasible for Americans without increasing taxpayer costs, the pay could be doubled if the number of research jobs were cut by half. For example, a $16,000 a year university research job could be increased to $32,000. Having our brightest American undergraduates doing research could make college affordable if they were getting paid. This would have the added benefit of reducing the number of Americans needing taxpayer funded financial aid.

US UNIVERSITIES

Our universities ought to be focusing on educating young Americans and keeping our nation strong and competitive. The demographics of our professors should be in line with our nation's demographics. Universities should not be used as propaganda machines promoting outsourcing and offshoring, but rather should be educating our children to be critical thinkers exploring the risks and long term implications to our nation and their future.

The FASFA and other policies discriminate against middleclass Americans. College costs for American youth have soared to levels beyond reason. Americans should not have to use home equity loans or their retirement savings to pay for excessive college costs. We need to focus on providing college to our top students not to favoring students from foreign countries, and not to favoring the children of illegal aliens and new immigrants over the children of the descendents of the people who sacrificed to build our country. The "temporary" H-1B program started in 1990 turned 20 years old in 2010. The children of people who entered the US under the fraudulent H-1B and other visa programs should not be favored in college admissions and financial aid over the children of the Americans who they unjustly displaced.

MEDIA COVERAGE ESSENTIAL

Americans unfairly lost jobs they needed to provide for their families, they lost savings needed for college and retirement, they lost their homes, and more while our media remained sadly, eerily, disturbingly silent. We Americans have a right to a free press dedicated to informing the American public. American citizens have the right to know what is going on, and Americans have a right to decide what needs to be done. Our media failed to adequately cover critical stories and in some instances cruelly ridiculed Americans and politicians trying to defend our jobs and our country. It appears the media played a role in the H-1B visa, the dotcom and the US banking crisis that ranges from misleading Americans, to failure to cover stories vital to Americans, and even to the extent of suppressing news stories. Americans lost their jobs to H-1Bs when they had never heard of the H-1B visa. Americans lost their investments when our media failed to warn them about dishonest executives and IT analysts. Executives and other insiders in control of our media should be held accountable and required to put money they unjustly gained into a fund to cover the cost of restructuring our media back into the control of American management and analysts who will look out for the best interests of US citizens.

US STOCK MARKET REFORM

Hardworking Americans who saved to provide for their families' futures were scammed by dotcom companies, financial institutions, and more. There needs to be broad scale investigations of people who extracted more than $500,000 from the US stock market from 1980 to present to determine if they extracted undue gain from the stock market by misleading the American public. Special emphasis needs to be focused on dotcom and financial stocks. In particular executives and insiders need to be identified who sold stocks that were highly inflated that then plummeted dramatically causing the American public to lose millions/billions of dollars.

Money and property recovered from insiders who perpetuated scams should go into a fund that helps hardworking Americans who were harmed. The focus needs to be on economic recovery such as financing American startup businesses that employ American workers, helping families that lost homes obtain a home, families that lost college savings to obtain grants for college, and more. This must be an open equitable process managed by a people of integrity and skilled in managing finances.

IT IS TIME TO REPEAL HARMFUL LEGISLATION

Our government passed legislation harmful to the American people whom they are sworn to protect. Some of the legislation that needs to be repealed includes:

1) Legislation that enables multimillion dollar executive bonuses subsidized at taxpayer expense and/or from displacing Americans with foreign workers.

2) US citizens should not be taxed to subsidize foreign students, particularly students from countries where the US has a trade deficit.

3) Laws allowing foreign students who graduate from US universities to stay and seek jobs in the US. The 26 month (2 ½ year) period allowing foreign graduates of US universities to seek employment in the US should be repealed?

4) The H-1B, L-1B and other harmful visa legislation.

5) Offshoring tax incentives.

6) Federal and state laws that deny shareholders justice when executives mismanage companies to take excessive compensation.

NEW LAWS NEED TO BE PASSED

Our government needs to pass laws that adequately protect American workers and our economy. And it needs to restore Americans who were unfairly harmed by visa programs and offshoring. For example, new legislation needs to include:

1) There needs to be a freeze on granting high tech worker green cards. And, an audit of the green cards already granted.

2) There needs to be a cap that dramatically reduces the number of foreign students admitted to study in the US. Foreign students should have to pass background checks to attend US universities where sensitive government and business research is done. Foreign students should not have access to, much less be paid to do, research on US homeland security projects.

3) Restrictions on corporate outsourcing and offshoring that harm the US economy and/or jeopardize US national security. Prior to the passage of any new visa legislation Americans being impacted should be given a platform to speak—not just the executives.

4) The H-1B legislation was passed under the guise these visa workers were temporary until Americans were trained. Therefore, laws need to be passed that require companies to post all jobs filled by H-1Bs and other visa workers to give Americans an opportunity to apply. Just as the Americans were required to train foreign workers taking their jobs, the visa workers need to be required to train the Americans as needed.

AMERICANS HAVE A RIGHT TO KNOW

Americans have the right to know who the executives in our universities, corporations, federal government, and state governments are that caused Americans to lose jobs. And, businesses, universities, and government agencies need to be required to disclose information to American citizens such as:

1) What happened to our media ownership that caused important stories about US citizens losing their jobs to not be covered? What role did the Media play in creating our current economic crisis? Who is responsible?

2) How many visa workers and foreign offshore workers are employed by major US media including technology journals and US market research companies? Did they write articles to persuade US businesses and banks to transfer jobs and money to their country of origin?

3)   Did H-1Bs employed by big US accounting firms play a role in misleading American investors during the dotcom boom and subsequently in the banking financial crisis? Did H-1Bs and other foreign workers manipulate financial reports that awarded multimillion dollar bonuses to executives for displacing Americans with foreign visa workers? Were H-1Bs working for Arthur Anderson connected to the Enron financial reporting deceptions?

4)   Should US universities be required to disclose the list of companies to which they licensed patent rights for US taxpayer funded research discoveries? Were these US companies employing foreign workers or outsourcing, or foreign owned companies? How many professors have gotten rich from side businesses receiving tax money for research and hiring foreign students and visa workers?

5)   How many foreign students are currently in our universities? How much is this costing US taxpayers? How many have received scholarships or other money from outsourcing companies? How much taxpayer funded research is channeled to foreign graduate students?

6)   Who were the instigators of the H-1B fraud—including US business executives, Indian "Mafia" members, university professors and others?

7)   Who were the US executives displacing Americans with foreign workers? Note: The Institute for Policy Studies and United for a Fair Economy did extensive research and analysis identifying executives they claim got pay increased that correlated with outsourcing.

8)   Who were the politicians responsible for sponsoring the H-1B legislation in 1990, and subsequently all the quota increases? In particular who were the 40 Congressmen who deceptively passed the Drier bill in 1998? Who financed their campaigns?

9)   Who got rich off the dotcom, recall that 100,000 Indians became millionaires and many of the venture capitalists getting rich financing their startups were white. Who got rich during the war in Iraq, recall an additional 100,000 Indians became millionaires, and many white executives including those in the financial industry took bonuses in the millions. Did they make money off the war?

10) Should data collected on H-1B applications be released and posted on the web for public access?

AMERICANS HAVE A RIGHT TO DECIDE

1) Should Americans who opposed H-1B visas be given media coverage? Should investigations of corruption be televised? Should media be required to let American families harmed by H-1B legislation be given an opportunity to tell their story?

2) What groups should receive US education and business minority benefits?

3) Should Americans displaced by H-1B's receive college educational tax credits for their education and/or the education of their children?

4) Should it be illegal to coerce Americans into signing severance agreements that forbid them to talk to the media when they are displaced by foreigners?

5) Should Americans be taxed to supplement foreign students? Should Americans be taxed to fund research projects done by foreign students?

6) Should foreign outsourcing companies be permitted to "import" foreign visa workers into the United States? Should foreign outsourcing companies be banned from operating in the US?

7) The H-1Bs were supposed to be temporary employees. Should all H-1B jobs be posted, so Americans have an opportunity to apply?

8) During layoffs should companies be required to layoff "temporary" H-1B and other visa workers before Americans?

9) Should economic stimulus money be directed to help Americans who lost their jobs due to layoffs create small businesses that hire Americans?

10) Should government jobs, with rare exceptions, go to American citizens? Including Defense research? Energy research? Tax Return Processing?

11) What would be a constructive strategy for righting stock market and banking fraud? What laws are needed to help prevent future fraud?

There is much that needs to be done. Every concerned American needs to write to our Congress and find a productive role to participate in restoring our nation. The biggest mistake we could make would be to allow this to deteriorate into chaos and harm more innocent people. "United We Stand, Divided We Fall" was the call to liberty by our forefathers (The Liberty Song by John Dickinson). Americans need to unite together to heal our country and remove corruption from our universities, businesses, and government.

Bibliography

Referenced sources are arranged in numeric order according to the reference numbers located in [brackets] in the document text. This book is the culmination of extensive research; only sources referenced in this book are included in this bibliography. Therefore, you will see breaks in the number sequence such as: reference number "6" followed by reference number "8", because reference number "7" in the complete documents list was not used in this book.

Note: Web addresses do not include the www prefix, and only contain the first part of the path. This address information or a search engine query for the title should be sufficient to help locate the articles and websites. Note also that some articles may have been removed, and some websites may have been changed from the time the research was done.

1: Rupert Cornwell, *Interview: Professor JK Galbraith*, The Independent, July 1, 2002.

2: Holly Sklar, *Up, Up and Away: CEO Compensation*, www.inequality.org, June 22, 1905.

3: David Batstone, *CEO Compensation Keeps Rising*, www.worthwhilemag.com, May 29, 2004.

4: Ed Frauenheim, *For CEOs, Offshoring Pays*, builder.com.com, September 1, 2004.

5: Studies, *New CEO/Worker Pay Gap Study*, Institute for Policy Studies and United for a Fair Economy, 2001.

6: Sarah Anderson, John Cavanagh, Chris Hartman, Scott Klinger, and Stacy Chan, *Executive Excess 2004 Campaign Contributions, Outsourcing, Unexpensed Stock Options and Rising CEO Pay*, Institute for Policy Studies and United for a Fair Economy, August 31, 2004.

8: Bruce Nussbaum, *Can You Trust Anybody Anymore?*, Business Week online, January 28, 2002.

9: Geoffrey Colvin, *Executive Pay The Great CEO Pay Heist*, www.fortune.com, Web Date: January 23, 2004.

10: Houston, *Top Enron Accountant Said Surrendering*, Earthlink Business News, January 22, 2004.

11: Kurt Eichenwald, *Big Paychecks are Exhibit A at C.E.O. Trials*, The New York Times, June 19, 2005.

12: Associated Press, *Senate Votes to Add More Visas for Foreign Workers*, Dallas Morning News, May 19, 1998.

13: Jeri Clausing, *Senate Passes Bill Increasing Foreign Worker Visas*, New York Times, May 19, 1998.

14: Jim Puzzanghera, *Senate Votes to Boost High-Tech Visas*, San Jose Mercury News, May 18, 1998.

15: Louis Freedberg, *Senate Oks High-Tech Worker Bill*, San Francisco Chronicle, May 19, 1998.

16: Steven Weiss, *04 Elections Expected to Cost Nearly $4 Billion*, opensecrets.org, October 21, 2004.

21: Robert R. Prechter Jr., *Conquer the Crash*, John Wiley & Sons, LTD, Hoboken, New Jersey, June 24, 1905.

22: *Highly Charged Visa Bill*, opensecrets.org, August 3, 1998, Web Date: January 30, 2002.

24: Dr. Norman Matloff, *Debunking the Myth of a Desperate Software Labor Shortage*, heather.cs.ucdavis.edu, July 8, 2001.

26: Dr. Norman Matloff, *Modern Day Slaves*, netslaves.com, December 30, 2000.

27: Gary Cohn and Walter F. Roche Jr., *How Many Visas? Uh, we don't know*, Sunspot/zazona.com, February 21, 2000.

28: Rescue American Jobs, *Amazing Facts and Statistics: Non-Immigrant (Temporary) Foreign Work Visa Programs and Workers*, rescueamericanjobs.org, Web Date: May 26, 2005.

29: Rep. Tom Tancredo, *H-1B Visas -- A Time to Cut Back*, h1bprotest.com, December 30, 2002.

30: Pradipta Bagchi, *Visas for business or bondage?*, y-axix.com, July 6, 2000.

31: Kim Berry, *Does the U.S. still need H-1B programmers?*, prestwood.com, Web Date: November 1, 2002.

32: *H-1B visa: Your trip may be harrowing*, The Times of India, April 11, 2001.

33: U.S. Border Control, *High Tech Worker Tells His Story*, usbc.org, March 7, 1998.

34: AFL CIO, *H-1B Fact Sheet Why S. 2045 Should be Defeated*, dpeaflcio.org, 2001, Web Date: July 20, 2005.

35: Jeff Nachtigal, *Can You Find a Job for my Friend?*, washtech.org, October 7, 2002.

36: Chris Currie, *IEEE-USA/Harris Poll: U.S. Public Overwhelmingly Opposed to H-1B Visa Expansion*, ieeeusa.org, September 16, 1998.

37: Programmers Guild, *How to Underpay H-1B Workers*, programmersguild.org, Web Date: July 20, 2005.

40: Associated Press, *H-1B Visa Demand Rises*, asianweek.com, February 7, 2002.

41: INS, *Characteristics of Specialty Occupation Workers (H-1B)*, U.S. Immigration and Naturalization Service, February 1, 2000.

42: Rachel Konrad, Staff Writer, *H-1B Visas Jump in 2001*, news.com.com, January 22, 2002.

43: Rob Sanchez, *H-1B Newsletter Get the Facts on H-1B*, zazona.com, June 28, 2002.

44: Ed Frauenheim, *Scourge of Silicon Valley --4*, salon.com, October 19, 2000.

45: Ed Frauenheim, *Scourge of Silicon Valley --5*, salon.com, October 19, 2000.

46: Linda Kilcrease, *Problems with the H-1B Expansion and T-Visas*, zazona.com, May 4, 2001.

47: Dr. Gene A. Nelson, *A Brief History of H-1B*, zazona.com, May 4, 2001.

49: Kevin Hattori, CNN Reporter, *Economy and Job Market in Silicon Valley*, ieeeusa.org, September 14, 2002.

51: Barbara Rose, Chicago Tribune, *Tech Veterans Squeezed Out: Overseas Hiring, Ageism Blamed*, seattletimes.nwsource.com, March 14, 2002.

52: Diane Alden, *H-1B: Bombing the Middle Class*, newsmax.com, February 11, 2003.

54: Tech Law Journal, *Senate Holds Hearings on H-1B Visas*, techlawjournal.com, February 25, 1998.

55: Martin Desmarais, *Lawsuit Slams Sun's 'Bias' for Indian H-1B Workers*, indusbusinessjournal.com, April 1, 2003.

56: Rachel Konrad staff writer, *"Body Shop" must pay fees in H-1B Lawsuit*, news.com.com, April 25, 2001.

58: Peter Brimelow, *New H-1B Scandal - Tax Evasion!*, vdare.com, September 24, 2000.

60: *A Legislative History of H-1B and Other Immigrant Work Visas*, zazona.com, August 11, 2004.

61: Margaret Quan, *High-tech Jobs Down by 560,000 since 2001*, theworkcircuit.com, March 19, 2003.

62: Margaret Quan, *IEEE USA Presses Congress on Visa Curbs*, theworkcircuit.com, March 26, 2003.

63: Phyllis Schlafly Report, *What the Global Economy Costs Americans*, eagleforum.org, June 3, 2003.

64: Dr. Norman Matloff, *Professor Norm Matloff' On Push to expand H-1B Visa Program*, itpaa.org, April 21, 2002.

65: Dr. Norman Matloff, *ITAA Opposes Giving Americans Hiring Priority*, engology.com, January 27, 2005.

66: Greg Levine, *Welch: GE Ex-CEO Blasts Outsourcing Opponents*, forbes.com, May 11, 2004.

67: Winston Chai, CNETAsia, *India: IT outsourcing aids U.S. Other economies*, asia.cnet.com, July 14, 2003.

68: David M. Halbfinger, *Outsourcing Kerry Urges Voters to Look Past Bush's 'Last-Minute Promises'*, New York Times, September 4, 2004.

69: Dean Baker and David Rosnick, *Bad Sources on 'Insourcing'*, cepr.net, March 24, 2004.

71: *American IT Pros Sue, Bangalore Shivers*, timesofindia.indiatimes.com, March 22, 2004.

72: Rachel Konrad, AP Staff Writer, *Outsourcing Backlash Brewing*, cbsnews.com, January 19, 2004.

73: *Hard Times in Silicon Valley*, cbsnews.com, July 14, 2003.

74: *Hire American Citizens*, hireamericancitizens.org, June 11, 2003.

75: Jim Ericson, *The Offshore Value Chain*, line56.com, March 27, 2003.

80: RTTS Services - Outsourcing Statistics, *Statistic Related to Offshore Outsourcing*, rttsweb.com, May 27, 2005.

81: Paul Craig Roberts, *Outsourcing: A Greater Threat Than Terrorism*, newsmax.com, April 22, 2005.

83: Andy McCue, *Gartner: Outsourcing Costs more than in-house*, news.com.com, March 4, 2005.

84: Ed Frauenheim, Staff Writer, CNET News.com, *Study: Software makers head offshore*, news.com.com, July 21, 2003.

86: Chidanand Rajghatta, *US gives India Assurance on Outsourcing*, FreeRepublic.com, June 14, 2003.

88: Board of Directors, *IEEE USA: Position Offshore Outsourcing*, ieeeusa.org, March 1, 2004.

90: *Outsourcing to India*, gnp.org/india, Web Date: March 31, 2003.

91: Todd Jatras, *Can India Retain Its Reign As Outsourcing King?*, forbes.com, February 28, 2001.

95: The Economic Times Online, *US IT Biggies Recalling BPO jobs*, economictimes.indiatimes.com, April 28, 2004.

96: Abhay Vaidya, *H-1B Cap No Big Issue for IT Firms*, economictimes.indiatimes.com, October 31, 2003.

98: The Economic Times Online, *India BPO guy: Hero or Villain?*, economictimes.indiatimes.com, April 28, 2004.

100: David Zielenziger, Reuters, *Corrected - US Companies Quietly Moving More Jobs Overseas*, money.excite.com, December 24, 2003.

101: Hughes Software Systems, *Area Companies Reaping Benefits of Outsourcing*, hssworld.com, June 28, 2001.

102: Ed Frauenheim, Staff Writer, CNET News, *U.S. Firms Move IT Overseas*, news.com.com, December 11, 2002.

104: Ed Frauenheim, *IT Services Firms Eye Foreign Labor*, CNET News.com, January 30, 2003.

105: Jennifer Bjorhus, San Joes Mercury News, *USA: Slowdown Sending Tech Jobs Overseas*, corpwatch.org, October 21, 2002.

106: Public Citizen, *How Many Jobs Are Involved?*, citizen.org, Web Date: May 27, 2005.

108: Business News, *Documents' Honeywell plans to add 5,500 aerospace jobs overseas*, start.earthlink.net, December 7, 2004.

113: Ed Frauenheim, *Coding: Should it Stay or Should it Go?*, CNET News.com, July 22, 2003.

115: Manufacturing & Technology News, *Engineers Fear Offshore Outsourcing is Contributing to High Jobless Rates*, manufactuingnews.com, November 4, 2003.

117: The Hindu Business Line, *Sun Grows 70 pc, Expands India Presence*, blonnet.com, June 29, 2000.

118: Express Computer India, *Sun Microsystems India turns up the heat on competition*, expresscomputeronline.com, December 24, 2001.

119: *India to See R&D Outsourcing Boom*, rediff.com, April 26, 2004.

121: Rashmi Sharma Singh, *H Workers in Limbo*, indolink.com, January 30, 2001.

122: Terry Atlas, *Bangalore's Big Dreams*, U.S. News & World Report, May 2, 2005.

123: K.C. Krishnadas, *India's Tech Industry Defends H-1B, Outsource Roles*, Electronic Engineering Times.com, July 10, 2003.

124: India Business Opportunities, *Electronics & Information Technology*, ficci.com/ficci/india-profile, Web Date: November 4, 2002.

125: United Press International, *High-tech Industry Fires Americans, Hires Indians*, newsmax.com, March 20, 2003.

126: Associated Press, *Dell to Stop Using Tech Support in India*, earthlink.net, November 24, 2003.

128: *Regional Advantage Notes - ITEC 1210 (IT Revolution)*, greenvertigo.net, November 1, 2001.

129: Ron Schneiderman, *Outsourcing: How Safe is Your Job?*, Electronic Design, May 10, 2004.

132: Geoffrey James, *How Companies Court Disaster in Outsourcing Deals*, computerworld.com, October 30, 2000.

134: The Economic Times Online, *India Jobs Offer Tax-Breaks to US, Inc.*, economictimes.indiatimes.com, April 6, 2004.

135: Christopher H. Schmitt, *Wages of Sin - Why Lawbreakers still win government contracts*, U.S. News & World Report, May 13, 2002.

137: Washington Technology, *Top 100*, Washingtontechnology.com, May 7, 2001.

138: Mike Fabrizi and Dave Michelson, *Outsourcing SWEE '98*, miter.org, January 1, 1998.

140: Jamie Horwitz, *White -Collar Meltdown*, dpeaflcio.org, June 4, 2004.

141: *Shipping Jobs Overseas: How Real is the Problem*, aflcio.org, Web Date: May 27, 2005.

142: David Cay Johnston, *Americans' Income Shrank for 2 Consecutive Years...*, dailyreckoning.com, Web Date: August 23, 2004.

143: Rescue American Jobs, *American Jobs for Americans First - Amazing Facts*, rescueamericanjobs.org, Web Date: September 23, 2003.

144: Rep Tom Tancredo Congressional Testimony, *Enforcing Immigration Laws Would Create 10 Million Jobs!*, rescueamericanjobs.org, June 18, 2003.

153: *Here is a list of Some of the Largest India Owned Bodyshops*, zazona.com, Web Date: September 6, 2004.

154: Edwin S. Rubenstein, *Can Immigrants Save Social Security?*, zazona.com, December 5, 2003.

155: Christian Kasica, United for a Fair Economy, *Bush Tax Cuts = Tax Shifts*, fair.economy.org, April 7, 2004.

156: Citizens for Tax Justice, *Surge in Corporate Tax Welfare Drives Corporate Tax Payments to Near Record Low*, ctj.org, April 17, 2002.

161: Embassy of India, *India's Information Technology Industry*, indianembassy.org, Web Date: May 27, 2005.

170: Albert H. Teich, *R&D in the Federal Budget: Frequently Asked Questions*, aaas.org, Web Date: August 23, 2005.

175: Gretchen Hyman, *India, the Jewel in Oracle's Crown*, siliconvalley.internet.com, July 31, 2002.

176: U.S. Commercial Service India, *Computer and Software Services*, buyusa.gov, November 6, 2002.

184: Mary Mosquera, *TechNet Targets Permanent R&D Tax Credit*, techweb.com, February 24, 1999.

186: Dr. Norman Matloff, *H-1B/L-1/Offshoring e-Newsletter*, engology.com, April 4, 2005.

187: Anthony Spaeth/New Delhi, *Golden Diaspora*, indianembassy.org, March 7, 2001.

188: Wikipedia, *Vinod Khosla*, wikipedia.org, Web Date: August 15, 2005.

189: The Hindu, *3 Indians on Forbes Midas List*, hinduonnet.com/thehindu, February 15, 2005.

190: Desi Flavor, *Plugging India's Brain Drain*, jgohil.typepad.com/desiflavor, June 2, 2004.

191: A P Kamath in Chicago, *TiE Company Forum to Discuss Biz Strategies, Models*, rediff.com, September 20, 1999.

192: *Interesting facts about India and Indians!*, hindustanlink.com, 2000.

194: DeAnne DeWitt, *Petition to Abolish the H-1B Visa Program: Permanent Pinkslips*, zazona.com, 2002.

195: *TechNet Members thank President Bush for his leadership in enacting a strong bi-partisan economic stimulus package*, technet.org, March 15, 2002.

196: Rick White discussion moderated by Cynthia L. Webb, *After the Election: Key High Tech Issues*, washingtonpost.com, November 23, 2004.

197: Leon E Panetta, *Lessons Not Learned: California's $35 Billion in Red Ink Calls for Fearless Leaders*, panettainstitue.org, January 12, 2003.

205: Eric Chabrow, *IT Innovation Drives Homeland-Security Efforts*, informationweek.com, February 25, 2002.

208: President George W. Bush, *Securing the Homeland Strengthening the Nation*, whitehouse.gov/homeland, March 5, 2002.

220: Michael Singer, *DOD Taps Verity for Military Intelligence*, siliconvalley.internet.com, July 23, 2002.

221: *U.S. Leads Science and Engineering but for How Much Longer*, Machine Design, October 7, 2004.

224: Hearing of the Immigration and Claims Subcommittee, *Oral Testimony of Gene A,. Nelson, Ph.D. Regarding U.S. High Tech Workforce*, zazona.com, August 5, 1999.

226: David Kirkpatrick, Fortune.com, *Will the U.S. Fall Behind in Tech?*, cnn.com, October 23, 2002.

228: Ashank Desai, *Making of a Software Superpower*, timescomputing.com, March 31, 1999.

229: Jim Montague and Mark Hoske, *Calmer Waters?*, Control Engineering, May 1, 2003.

230: George J. Borjas, National Review, *Rethinking Foreign Students: A Question of National Interest*, ksghome.harvard.edu, June 17, 2002.

235: Kellogg School of Management, *Academics & Faculty, Mohanbir Sawhney*, www1.kellog.northwestern.edu, July 1, 2005.

236: *How Divine was this Venture?*, siliconindia.com, January 2, 2001.

237: David Whitford, *Press Coverage, The Intellectual Capitalist*, splitthedifference.com, April 17, 2000.

238: Marc Ballon, Los Angeles Times, *Professors Profiting from Practicing What They Teach*, kellogg.northwestern.edu, July 16, 2000.

239: Mohanbir Sawhney, *Getting to Global*, Profiting from Transparency, October 2, 2003.

240: Des Dearlove and Stuart Crainer, The Conference Board, *The Indians Are Coming, How Management Thinkers From India are Changing the Face of American Business*, conference-board.org, July 1, 2005.

242: About Us, *Editorial Board of siliconindia*, siliconindia.com, 2000.

244: Chidanand Rajghatta, *Wireless Whisper: Design network begins to take over telecom world*, indianexpress.com, July 13, 2000.

245: The Economic Times Online, *US Professors: New Age Ambassadors of India Inc.*, economictimes.indiatimes.com, April 8, 2004.

246: Michael Dorgan, *Chinese Families Pay Big Money for U.S. Student Visas*, americanvisas.com, April 2, 2000.

249: National Science Foundation, *Foreign Doctoral Recipients with plans to Stay in the United States*, nsf.gov, Web Date: February 27, 2005.

250: Tom Biggs, Senior Hardware Engineer, Hammerhead Systems, *Don't Blame Students for Declining EE Grad Numbers*, Electronic Engineering Times, March 14, 2005.

252: Federation for American Immigration Reform, *Foreign Students in the United States*, fairus.org, November 4, 2004.

253: Tom Walsh, *University of Michigan Center in India Aims to Help U.S.*, thebatt.com, May 19, 2004.

254: George Borjas, *An Evaluation of the Foreign Student Program*, cis.org, June 1, 2002.

255: Paul Craig Roberts, *War, Outsourcing and Debt. Delusion Rules*, axisoflogic.com, September 30, 2004.

256: Chidanand Rajghatta, *Brain Curry: American Campuses Crave for IIT of Glory*, indian-express.com, December 7, 2000.

261: Associated Press, *U.S. Flunks Higher Education Affordability*, earthlink.net, September 15, 2004.

262: Leslie D'Monte, *MIT Media Lab in India*, zdnetindia.com, February 15, 2001.

263: College Savings Bank, *College Costs*, collegesavings.com, Web Date: January 12, 2003.

264: June Kronholz, *Who Can Fix Higher (Cost) Education*, The Wall Street Journal, August 1, 2004.

267: Joseph Farah, *The Prince and The Media*, wnd.com, November 7, 2001.

271: The Daily Reckoning, *Rude Awakening*, dailyreckoning.com, May 27, 2005.

272: Numbers USA, *Did Congress Intend a huge Increase in Numbers after 1965?*, numbersusa.com/overpopulation, Web Date: February 27, 2005.

281: *Washington Largest Gathering of Indian Americans at State Banquet*, evishwagujarati.net, November 1, 2000.

286: David M Boje, *Enron is Theatre*, cbae.nmsu.edu, September 21, 2002.

288: Sanjeev Srivastava in Bombay, *India's High-Tech Hopes*, bbc.co.us, March 17, 2000.

289: Melanie Warner, *The Indians of Silicon Valley*, Fortune, May 15, 2000.

290: CBS Worldwide Inc., *Pump and Dump*, cbsnews.com, October 19, 2000.

292: *Investment Scams: Pump and Dump*, investopedia.com, Web Date: July 13, 2005.

293: Dvorak, *Dot Conned and The American Way*, dvorak.org, March 8, 2005.

294: Stock Market Crash!, *The Nasdaq Bubble*, stock-market-crash.net, Web Date: July 13, 2005.

295: *The Dot-Com Crash: March 11, 2000 to October 9, 2002*, investopedia.com, Web Date: July 13, 2005.

296: Alan Stewart and Paul McLaughlin, CA Magazine, *The Dirt on the Dot.Cons*, kkc.net, July 1, 2001.

297: Associated Press --Curt Anderson contributed, *Ex-Computer Associates CEO Kumar Indicted*, earthlink.net, September 23, 2004.

298: Robert L Grant, Dow Jones Newswires, *Lay, Other Enron Directors' Seats on Boards Face Scrutiny*, quicken.com, January 25, 2002.

299: Rob Spiegel, *Dot Com Crash: Whose Fault is it Anyway?*, theezine.net, December 8, 2001.

300: Manjeet Kripalani and Pete Engardio, *The Rise of India*, BusinessWeek, December 8, 2003.

301: Mike Yamamoto, staff writer Cnet News.com, *Will India Price Itself out of the Offshore Market?*, freeborders.com, March 29, 2004.

302: Richard Armstrong, *H-1B Myth: The Best and the Brightest*, americanreformation.org, Web Date: December 4, 2002.

303: Manjeet Kripalani in Bombay, with Pete Engardia and Leah Nathans Spiro in New York, *India's WHIZ KIDS (int'l edition), Inside the Indian Institutes of Technology's star factory*, businessweek.com/1998/49/b3607011.htm, November 25, 1998.

304: IndiaExpress Bureau, *Those Magnificent Indians in Forbes List*, indiaexpress.com, September 23, 2000.

305: The Red Herring Magazine, *The Bucks Start Here: The Leading Venture Capital Firms of 1996*, Frontenac Company, June 1, 1997.

306: *Investor Entrepreneur Forum at siliconindia Annual Conference 2001*, siliconindia.com, 2000.

308: CBS Worldwide Inc., *Out of India*, cbsnews.com, January 11, 2004.

309: Ela Dutt, *7 Indian Americans Among 'Forbes' 400 Richest*, timesofindia.com, September 24, 2000.

310: *TiE-Rockies Speakers 2000-2001*, tie-rockies.org, Web Date: May 14, 2002.

312: Alex Salkever, The Industry Standard, *The Curry Network*, tie-carolinas.org, January 24, 2000.

315: Special Correspondent, *IIT Alumni Gesture to the Alma Mater*, the-hindu.com, December 9, 1999.

319: Raja Bose, Times News Network, *NRI Hunts for Talent in India*, indiaday.org, November 19, 2003.

320: Hindustantimes.co, Press Trust of India, *Eighteen Indian Companies in Forbes' List*, indiaday.org, November 5, 2003.

321: Seema Hakhu Kachru in Houston, Rediff.com, *Indians Top US International Students Chart*, indiaday.org, November 3, 2003.

323: Lesly Stahl, *Imported from India*, 60 Minutes, March 2, 2003.

324: *Rebuttal from Norm Matloff*, hireamericancitizens.org, July 1, 2003.

327: Dr. Norman Matloff, *Bias at CBS*, itaa.org, September 21, 2003.

328: *The National Television Academy Announces the Nominees for the 2nd Annual Emmy Awards for Business and Financial Reporting*, November 2, 2004.

329: Dr. Norman Matloff, *Needed Reform for the H-1B Work Visa: Major Points*, heather.cs.ucdavis.edu, May 7, 2003.

330: Chidanand Rajghatta, *Where Integrated Chip means Indians, Chinese*, indian-express.com, February 23, 2000.

331: Kevin Wu, New York City, *The Silicon Valley Indians*, bebeyond.com, 2002.

332: *Organizational Profile: The IndUS Entrepreneurs (TiE)*, larta.org, June 14, 2001.

333: Vanessa Richardson, *The 'Indian Mafia' Muscles onto the Web*, redherring.com, December 14, 1999.

334: Vishwas Varghese, *Information Superpower India?*, swordoftruth.com, May 20, 2000.

335: Y--Axis: Recruit from India, *The Indian Software Industry*, y-axis.com, Web Date: November 4, 2002.

338: Sreeni Meka's Immigration Issues, *Who Uses High-Skill Visas*, angelfire.co, Web Date: November 4, 2002.

339: *Top 100 H-1B sponsors for this year*, h1bsponsors.com, Web Date: July 9, 2001.

341: Melanie Warner, Fortune, *Could Telecom be Carlyle's New Defense*, openflows.org, March 18, 2002.

342: *US Congress Heaps Praise on IITs*, in.rediff.com, April 28, 2005.

344: Spencer E. Ante, New York, *The Secret Behind Those Profit Jumps*, BusinessWeek, December 8, 2003.

345: *TiE-NY -- Membership*, spidersweb.com/tie, Web Date: October 6, 2005.

346: TiE New York Chapter, *Santanu Das, CEO, Transwitch*, spidersweb.com/tie, Web Date: October 6, 2005.

347: Viji Sundaram, India-West Staff Reported, *India West: Kanwal Rekhi Joins ISN Advisory Board*, isn.org, May 4, 2001.

348: Murali Krishna Devarakonda, *Kanwal Rekhi advises Laid-off H-1B workers not to Leave*, isn.org, April 29, 2001.

349: *Kanwal Rekhi School of Information Technology*, it.iitb.ac.in, Web Date: September 27, 2005.

350: Emeral Yeh, *Kanwal Rekhi Biography 2001*, asianpacificfund.org, Web Date: September 27, 2005.

351: David Mildenberg, *Networking Godfather to Visit Triangle*, bizjournals.com, September 25, 2000.

354: Sean Gregory, *Rainmaking 101*, Time Bonus Section, November 1, 2004.

355: William K Tabb, *New Economy ...Same Irrational Economy*, monthlyreview.org, April 2, 2001.

357: Kamla Bhatt, *From Meerut to Silicon Valley: The $11-billion Story*, rediff.com, May 3, 2000.

358: IANS san Jose, *Dotcom Shakeout has Set Things Right'*, hindustantimes.com, December 11, 2000.

359: Ajay Singh, *Upstarts How India's dotcom Pioneers Staked their Claims in Silicon Valley Your Space*, asiaweek.com, November 23, 2001.

360: Pallava Bagla, *Indian Schools Cash In on Silicon Valley Wealth*, wbln0018.worldbank.org, May 11, 2000.

361: Priya Ganapati, *Giving Back to the Alma Mater, IIT Alumni Style*, iitbombay.org, February 1, 2002.

362: Associated Press, *Tech Downturn Doesn't Slow H-1B Visas*, apnew.excite.com, January 28, 2002.

363: Brian Sullivan, *Emotions Run Hot on H-1Bs*, computerworld.com, April 29, 2002.

364: Thomas W. Hazlett, Special to ZDNet, *Why Are We in a Broadband Recession?*, excite.com, July 30, 2001.

365: Robert Thompson, LookSmart, *Scrutinizing the Scrutineers: How accurate are high technology's pithy pundits?*, findarticles.com, September 1, 1998.

366: Namita Bhandare, Dew Delhi, *Indian CEOs Still Riding High in US Despite Two Exits*, hindustantimes.com, April 12, 2001.

367: Non-Resident Indians, *Forbes 500 Honors Indian Entrepreneurs*, welcome-nri.com, January 1, 2000.

369: *The Greedy Bunch*, fortune.com, September 2, 2002.

371: Penelope Patsuris, *Forbes Dropoffs*, forbes.com, June 22, 2001.

372: AnnaLee Saxenian, *Silicon Valley's New Immigrant Entrepreneurs*, The Center for Comparative Immigration Studies, University of California, San Diego, May 1, 2000.

373: Denver Business Journal, *Qwest lawsuits Settled*, bizjournals.com, February 18, 2004.

374: Sunil Thomas, *Call the Hotline Software Piracy*, India's No. 1 Weekly News magazine, April 30, 2000.

377: Anonymous, *I am Proud to be a Indian are You?*, geocities.com, Web Date: November 4, 2002.

378: Shyamanuja Das and Ch Srinivas Rao, *Tech Start-ups: Indus Valley, Circa 2002*, CIOL Cybertimes, voicendata.com, September 7, 2002.

379: NPR-- All Things Considered, Outsourcing entrepreneurs going back home to export American jobs, *neoIT-Atul Vashistha Discusses Outsourcing*, neoit.com, March 16, 2004.

387: CNN Tonight, *Harvey Pitt Announced SEC will bring in McKinsey Mgt Consulting to perform a Top to Bottom Analyis of SEC Operations*, h1bvisasucks.com, July 18, 2002.

388: Broc Romanek, *270-Page Report on SEC's Weaknesses*, thecorporatecounsel.net, December 1, 2003.

389: Organizations and Scofflaws that Shill H-1B, *Public Policy Institute of California (PPIC)*, zazona.com, Web Date: October 17, 2005.

390: INDOlink-International and NRI News, *Silicon Spice Acquired by Broadcom for $1.2 Billion*, indolink.com, August 7, 2000.

392: Former and Current Employees of Intel, *Licensed to Cheat: Intel threatens politicians and Clinton to increase H-1B quota*, faceintel.com, August 17, 1998.

395: *Despite Tech Crash, Premji Remains Richest Indian*, newsindia-times.com, June 29, 2001.

397: Philip Martin and Peter Duigan, *Recent Immigration Patterns*, Hoover Press, 2003.

398: Michael Lehman President Flinchbaugh Engineering, York Pa., *Line Transfer: An Alternative to Offshore Manufacturing*, Machine Design, October 7, 2004.

400: Y-Axis The H-1B Co., *Statistics and Trivia*, y-axis.com, Web Date: September 26, 2005.

404: *Let the Brain Drain Increase*, isa.org, October 29, 2003.

421: Financial News, *i2 Settles Class Action and Derivative Lawsuits*, biz.yahoo.com/bw/040510/105480 1.html, May 10, 2004.

422: *Interview of Prime Minister Dr. Manhohan Singh on Charlie Rose Show*, indianembassy.org/pm/pm Charlie rose sep 21 04.htm, September 21, 2004.

431: Janet Kornblum and Alex Lash, *Pockets Run Deep for Java*, news.cnet.com, August 20, 1996.

432: Jill Steinberg, *Java Gets $100 Million Endorsement*, javaworld.com, September 1, 1996.

440: Project on Government Oversight, *Government Contractors Wield Influence Through Revolving Door, Campaign Contributions*, pogo.org, June 29, 2004.

451: Wayne Labs, Contributing Editor, *The Shifting Design Cycle*, Electron Design, October 20, 2005.

452: David Roman, *Dispiriting Days for EEs*, Electronic Engineering Times, November 14, 2005.

453: David Lammers, *Alarming Export: Engineers*, Electronic Engineering Times, November 14, 2005.

455: M.R. Rangaswami, Co-founder, Sand Hill Group LLC, *The Next Wave of Software Business Strategy*, sterlinghoffman.com/newsletter/articles/article 103.html, Web Date: November 5, 2005.

461: Richard B. Johnson, Project Engineer, Analogic Corp., Peabody, Mass, *I Created Jobs to Keep Americans Employed*, Electronic Engineering Times, July 11, 2005.

462: David Roman, *Firms Grab Large Piece of Venture Pie*, Electronic Engineering Times, January 30, 2006.

463: Ben Stocking, Mercury News, *The TiE That Binds*, slomedia.com/filles/press/20001127, November 27, 2000.

464: Dr. Norman Matloff, H-1B/L-1/offshoring e-newsletter, *More on the CMU/TCS Connection*, heather.cs.ucdavis.edu, February 25, 2004.

467: Arthur J Pais, *Jessie Jackson is Blowing Smoke,' Says TiE's Rekhi*, rediff.com, June 4, 1999.

468: Gary Cohn and Walter Fl. Roche, Baltimore Sun, *Indentured Servants for High-Tech Trade Labor*, ailf.org/pubed/n022100a.htm, February 21, 2000.

469: The Official Website of the Department of IT and Biotechnology, Government of Karnataka, *TiE Con - Speakers Profile*, bangaloreit.com/html/itscbng/tieconspeak.htm, 2000.

473: School of Government, *What are the Qualifications to be Considered an M/WBE?*, iog.unc.edu/programs/purchase/mwbe/contractos.htm, Web Date: January 16, 2006.

477: Anthony Kujawa, Washington File Staff Writer, *Foreign Student Enrollment at U.S. Graduate Schools Up in 2005*, usinfo.state.gov, November 7, 2005.

478: Wikipedia, *James Gosling*, http://en.wikipedia.org/wiki/James Gosling, Web Date: December 21, 2005.

479: Daniel Brook, *Are Your Lawyers in New York or New Delhi?*, legalaffairs.org, June 1, 2005.

482: Wikipedia, *AnnaLee Saxenian*, http://en.wikipedia.org/wiki/AnnaLee Saxeian, December 10, 2005.

484: Michael Fitzgerald, *Is U.S. Losing the Innovation Arms Race*, cioinsight.com, June 5, 2005.

488: Edwin S. Rubenstein, The Hudson Institute, *Trade Drag?*, americanoutlook.org, June 1, 2001.

491: Jim Turley, editor in chief of Embedded Systems Design, *Engineering Shortage? Get Real*, Electronic Engineering Times, January 16, 2006.

492: Sadanand Dhume, *Hyderabad's Harvard: A University Built on an Arid Plain with Funds from Overseas Indians ...*, fas.ulaval.ca/personnel/vernag/EH/F/cause/klectures/hyderabad harvard .htm, August 8, 2002.

494: Dr. Norman Matloff, *Johnny Can So Program*, news.com.com, May 10, 2005.

503: Jeffrey Pfeffer, *The Hidden Cost of Outsourcing*, cnnmoney.com, March 1, 2006.

504: Paul Craig Roberts, *Nuking the Economy -- Forget Iran --Americans Should be Hysterical About This*, baltimorechronicle.com/2006, February 13, 2006.

505: Jeannine Aversa, AP Economics Writer, *Bush Concedes Outsourcing Hurts Workers*, latimes.com/business/investing/wire/sns-ap-bush-outsourcing, March 3, 2006.

510: DiamondCluster International, Inc, *2005 Global IT Outsourcing Study*, diamondcluster.com, 2005.

512: S.L. Bachman, Pacific Council on International Policy, The Western Partner of the Council on Foreign Relations, *Globalization in the San Francisco Bay Area: Trying to Stay at the Head of the Class*, January 2, 2003.

513: ABC News Internet Ventures, *A Billion Reasons to Care About India -- India is a Global Force to Be Reckoned With-- Its Economy is Booming*, abcnews.go.com/GMA, March 1, 2006.

515: David Roman, *Bush's Budget, Up Close*, Electronic Engineering Times, February 27, 2006.

516: IndiaTimes News Network, *Employee Files Class Action Suit Against Tata America*, economictimes.indiatimes.com, February 15, 2006.

517: Wikipedia, *Spencer Abraham*, http://en.wikipedia.org/wiki/Spenser Abraham, Web Date: March 8, 2006.

518: *Senator Spencer Abraham*, opensecrets.org, December 31, 2000.

523: multiple authors, *Technology Without Borders Global iit2005 Conference*, iit2005.org, 2005.

528: Nicolas Mokhoff, *Have Engineers Come to Accept the Offshoring Phenomenon?*, Electronic Engineering Times, August 21, 2006.

529: David Roman and Junko Yoshida, *State of the Engineer -- The Young and the Restless*, Electronic Engineering Times, August 21, 2006.

531: Xinhua News Agency, *More Chinese Postgraduate Applicants Enrolled in US Universities*, china.org.cn, November 21, 2006.

537: David Wallechninsky, *Is America Still Number 1?*, Parade, January 14, 2007.

540: T.V. Mohandas Pai, Director and CFO, *The Infosys Financial Model*, infosys.com/investor/transcript/the infosysfinancial model.pdf, 2002.

549: Jim Whitehead, *Advice for Foreign Students Wishing to Pursue Graduate Study in Computer Science at UCSC*, cse.ucsc.edu, December 8, 2005.

552: *Dot.com Job Cuts Soar*, money.cnn.com, April 27, 2001.

557: William Aspray, Frank Mayadas, Moshe Y. Vardi, Editors Association for Computing Machinery, *Job Migration Task Force*, acm.org/globalization report/summary, Web Date: March 11, 2006.

558: *TechNet: Who We Are, Meetings with US Politicians, and Members*, technet.org, Web Date: March 22, 2006.

559: Mother Jones, *John Doerr (with Ann), Donor Profile*, matherjones.com, March 5, 2001.

560: NNDB Tracking the Entire World, *John Doerr*, nndb.com/people, Web Date: March 23, 2006.

565: Marcus Courtney, WashTech News, *Congress Considers Massive H-1B Visa Expansion, Gates Tells Congress It's Microsoft's Top Priority*, washtech.org/news/legislative, March 21, 2006.

566: Michael A. Banak, PE, Crosstalk Town Hall, *Similar Fate Awaits H-1Bs Who Displaced American EEs*, Electronic Engineering Times, June 12, 2006.

567: Sudhir Shah, Global Indian Takeover, *Worried About H-1B Visa? Take the L1 Route*, economictimes.indiatimes.com, March 20, 2006.

568: Leslie Stahl, *North of the Border*, CBS News, "60 Minutes", October 3, 1993.

581: Associated Press, International Herald Tribune, *Doctors strike at Indian Hospitals to Protest Affirmative Action*, iht.com, May 14, 2006.

586: Sandip Roy - Chowdhury, *Major US Companies are Setting Up Offices in India for Software Development. Is the Outsourcing of Jobs to India a Temporary Phenomenon?*, indiacurrents.com/news, August 4, 2003.

587: Stephanie Crane, Tech Knowledge, *India's Outsourcers Gain Traction*, businessweek.com, October 29, 2004.

588: Reuters, *Infosys Shares Up On Strong Profit*, cnn.worldnews, July 12, 2006.

592: *TiE Website*, tie.org, Web Date: October 17, 2006.

594: Grant Gross, IDG News Service, *Tech Worker Group Files Complaints Over H-1B Job Ads*, infoworld.com, June 22, 2006.

597: BusinessWeek Online, *The Future of Technology: The Big Trends Ahead and Our Ranking of the Top 100 Info Tech Companies*, businessweek.com, 2005.

601: Wikipedia, *N.R. Narayana Murthy*, wikipedia.org/wiki, Web Date: April 15, 2006.

602: VC Circle :: Early Stage/Angel, *Kanwal Rekhi Raising $150-$175 Million India-specific Fund*, vccircle.com/blog/EarlyStageAngel, February 13, 2006.

603: Rep Tom Tancredo, *Representative Tom Tancredo's Speech Before the House of Representatives July 13, 2003*, american-champions.org/Presentations, July 13, 2003.

604: Kim Gerard, *TiE -- The Secrets of Success*, tie-asia.org/events, Web Date: November 1, 2005.

611: *There are Three Types of Student Visas*, going2usa.com/education/studentvisa.html, Web Date: February 28, 2007.

612: *Exchange Visitor (J) Visas*, travel.state.gov/visa/temp/types, February 28, 2007.

613: *ECFMG J-1 Visa Sponsorship Fact Sheet*, ecfmg.org/evsp/j1fact.html, September 24, 2004.

615: Ron Schneiderman, Contributing Editor, *Offshoring. Outsourcing. Out of Work.*, Electronic Design, October 20, 2005.

618: Wikipedia, *Non-Resident Indian and Person of Indian Origin*, en.wikipedia.org/wiki/Non-resident Indian and Person of Indian Origin, Web Date: March 9, 2007.

619: Rick Merritt, *Where are the Programmers?*, Electronic Engineering Times, March 12, 2007.

621: John Edwards, Contributing Editor, *Military R&D 101*, Electronic Design, September 1, 2006.

625: US India Political Action Committee, *USINPAC*, http://www.usinpac.com, Web Date: April 9, 2007.

626: Josh Shaffer, Staff Writer, *A Little India, here in Raleigh*, The News and Observer, April 29, 2007.

627: Christopher Reynolds, Los Angeles Times, *New Eyes on an Old Chinatown, San Francisco's miniature country offers wisdom still*, The News and Observer April 29, 2007, April 29, 2007.

628: The News and Observer, *Duke Business School Hit by Cheating Scandal*, tmcnet.com, April 30, 2007.

632: Vivek Wadhwa, Duke University,WRAL.com, *America's New Immigrant Entrepreneurs*, localtechwire.com/business, Web Date: May 3, 2007.

634: Emily Flynn Vencat, Newsweek International, *Education: Why Everyone Cheats Now*, msnbc.msn.com/id/, May 27, 2006.

635: Alan Finder, The New York Times, *34 Duke Business Students Face Discipline for Cheating*, www.nytimes.com, May 1, 2007.

640: Show 321 Transcript, *Sizing Up the Competition*, foreignexchange.tv, May 25, 2007.

644: Website, *Open Silicon Valley*, opensiliconvalley.com, Web Date: September 21, 2007.

649: Wikipedia, *M.S. Krishnan*, wikipedia.org/wiki/M. S. Krishnan, December 30, 2007.

653: *TiE has Helped Create Businesses Worth More than $200 Billion*, startinbusiness.co.us/flowchart/tie.htm, January 1, 2000, Web Date: September 21, 2007.

659: website, *About Tie*, tienewdelhi.org/members, Web Date: July 27, 2007.

661: *IT Industry Finds Little to Like in Immigration Bill*, itbusinessedge.com, May 31, 2007.

662: *Engineers Learning People Skills, Too*, att.net/, Web Date: December 9, 2007.

665: *H-1B Visa*, wikipedia.org/wiki/H-1B visa, Web Date: January 2, 2008.

666: Patrick Thibodeau, *H-1B Video Shocker: 'Our Goal is Clearly not to Find a Qualified ... U.S. Worker'*, computerworld.com, June 19, 2007.

670: Posted by Ann All December 10, 2007, *Boeing Is Latest Company to Learn Importance of Outsourcing Management*, itbusinessedge.com, December 10, 2007.

685: Francis C. Assisi, *Skilled Indian Immigrants Create Wealth for America*, indolink.com, January 4, 2007.

686: Who's Who of Asian Americans, *Who's Who of Asian Americans: Biography of Vivek Wadhwa*, asianamerica.net, Web Date: April 5, 2008.

687: Vivek Wadhwa, Duke University, *Open Doors Wider for Skilled Immigrants*, businessweek.com, January 3, 2007.

688: Ela Dutt, *Indian Owns a Goldmine*, tribuneindia.com, May 16, 2008.

689: Gary Weiss, *Are You Paying for Corporate Fat Cats*, Parade, April 13, 2008.

690: David Jackson, *McCain Denounces 'Siren Song' of Protectionism*, usatoday.com, April 22, 2008.

693: Peggy Lim, *Fury Vented on Duke Student*, The News & Observer, April 27, 2008.

696: *McKInsey & Company -Wikipedia, the free encyclopedia*, en.wikipedia.org, Web Date: May 14, 2008.

703: Sheila Riley, *Green-card Red Tape Sends Valuable Engineers Packing*, eeTimes, August 27, 2007.

704: Michelle Singletary, *Grad is Back Home. Now the Rules*, The News and Observer, May 25, 2008.

709: Suzanne Gamboa, Associated Press Writer, *Labor Dept. Probes Work of Major Immigration Law Firm*, usatoday.com, June 24, 2008.

711: my.att.net/scprits/editorial.dll, *California Sliding Toward $41.8B Budget Deficit*, Associated Press, December 11, 2008.

716: andhra-pradesh-news, *Hyderabad Police Arrest 25 Foreign Students for Overstaying*, newkerala.com, October 22, 2008.

719: Rhys Blakely in Bombay, *Madoff Tipster Blasts SEC, Says He Feared for His Safety*, foxnews.com, February 4, 2009.

720: Tony Brown, *Why Indian H-1Bs Are Not Superior And Aframericans Are Not Cry Babies*, zazona.com, September 7, 2001.

721: Manjeet Kripalani in Bombay, *Private Equity Pours Into India*, businessweek.com, June 20, 2005.

722: Richard Behar, *World Bank's Web of Ties to 'India's Enron'*, foxnews.com, January 12, 2009.

723: Stephanie Armour, USA Today, *2008 Foreclosure Filing Set Record*, usatoday.com, January 14, 2009.

724: *Syntel*, wikipedia.org, Web Date: August 9, 2008.

725: *Mastech*, igatemastech.com, Web Date: August 9, 2008.

726: Mary Beth Marklein, *U.S. School's Foreign Enrollments Soar*, usatoday.com, November 16, 2008.

727: Grant Gross, IDG News Service, *Foreign Students Get Longer U.S. Stay*, pcworld.com, April 12, 2008.

728: Hadley Gambie, *As Economy Slumps, Firms Line Up to Hire Skilled Foreign Workers*, foxnews.com, March 19, 2009.

729: Associated Press, *Microsoft to Slash 5,000 Jobs, Misses on Profit*, usatoday.com, January 22, 2009.

730: Patrick Thibodeau, *H-1B, Offshoring Supporters Get Key Obama Administration Posts*, computerworld.com, February 3, 2009.

731: Patrick Thibodeau, *Why Obama May Back the H-1B Increase Even In a Recession*, computerworld.com, November 6, 2008.

732: *New Jobless Claims Jump Unexpectedly to 669,000*, foxnews.com, April 2, 2009.

733: Susan Page, *24 Million Go From 'Thriving' to 'Struggling'*, usatoday.com, March 9, 2009.

735: Lalit K Jha in Washington, *H-1B: Indian CEOs Meet Obama Team*, business.rediff.com, March 19, 2009.

737: Associated Press, *Lawmakers Prosper Despite Economic Slump*, usatoday.com, June 16, 2008.

739: Associated Press, *Microsoft Lays Off Thousands, Hints at More to Come*, foxnews.com, May 6, 2009.

740: Jesse James Deconto, Staff Writer, *Protest Stops Tancredo's UNC Speech*, newsobserver.com, April 15, 2009.

741: Marianne Kolbasuk McGee, *Should H-1B Employers Pay for US Students' Degrees*, informationweek.com/blog, November 1, 2006.

742: Vivek Wadhwa, TechCrunch blog, *Free the H-1Bs, Free the Economy*, techcrunch.com, August 30, 2009.

743: Christian Dugas, USA Today, *College Graduates Struggle to Repay Student Loans*, usatoday.com, May 12, 2009.

744: Emily Bazar, USA Today, *More of the World's Talented Workers Opt to Leave USA*, usatoday.com, September 20, 2009.

745: Dr. Norman Matloff, *Globalization and the American IT Worker*, Communications of the ACM, November 1, 2004.

746: Dr. Norman Matloff, *Offshoring What Can Go Wrong?*, IT Pro, July 1, 2005.

747: Arthur Hu, *Norman Matloff, The Hatchet Man of Asian Immigration*, arthurhu.com, Web Date: October 6, 2009.

753: The Associated Press, *Supreme Court Turns Down Appeal From InfoSpace Founder*, seattletimesnwsource.com, March 9, 2009.

754: *US Embassy Alerts Cops on Fake Student Visa Rackets*, telugudreams.com/News/NewsDetails, January 17, 2010.

755: Stephen Labaton, *S.E.C.'s Embattled Chief Resigns in Wake of Latest Political Storm*, nytimes.com, November 6, 2002.

756: Associated Press, *Settlement is Approved in Qwest Lawsuit*, Salt Lake City, Desert News, September 30, 2006.

766: Peter S. Goodman, Washington Post, *How China is Making the Pen as Mighty as the PC*, umsl.edu, December 12, 2002.

770: Eryn Brown and David Kirkpatrick, Fortune, *The Reverse Brain Drain*, umsl.edu, November 11, 2002.

774: Paula Musich, eWeek, *Offshore Upstarts*, umsl.edu, September 23, 2002.

776: Knowledg@Wharton, *The Case For and Against, Shifting Back-Office Operations Overseas*, umsl.edu, October 9, 2002.

778: Jack Anderson and Douglas Cohn, *SEC Needs New Leader*, ljworld.com, July 20, 2002.

779: *Testimony of Vivek Wadhwa To the U.S. House of Representatives Committee on Education and the Workforce*, May 16, 2006.

780: Professor Norm Matloff's H-1B Web Page, *The H-1B is Fundamentally about Cheap Labor*, heather.cs.ucdavis.edu, Web Date: January 18, 2010.